AGING, DE
COMPLE

JOHN DEMOS · LEON EDEL · ERIK H. ERIKSON

LESLIE FIEDLER · TAMARA K. HAREVEN

ROBERT KASTENBAUM · ROBERT KOHN

JUANITA KREPS · PETER LASLETT

FRANCIS V. O'CONNOR · ROBERT F. SAYRE

AGING, DEATH, AND THE COMPLETION OF BEING

edited by DAVID D. VAN TASSEL

UNIVERSITY OF PENNSYLVANIA PRESS · 1979

Library of Congress Cataloging in Publication Data

Main entry under title:

Aging, death, and the completion of being.

Includes bibliographical references and index.
1. Old age—Congresses. 2. Aging—Congresses.
3. Death—Congresses. I. Van Tassel, David Dirck,
1928-
HQ1061.A4575   301.43′5   78-65111
ISBN 0-8122-7757-0

TO MERLE E. CURTI

CONTENTS

3   AGING AND DEATH AS UNIVERSAL EXPERIENCE: LITERARY AND ARTISTIC PERCEPTIONS

DAVID D. VAN TASSEL

INTRODUCTION

The following papers were written for and delivered at a conference on "Human Values and Aging-New Challenges to Research in the Humanities," held in November 1975 on the campus
of Case Western Reserve University. The conference and the
project of which it was a part were funded by the National
Endowment for the Humanities in order to stimulate research in
the disciplines of the humanities on the subject of aging. The
assumption behind the conference and the project was that
scholars in the humanities could extend knowledge in their disciplines and enhance our present understanding of aging, old age,
and death by mining the vast and rich vein of human experience
recorded in centuries of history, literature, myth, folklore, and
art. Clearly, twentieth-century civilization has discovered old age
as a social, economic, and health problem of growing proportions.
Old age as a problem has been studied by social and biological
scientists through miles of questionnaires and computer print-
outs, laying bare in cold statistics the lives, the pains, and the
hopes of the contemporary generation of elderly, or through the
microscope, peering at colored slides of aging cells, or through
analyses of case studies of diseased or troubled patients. Yet few
of these studies have been informed by a humanistic perspective
drawn from the materials of the experience of mankind, which
could and should be located, brought to life, and refined by
scholars in the humanities, including historians, philosophers,
literary scholars, art historians, and many others. In 1973, when
this project began, there were few humanists working in this

field, and little existed in the way of published research, either in monograph or article form. Why? Perhaps because, although old age has been a part of the human condition and the family life cycle since the dawn of conscious time, there was no material; perhaps, as the social scientists assumed, this was a phase of life faced only by the twentieth century; but someone had to find out. And by the time the reader sees this volume, not only will its contents bear out the truth of the assumption that such a vein of material exists, but numerous books and articles by humanists will have seen print, and at least three other volumes of essays will be coming out of the project.

At first glance, there may appear to be little relationship between the disciplines represented by the authors or the topics of the papers, but running through the entire volume are several themes important to humanists and just beginning to dawn on the intellectual horizons of gerontologists. The first theme is that aging is a lifelong process, that therefore old age does not begin on the day of retirement at the age of sixty-five. Indeed, the definition of old age itself is problematic: is it determined chronologically, or physiologically, or mentally, or environmentally, or culturally, or economically? Old age may not be a phase of life as identifiable as adolescence, but growing old is a process that occurs to every person every minute, every hour, every day, and every year that passes; and old age—how it is received and how it is perceived—is a function of the life that the person has lived.

The second theme that runs through most of the essays in this volume is that in the present generation old age has become inextricably associated with death, the termination of the aging process, the final completion of being. This is simply the product of a higher standard of living, better nutrition and lower infant mortality rates, so that during the past fifty years the chances of a young person's growing to a ripe old age and dying of a disease associated with old age have been enhanced manyfold. In the eighteenth century it was an accepted fact of life that death was ever-present, and it was the exceptional person who was able to live out his biblical three score and ten. Now, however, the way we treat dying and death affects our view of old age. It will become clear, as one reads these essays, why the subject of death intrudes itself in a volume on age and aging.

The first part of the book consists of essays by a pathologist, an economist, a psychiatrist, and a psychologist. These essays briefly and simply lay out the contemporary situation and the state of the art, as it were. But each one throws down the gauntlet to the humanist, challenging the humanities to identify cultural values; to trace the origins of present attitudes and myths; to produce a philosophy upon which a system of ethics can rest; to identify models in literature and history of good and bad old age; to identify the literature, poetry, art, and music of solace, of inspiration and revelation, which people have always sought in the fine arts; and, finally, to identify the cultural sources of attitudes toward old age and death so that we may be freed, as Robert Butler put it, of a blind "age-ism."

Robert Kohn, a pathologist whose specialty has been the study of the biological process of aging, points out that aging is a continuous physiological process with a chronological limit, and that while there are many theories of why human organisms age, there is still little agreement. With no hope yet of finding Ponce de Leon's long-sought fountain of youth, there will not be in the foreseeable future a society of Methuselahs or Swift's Struldbrugs. On the other hand, medicine has achieved many breakthroughs, and if a cure for cancer is found, two years will be added to life expectancy at birth, while prevention of deaths due to atherosclerosis will increase the human lifespan by seven or eight years. Therefore, what has occurred and what may be expected in the future is that men and women will have a relatively healthy and vigorous old age for twenty years beyond the normal retirement age of sixty-five. Dr. Kohn challenges the humanist to improve the quality of life and the intellectual and cultural sphere of those last twenty years, during which the physician and nutritionist have furnished us with hope of relative good health and vigor.

Juanita Kreps, an economist and now secretary of commerce in President Carter's cabinet, points out that those additional twenty years constitute an economic problem and an additional area for humanistic endeavor. The work ethic has been very strong in Western civilization, and yet our population of dependent retired people is growing and overburdening an economy that values only economically productive work. The economic system will not change until the value system changes. The economist works within a system determined by society and can only assess what can and ought to be done to achieve certain social goals. These goals are arrived at by people who have been affected by the standards of their culture. It is the humanist who can lay bare the assumptions, the attitudes, the makeup, of the value system of the culture.

Erik Erikson, in his essay "Reflections on Dr. Borg's Life Cycle," admirably illustrates the theme that the growth and change of the personality is a lifelong process. Freud asserted that once the libido has settled into its final form early in a person's life, personality change is the result of a compromise between the instinctual forces of Eros, whose powers decrease with advancing age, and Thanatos, whose powers force the individual toward the portals of death and despair. Erikson, on the other hand, in his seminal volume *Identity and the Life Cycle*, posits a theory of personality development that encompasses the entire lifespan of the individual.[1] He insists that the concept of growth and change occurring continuously in the individual and in society is a necessary prerequisite for the satisfactory resolution of the crises that arise at each stage of a person's life. The crises and resolutions occurring throughout the successive stages involve the emergence of new attitudes, ego strengths, or virtues. If the individual has successfully progressed through and resolved the five crises that occur through late adolescence, he or she should be ready to face the emergence or submergence of the last three ego strengths or virtues: love, care, and wisdom. These virtues correspond to the last three stages of Erikson's developmental theory and involve choices between intimacy and isolation, generativity and stagnation, integrity and despair. In his essay, Erikson deftly utilizes the screenplay of Ingmar Bergman's film *Wild Strawberries* to present his conception of the life cycle. He finds his stages or crises illuminated by a memoir reaching from old age "through a man's resolved adulthood to the dim beginnings of his awareness as a child." Here we find the literary drama and the visual symbols of the film interacting with the social-science theory through the wholeness of the human life cycle, stage by stage Erikson believes this cycle should be interpreted for a new generation of adults, compelled to comprehend, perhaps with occasional distaste and horror, what adulthood and old age are all about. In the first section of his essay Erikson alternates brief descriptions of the screenplay's main scenes and themes with statements of how they relate to his "stages" of life. In the second section, he deals more fully with his conception of the human life cycle, particularly the last of the crises of life, a struggle between integrity and despair, which must be resolved in order to achieve the completion of being, the final strength: wisdom.

Robert Kastenbaum, a psychologist who has studied and written a great deal on death and dying, outlines some current trends and some popular myths, and then develops from these trends and myths a scenario in which life is meaningless because death is meaningless and old age is not economically feasible. He suggests an alternative scenario that seems to him eminently more desirable. But again, it is to the humanist that he turns and says, "You must alter the values and the attitudes that will affect the future."

The humanists who respond, beginning with the historians, ask what happened to old people in the past? Was there a time when the old were revered because of their years? Was there a time when the family structure was such that the oldest members retained power?

Peter Laslett, who has made extensive studies of preindustrial English families in the seventeenth century, argues that old people, who were few in number, were nevertheless not necessarily held in esteem simply because of their years, nor was the extended family structure, which would have taken care of its older members, the dominant family organization in preindustrial England. He therefore cautions that an excessively legitimatory use of the past, "drawing upon it only to justify a proposed change in the contemporary world" by appealing to what he calls "the world we have lost"—a vanished golden age—must be avoided. History should be used to free us of the past, to arrive at new solutions for an entirely new situation.

John Demos, an American colonial historian, reaches some of the same conclusions as Laslett in his microcosmic look at the situation of the elderly in seventeenth-century New England, but suggests some differences and raises some provocative questions.

He finds in the literature that the ideology and the rhetoric of the Pilgrims and the Puritans put age in a place of honor. In the area of behavior, however, where the evidence is less substantial, he finds that old people either were not treated well or were treated well on grounds other than their years. He suggests that the Puritans—always somewhat insecure, living in a constant state of tension and conflict—were even less able than modern society to cope with the narcisstic imbalance that growing old always creates. They were also unable to "see" the elderly in a way that encompassed "the full richness of human individuality," in part because the old person was something of a stranger in the seventeenth century, when only 3 percent of the population was aged sixty or over, and in part because of the Puritan belief that the ancient had reached old age because of either the attainment of grace or a pact with the devil. In either case, the awe was based on religion, which involved a theory of life and death, and not on respect for a particular individual.

The one constant in history is change. Tamara Hareven, a historian of the family, bases on this axiom an extremely provocative essay, which argues that growing old is not only a lifelong process, but a historical one as well. She challenges the historian and the humanist to synchronize the individual life experience with historical change. She concurs with Erikson in arguing that there is a symbiotic relationship between societal change and the biological rhythms of the individual. Therefore, to understand attitudes and behavior toward old age, or the attitudes and behavior of the old, one must explore individual development along with social change in an integrated approach that takes into consideration the entire life course, rather than in the horizontal examination of a specific age group.

In the final section—on the perception of age and death in literature and art—three literary scholars and an art historian reveal how a sensitivity to the aging process can enrich our understanding of the later works of artists and authors, as well as how literature and art can give us additional insights into the tragedy, the joys, and the fulfillment of old age. Leon Edel, the biographer noted for his definitive five-volume biography of Henry James, shows in his essay "Portrait of the Artist as an Old Man" that those last years that biographers usually dispatch with a chapter or a paragraph are often the richest in the material for understanding the whole life of a person, for it is at this stage that the "pain of growth, the anguish of aging have been surmounted; the radiance and suffering have ended in triumph and fulfillment, even if sometimes in penury and want." The biographer of the old person, Edel asserts, enjoys a privileged position in "clearer land, amid a finished forest," while the biographer of the young can only survey a "forest of saplings." He demonstrates this point through comparative portraits of two novelists and one poet, whose lives span the nineteenth and twentieth centuries. Leo Tolstoy, at the height of his fame and productivity, was plagued by despair, unable to accept old age, lacking faith in his art. It was a chronic crisis he was unable to resolve. Henry James, on the other hand, embraced old age with grace and achieved great maturity and a sense of completion. While Tolstoy questioned life and could not think of it in terms of disintegration and death, James accepted man's weaknesses and believed they might be transcended by cultivating the imagination. According to Edel, by giving supremacy to his imagination, James was a complete and finished artist while Tolstoy, who distrusted his imagination, only plunged himself back into chaos. James was able to accept life and its cruel dictates, and for him aging was yet another important part of life. "He died in full belief in his art." William Butler Yeats, the third person and the only poet in Edel's trio, represents an artist who fully blossomed and developed only in his old age; although "Yeats accepted aging, he also defied it and *used* it." He expanded his mind and intellectual capabilities by growing, emotionally and psychologically, in order to combat those infirmities and frailties associated with the aging of the physical being. The poetry of his later life far surpassed anything he had written in his younger years.

The biographer, as Edel demonstrates, might well pay more attention to the latter years of his subject. But autobiography, too, can give an important insight into the various experiences of human aging. Robert Sayre, a literary scholar who has studied the autobiographies of other people, chose instead to utilize the materials more closely and intimately at hand, a part of his own autobiography and comparative biographies of his parents' lives and old age. He combines these in a sensitive but revealing personal essay with insights that go beyond the individual stories. Sayre's father, who came from a lower-middle-class background, reached early national success and wealth and retained throughout his life an active interest in social work and in the lives of other people. His mother, on the other hand, from a more aristocratic background, was dependent throughout her life. Sayre analyzes with great perception the effect of the presence of an elderly person, his father's Aunt Adelaide, in the household. His father doted upon his aunt and enjoyed her company, while his mother bore the burden of looking after the elderly but vital and active woman. As Aunt Adelaide grew older, Sayre's mother became younger. She obviously thrived on the unspoken competition that developed between them. When Aunt Adelaide died, Mrs. Sayre no longer needed to keep up, and she, in effect, died as well, although her old age was extended through a physical nervous disorder and life in a nursing home. The conclusion, however, is more universal: the way in which one ages and dies must be a matter of, or a function of, how one lives.

On the other hand, Leslie Fieldler, a literary critic and scholar, takes a more traditional approach in examining the tension that Freud set up between Eros and Thanatos. He examines those myths in literature that permeate the tales about old men. For Fiedler, such mythical old men appear to represent the tension between carnal love and physical death that determines the basic rhythm of life. Thus, any depiction of their plight brings us to a renewed awareness of the central absurdity of being human, a theme that underlies both comedy and tragedy, and that "arises out of the conflict between the desire we cannot deny without denying the very wellspring of our existence, . . . and the fragility of the flesh upon which the satisfaction of that desire depends." He examines the whole range of the myth in stories and folklore, novels, and films such as *Lolita* and *The Blue Angel* and returns to Shakespeare, who grappled all his life "with the problem of 'crabbed age' in love with youth, and who in *The Tempest*, came as close as any man can to transcending the dilemma that relationship" poses. Shakespeare, from the beginning of his career, had confronted that dilemma in two primary mythical forms: "the love of an older man for an unattainable boy, and the strange unwillingness of fathers to release their nubile daughters to marriage and motherhood. . . . Only late in his life does Shakespeare become fully aware that . . . the continual father-daughter crises of his plays" rested chiefly on the father's inability to recognize in himself a fatal reluctance to relinquish his daughter to someone of her own age and generation. Fiedler concludes that the myths of father-daughter incest and pederasty are complementary, since the dream of embracing death in the form of a beardless boy and that of postponing it indefinitely in the arms of an ever-renewed bride both represent the refusal to grow old, or to accept man's fate.

While Sayre concludes that the way we live determines the way we accept old age, there is, it should be noted, a corollary: that is, the way man views death affects his view of aging and old age. This corollary is important to the twentieth century, especially in the Western world, since death is no longer constantly faced and distributed over the lifespan as in the past. The death of a child or a young person, for example, has become an unacceptable tragedy, not a part of life. To a large extent the fear of death, or the anxiety associated with it, is also a product of contemporary culture and is not universal. Even within the Christian tradition, there is a wide variety of attitudes toward death, as revealed by Philippe Ariès, the French social historian, in his book *Western Attitudes Towards Death.*[2] Among nineteenth-century poets, for example, we see a consistent concern about death and a variety of alternatives to the fear of death. Some poems depict death as a gentle or peaceful sleep, an awakening, or a liberation from the earth. Other poems romantically glorify death, while still others see death as a welcome relief from a life that may lack peace and contentment. Like others, Kastenbaum in his second scenario implies that if death were viewed as the ultimate celebration of life, then old age and death would be embraced as a period of growth, fulfillment, and culmination: "the completion of being."

In the final essay, Francis V. O'Connor, an art historian and critic, suggests three ways in which painting may be utilized—and through painting we may infer all art forms from sculpture to music and dance—for the sustenance of the elderly, for the study of aging and old age, and for the increase of knowledge within the discipline. He does this by a case study of the paintings of a ninety-six-year-old man, Albert Berne. O'Connor insists that the act of creativity, of being an artist, should be open to and encouraged in men and women of diverse backgrounds and levels of education so that they may participate "fully, freely, and creatively in human consciousness and in human society according to their capacities to attain and live with a personal sense of wholeness and identity with which to encounter their extinction" so that they may embrace death without dread. There are, of course, countless examples, from Winston Churchill and Grandma Moses to Albert Berne, of prominent men and women, educated and with means, who have taken up painting, in their old age. But Kenneth Koch in a recently published book, *I Never Told Anyone: Teaching Poetry Writing in a Nursing Home*, has demonstrated O'Connor's assertion that not only can men and women, from any background, and at any age, achieve great self-satisfaction and self-expression through artistic creation, but some can produce very good poetry.[3] O'Connor also suggests that there are insights to be found in the later paintings of older artists. Such paintings may be the "visual Rosetta stone by which we can begin to translate the hieroglyphs of the aging psyche." He explores, with the aid of his knowledge of art history and the psychology of symbolism, the symbols displayed in the paintings created during the final six months of Berne's life, during which he produced a painting every day. Finally, O'Connor's essay suggests that while art historians have noted the difference between the productions of the artist as a young man and those of the artist as an old man, no one has yet really studied this phenomenon. Therein lies a whole new field.

In fact, this volume merely suggests the richness that lies as yet untapped in the total experience of human aging, recorded throughout our cultural past and that of other civilizations. It suggests the insights that may be revealed through an interplay between the theories, knowledge, and methods of the social scientist on the one hand and the humanist's insights, knowledge, and attention to the individual and to values on the other.

It would be remiss of the editor not to acknowledge the hard work and continual support of the many people who made possible the exciting conference of 1975, of which this volume becomes a physical artifact. Richard Hedrich, Coordinator of the

Program of Science, Technology, and Human Values of the Office of Planning and Analysis of the National Endowment for the Humanities, was always available and helpful. He was an active and constructive observer during the first and second conferences of the project, which was supported by the National Endowment for the Humanities. Mary Jevnikar, secretary for the project, made herself invaluable, not only to the editor for typing of manuscripts and dealing with details of arrangements, but to all the participants, who came to depend upon her ebullient good spirits and willingness to aid with even the smallest problems. Judith Cetina, research assistant for the project, carefully checked all of the manuscripts and footnotes; however, without the superb editorial work of Katherine Soltis of Case Western Reserve University and Jane Barry of the University of Pennsylvania Press, this volume would not now be as clear or as consistent in style. If, in spite of all this aid, there are errors of fact, judgment, or organization, these are the sole responsibility of the editor.

Notes

1. Erik Erikson, *Identity and the Life Cycle* (New York: International University Press, 1950).

2. Philippe Ariès, *Western Attitudes Towards Death: From the Middle Ages to the Present,* trans. Patricia R. Ranum (Baltimore: Johns Hopkins Press, 1974).

3. Kenneth Koch, *I Never Told Anyone: Teaching Poetry Writing in a Nursing Home* (New York: Random House, 1976).

1 AGING AND DEATH IN CONTEMPORARY SOCIETY

MYTHS AND REALITIES

ROBERT KOHN

BIOMEDICAL ASPECTS OF AGING

A biological aging process is defined as a normal process, in that it occurs in all members of a population. It is progressive and irreversible, and progressive and irreversible processes are generally harmful. Humanists may not be interested in phenomena that occur in everyone, but may be more concerned with certain exceptional people who have been unusual over their entire lifespan. Humanists may not find it feasible, or even desirable, to generalize about aging.

Of all the biological aging processes, we are interested in discovering and understanding those that cause predictable and characteristic deterioration and dying-out of all members of a population, even those with the best nutrition, environment, life style, and genes, in spite of all efforts to keep them alive and healthy. The most useful approach is to start with the most general observation at the highest level of organization, and attempt to work through cause-and-effect sequences to the molecular and tissue levels, where the most basic processes are occurring. The most general observation is, of course, that a population is dying out.

One reads in the newspaper that the human lifespan is increasing because of the great progress we have made in the last century, and that people born in the years 2000 to 2020 will live to be 140 years old. That is just not true. The human lifespan is a fixed, biological phenomenon. The variations in different societies and different cultures through history have been confined to that proportion of the population that can live out the human lifespan. In the past, primarily because of infection, many deaths occurred very early, as is true in undeveloped countries today. As societies become more highly developed, and more progessive, the people stop dying young of infectious disease, and live to die at an older age from degenerative disease. The survival curves continue to get more rectangular: more people live to an older age and then die off more rapidly. This is what progress has meant in terms of health and vital statistics. In analyzing the causes of changes in the survival curves, we see that the changes are not primarily the result of anything that medicine does, but rather are a result of changes in the standard of living—especially in sanitation and nutrition. The percentage of people who live to be five years of age has risen enormously in the past seventy or eighty years. The percentage of seventy-year-old people who live to be seventy-five has changed very little. Throughout history, and in various societies today, once individuals have lived through the dangerous young years, once they get to be sixty-five, they are at an age where very little has changed. They are in the same position now as they always were, and in the same position in the United States as they are in the less developed countries.

Moreover, there are limits to progress. The Swedish female population is one of the healthiest in the world; Swedish women enjoy the best health that can be attained in any culture. But this pattern of health, of life expectancy, has not changed substantially in about twenty years. This is but one sign of the end of progress in public health and vital statistics. By 1955 the limits of progress had been reached in terms of vital statistics, and nothing is going to change until we understand why the aging population is dying. Those interested in the biology of aging want to know the processes occurring over the lifespan that cause this very rapid dying-out of the old population. Of course, to gain information on mechanisms of death, we have to look at the diseases. We can plot mortality data as the log of deaths per 100,000 people at each age, for all causes, and for each of the major diseases. When we plot deaths in the population by this method, we get a straight line for all causes. This relationship was discovered in 1832 by an English actuary, Gompertz, and is characteristic of an aging population. What it means is that the rate and probability of dying goes up exponentially with increasing age. In other words, it doubles at regular intervals. Now, for a human population, the rate and probability of dying doubles every eight and one-half years after maturity. We can look at curves for the various causes of death to see if they are parallel to the curve for all causes, indicating a very close relationship to or dependence on aging, or if they fall away from the all-causes curve, indicating that there is no dependence, or just a partial dependence, on aging.

There are some interesting concepts to be derived from these kinds of data; for instance, we can calculate what would happen if we had no cancer in our society. If we could cure cancer, the all-causes curve would shift, and the life expectancy at birth of the whole population would be increased by about two years. If we had no deaths due to atherosclerosis, which is the main killer, the all-causes curve would shift even further, and life expectancy at birth would be increased by seven or eight years. Consequently, if these major killers did not exist, we would have, perhaps, only a nine- or ten-year increase in life expectancy at birth. The population would then die off from all of the other diseases, but particularly from accidents and respiratory infections, such as influenza and pneumonia.

In terms of aging, there are two types of diseases. The first includes those diseases that are aging processes themselves, occurring in everybody, progressive and irreversible. Diseases of the blood vessels—for example, arteriosclerosis—fall into this group. The second category comprises those diseases that have more serious consequences as individuals age, the best examples of which are influenza and pneumonia. In these cases, a given amount of damage due to pneumonia will have a much more serious effect on an older person. This relationship between a standard injury and the probability of dying can be worked out for a number of systems, and we find that it is a linear relationship. As the population ages after maturity, the numbers that will die from standard injury increase linearly. There is a progressive inability of the body to react to stresses and insults.

While it is interesting that these diseases differ from each other in terms of what causes them or in terms of changes in the tissues, they seem to have a relationship with age that is very similar. This leads one to suspect that there may be one underlying aging process, or a very small number of these, occurring in the tissues, and that the diseases may be complications of these basic processes. We can test this if, for instance, we start with a large number of females at birth, follow them over their lives, and plot the number dying of each disease as a function of age. Arteriosclerotic heart disease deaths give a modal value of eighty-five or eighty-seven years. Hypertensive heart disease deaths show a modal value of about the same age. Accidents and pneumonia are very close, showing a modal value of eighty-eight or eighty-nine years. Cancer is somewhat different in causing deaths at earlier ages. We do not have to concern ourselves with cancer if we want to deal with the most important causes of death in the aging population, because aging and death occur even without cancer.

The data suggest that even though these diseases differ widely from each other, they have some common, underlying change going on in the tissues. Arteriosclerotic heart disease is basically an inflammatory process of the vessel walls. Hypertension, or long-standing high blood pressure, infections, and accidents are different kinds of diseases representing different kinds of changes in tissues; but while they appear to have different causes, they result in death at about the same age. This suggests that basic aging processes underlying the diseases should be looked upon as comprising a 100 percent fatal disease inherent in everyone. We will not be able to do much about these diseases occurring late in life until we understand the basic aging processes. This information also indicates that the human lifespan is an intrinsic biological property of the species, and should be considered to be about eighty-seven years for females; males are not as healthy, and their lifespan is shorter. There is some distribution around the average value—obviously some people live longer and others shorter periods of time—but this is what the lifespan will remain until basic aging processes are understood and something is done about them.

We want to know now what processes in the tissues are causing atherosclerosis or arteriosclerosis and also making the individual more susceptible to death from pneumonia or accidents. Of course, the logical place to look for factors causing decline in resistance is the physiological processes—the machinery of the body. Measurements made of a number of functions of the

body—kidney functions, lung functions, and heart function—
show that all these deteriorate with age. It is safe to say that
every bodily function that can be measured shows a linear decline
with age after approximately twenty or twenty-five years of age.
From that point on, everything the body does that we can measure
gets progressively more sluggish and less efficient. We can assume
that there is a threshold level of physiological efficiency, below
which it becomes incompatible with life. Individuals can lose
many functions, but when they drop below a certain level, they
are not able to cope with insults and injuries that occur over the
whole lifespan, such as accidents, infections, and traumas of
various kinds. We can see that as the population gets older,
individuals begin to reach this threshold, and therefore they are
going to be dying from trivial insults that they could well have
survived at an earlier age.

These are measurements of overall functions in live human
beings, surveys of a fairly small number of processes that are
occurring in the tissues. These processes include the ability of a
muscle to contract, the ability of the vessels to dilate or constrict,
and the passage of materials between cells and blood vessels. If
we measure these at the organ level, we find the same kinds of
change with age. An example is the measurement of the heart
function, the cardiac output, or the amount of work done per
heartbeat. Although the whole population shows a downward
trend with age, there is a range with a considerable scatter of
values at every age. It is probable that such factors as nutrition,
exercise, and the environment determine where within this range
an individual at a given age is going to be.

Marked changes occur in the major blood vessels with age.
The volume of the aorta increases until a person is about sixty,
and then it loses its elastic qualities. This occurs in everyone.
There is a pervasive stiffening of the blood vessels throughout
the body. A measurement of the volume increase in the human
aorta under constant pressure—a measure of its stiffness—shows
a decline with age. The human arteries take on the properties of
iron pipes at about the age of eighty-five. This is detrimental
because of the arteries' role in the functioning of the cardio-
vascular system: when the heart beats, the arteries dilate and
energy is stored in the dilated artery; when the heart relaxes,

the blood vessels squeeze down again and drive the blood out into the distal circulation. When arteries stiffen, the system will not function well.

The reason individuals die out with increasing ease as they get older is that all of their physiologic processes at the organ and tissue levels are becoming less efficient. There is a general rise in efficiency up to maturity, and then a linear drop-off of about 1 percent a year. Thus, between thirty and eighty, an individual loses about 50 percent of the function of the various organs and tissues. For instance, as the lungs get progressively stiffer so that they fail to contract, the gas diffusion in the lungs decreases about 8 percent per decade.

We want to know why people develop arteriosclerosis. We want to know why all the physiologic processes decline, and what basic processes in the tissues are responsible. These changes with age that I have been describing are gross: they can be easily observed. One might suppose that when people interested in the chemistry of these processes are planning their research, there is uniform agreement on what types of systems to study or what kinds of experiments to carry out. This has not been the case. Aging is a controversial field, and every possible cause of aging is studied seriously by somebody who has a research grant to work on it.

There are a few main categories of theories about aging. First, there is a theory that the cells in the body are dying out. We might wonder *a priori* if this makes sense. If the cells of the body were dying out, and that was all that was happening, once an individual lost half his cells, he would be half as big as when he started. It has never been clear why this should be particularly debilitating, unless one makes various complicated assumptions that not only are cells from one part of the body dying out, but someplace else the cells are not dying out. Because, however, they are dependent on the cells that do die out, they cease functioning. It is contrary to the scientific method to accept a theory that requires so many assumptions. But more importantly, researchers have been looking at organs and counting cells, and it is evident that cells do not die out. There has been a controversy about the relationship between the loss of brain cells and aging. Although the media may report that all adults lose 100,000 brain cells each day, this has not proved verifiable. The subject has been reviewed, and the conclusion is that while there is a significant loss in some individuals with certain diseases, the loss of brain cells, if it occurs at all in most people, is probably trivial, and probably caused by diseases of the blood vessels to the brain. There is no reason to believe that it is an intrinsic biological property of brain cells to die and disappear.

The next theory is that a defect develops in cells so that they lose their capacity to function—to produce enzymes, for example, or to divide—and therefore the organs that contain them become defective. Although a great many studies have been made, nowhere has evidence been found to prove that there is any intrinsic, progressive, irreversible change in the ability of cells to divide or to replenish themselves. There are no age-related changes in the ability of cells to synthesize intracellular components. No differences have been proved in the ability of cells to respond to hormones. Some differences have been reported, but they are probably reversible and secondary to changes going on elsewhere in the body, particularly those changes linked to the generalized debility that goes with aging.

It is most likely that when basic mechanisms fail, it is not because of the cells themselves, but because of materials outside the cells, the connective tissue proteins. The best-known of these substances is collagen, which we know as leather. Collagen makes up about 30 percent of the total body protein. If we add some of the other connective tissue protein, we have 40 percent or more of the total body protein. These proteins are important, first because of the amount of protein they comprise, and second because they are not replaced at many sites of the body. Once formed, most of them remain for the life of the individual and are susceptible to change. These are highly polymerized materials, and polymers, such as plastic, rubber, and paper, characteristically become brittle, cracked, and fragmented with increasing age. This is caused by a chemical cross-linking or bonding of various molecules within the substance. Proteins like collagen are crucial in determining the mechanical properties of tissues, in holding tissues together, and in maintaining form. If it were possible to dissolve everything in the body and leave just the collagen, a person would still be recognizable, although perhaps a bit paler.

Collagen surrounds every cell and capillary. One can regard an organ as a matrix of this connective tissue in which cells are imbedded. For instance, collagen is the major protein of the lung, and is very important in maintaining the lung's elastic properties. Collagen as it relates to age has been examined by a variety of techniques. After maturity, human collagen becomes increasingly stiffer until about the age of fifty. After this point the stiffening slows down until old age. It is possible, if yet unproven, that there is a true cause-effect relationship between connective tissue changes and aging. We can generally explain aging in terms of tissues and organs becoming stiffer and more rocklike because of changes in the connective tissue protein. These changes mean that the heart is not going to be able to pump as well, that the blood vessels are going to be stiffer, that there is going to be more resistance to blood flow in the organs, that the delivery of nutrients to cells is going to become progressively defective, and that physiological processes will thus become sluggish. Artery walls have poor blood supplies even in young people, and this worsens with age. The progressive sluggishness in supplying the nutrients to artery wall cells and removing wastes results in inflammatory processes that we can recognize as atherosclerosis. Hypertension is caused by the stiffening of the walls of the blood vessels because of the stiffening of the collagen. Thus, it is possible to explain most of what concerns us about aging on the basis of what we know is happening to connective tissue proteins like collagen. The study of collagen and related proteins should receive a high priority in aging research. It is central to the question of why people age biologically.

JUANITA M. KREPS

HUMAN VALUES, ECONOMIC VALUES,
AND THE ELDERLY

> Strongly competitive societies in which too much emphasis is given to an individual's worth in terms of productive work and achievement, in which inactivity is somewhat suspect and leisure is highly commercialized and therefore expensive are not congenial environments in which to grow old.[1]

Economists never meant to lay exclusive claim to the concept of value. Nor did we mean to imply that the price tag attached to a good or service reflected its worth, save in a momentary, market sense. We would argue only that goods and services, and ultimately people's productive efforts, have different values to different buyers, that at a given time and location these subjective appraisals come to be translated into market prices that facilitate exchange. The fact that a price reflects the market value of, say, a day's work makes it easy to identify the economic value of the worker himself. Thus, it is not unusual to hear a man's worth expressed in dollar terms.

Even among economists there is some question as to whether the price paid for human labor is a reliable index of economic worth, or whether, more often than not, earnings either understate or overstate the value of a worker's contribution to output. The axiom that "a man gets what he is worth and is worth what he gets" assumes that competition in the market forces the employer to pay the worker a wage equal to the value of what he produces, or else he will go to work for another employer. A lack of competition or alternative jobs removes the assurance of a productivity wage. Conversely, it is difficult to explain some extremely high earnings except by reference to monopolistic position. In any case, the argument that earnings reflect productive worth says nothing about the value of the individual beyond this economic framework.

Nevertheless, there is a strong tendency to equate human worth with earnings. It is this tendency that renders the elderly valueless to society. Indeed, by the current-productivity standard a retiree merely consumes the output of others just as a child does; both must depend on others for their support. The important difference between retiree and child, this line of reasoning continues, lies in their potential. Whereas investments in the young person will "pay off" because he will become a producer, spending for the older dependent yields no future return. Hence, it is easy to develop an economic rationale for heavy investments in the education of youth. But the cost of supporting the aged is not recouped, and there is some tendency to view these expenditures as poor investments.

Economic Versus Human Values

The increasing use of lifetime earnings mitigates this dichotomy between potential and ex-post earnings. But the basic flaw in the view that earnings and human worth are synonymous turns on the assumption that a person is of no consequence save for the work he does, that his economic value (whatever someone will pay him to work) is the full measure of the human being. On reflection, we readily admit that such an appraisal grossly understates the sum of the qualities that make up the individual. Yet the habit persists of labeling useless those persons not currently productive, and questioning the wisdom of giving the needs of the elderly any special priority when at best they can merely maintain themselves in a state of declining physical and mental capacity.

Humanists can turn this distorted view around, first by insisting that productivity is not an acceptable measure of human worth, and second by specifying an alternative scheme for valuing human beings. The first is not difficult; it requires only a soapbox and a loud voice. The second is a matter for research, and it is to this pursuit that we should direct attention. To point up the need for humanists to study aging, one has only to show what is happening to the societal view of the elderly in the absence of such input. In particular, consider some popular views of time and its utility, of the value of work and the importance of productivity; and consider the ways in which these views condemn the aged to the least respected role in society. Finally, it is important to review the extent to which the loss of roles is accompanied by reductions in income and living standards.

THE VALUE OF TIME   "In the world of common-sense experience, the only close rival of money as a pervasive and awkward scarcity is time," wrote Wilbert Moore more than a decade ago.[2] The rivalry continues. Although for some the scarcity of time has long outstripped the need for money, it is still true that a large proportion of the world's people would trade time for money but are unable to do so; that is, they would work more hours for pay because they value goods more than time free of work. Included in this group are the unemployed and the partially employed; youths who would combine work with school; older people who would combine work with retirement. Included also are many full-time workers whose taste for the consumption of goods is stronger than their desire for leisure time.

Economists have reasoned that the appeal of additional money for buying goods over extra time for enjoying leisure is generally greater the smaller the income and the larger the amount of time still available for work. As working time increases, an added hour of work becomes more burdensome, and each succeeding hour of leisure foregone becomes more valuable. From this concept of marginal utility (the satisfaction gained from the least unit of a good), it follows that the person with days and months and years of free time has a view of leisure that is quite different from that of the fifty-hour-a-week worker. In the latter case, an additional week or month of vacation is highly prized. But in the former, when nonworking time is plentiful, little worth may be attached to a given portion of that time. Work, on the other hand, may have utility precisely because it is scarce, notwithstanding Freud's assertion that "work is not highly prized by men."[3]

Retirees are often drowning in free time, whereas some reasonable balance of work and leisure through the lifespan would be far more satisfactory. But in addition to the problem of temporal allocation, there are questions as to what is considered the best use of time. The usual view of time—that is, that its value depends on how "productively" it is used—pervades our decisions throughout worklife, when the use of each hour is scrutinized. Consider the sale of consumer goods designed to reduce the time necessary for cooking, travel (even for pleasure), or personal and household maintenance. Other activities, such as visiting the sick and caring for children and very old people, are coming to be institutionalized in such a way that they constitute work for pay. In the absence of such organization, the elderly in particular are likely to be neglected, for there is implicit in our reluctance to provide them adequate care the belief that giving attention to other people's needs would be more useful. Are the productive years of the aged not over? And does the allocation of time to their needs not waste the time of productive workers?[4]

In emphasizing the value of time spent in production, we confer on the worker the useful role and by implication diminish the importance of the nonworker and consign him to a pointless existence. When one loses sight of Aristotle's reminder that "the goal of war is peace; of business, leisure," it is easy to suppose that life with little work has little purpose. Persons without work to do, we reason, lead dismal lives.

> Mr. Creech, it is said, wrote on the margin of the *Lucretius* which he was translating. "Mem.—When I have finished my book, I must kill myself." And he carried out his resolution. Life . . . is a dreary vista of monotonous toil, at the end of which there is nothing but death, natural if it so happens, but if not, voluntary, without even a preliminary interval of idleness. To live wtihout work is not supposed to enter into our conceptions.[5]

Idleness would not be conferred in such abundance at the end of worklife if it were more freely available in earlier years. By concentrating free time on the old and the young, we have lengthened the two roleless periods, which have many of the same characteristics: minimum incomes, excessive amounts of free time, lack of status. Meanwhile, those in their middle years are harassed by heavy work commitments. Work satisfaction during this stage of life is diminished by the length of the workyear, just as the joy of free time declines when it becomes endless.

THE VALUE OF WORK   Although man lacks enthusiasm for work, Freud points out, "No other technique for the conduct of life attaches the individual so firmly to reality as laying emphasis on work; for his work at least gives him a secure place in a portion of reality, in the human community."[6] Contemporary authors stress the negative aspects of work, however; since most people work from economic necessity, work brings no sense of achievement. It is the pecuniary reward, not the urge to undertake work for its own sake, that motivates man.[7] Nevertheless, in society's view work remains the measure of the man; "it provides *the* standard of judging his worth."[8]

But if work determines man's worth, what happens when work ceases? Can a man rely on the contribution he made during work-life to sustain his identity during retirement? Does he continue to be known as a fine craftsman or a brilliant teacher long after he ceases to practice his trade? Perhaps so. Yet there is a curious tendency to view with approval those older persons who continue to work, and to deplore those elderly who just "give up." The press is particularly fond of praising eighty- and ninety-year-olds who go to work every day. Taking part in recreational programs or travel arrangements—in general, enjoying free time—appears to have much less public approval, even if one has supposedly earned the leisure.

During working life, the constant drive to produce, to use time wisely, to increase one's position or income through extra work, pervades all we do. Playwright Walter Kerr notes that:

> We are all of us compelled to read for profit, party for contacts, lunch for contracts, bowl for unity, drive for mileage, gamble for charity, go out for the evening for the greater glory of the municipality, and stay home for the weekend to rebuild the house.[9]

As a result of the individual's work ethic, the impact of technology that could increase productivity, and thus allow people the luxury of greater freedom from toil, is largely subverted. Steffan Linder indicts modern societies for the inability to turn the fruits of growth to the advantage of the people: "We had always expected one of the beneficent results of economic affluence to be a tranquil and harmonious manner of life, a life in Arcadia. What has happened is the exact opposite. The pace is quickening and our lives in fact are becoming steadily more hectic."[10]

The individual's failure to gain satisfaction from the work he does has been under renewed scrutiny in recent years. Worker alienation has come to be viewed as one of the many social ills calling for research and policy development. The distasteful shape that work has assumed under the drive for automation and increased efficiency has led to complaints of monotony, lack of worker control over the pace or content of the job, worker's inability to find meaning in the restricted range of tasks assigned to him. Finer and finer divisions of labor, applauded by Adam Smith and perfected by two centuries of efficiency experts, have allegedly robbed work of any breadth and workers of any workmanship. In contrast to Veblen's "savage state," in which workmanship—that is, the instinct to work efficiently—was dominant, "Success gradually came to be stated in terms of predatory exploit, and labor became dishonorable."[11]

Evidence on the meaning of work to the individual, by occupation, skill and educational level, and length of time on the job, is sketchy. The degree of satisfaction ranges from extreme alienation, as reported in the recent Department of Health, Education and Welfare study, to instances in which workers who can control their hours work far more than the minimum number, even when their earnings are unaffected by the amount of time worked.[12] Depending largely on where a worker falls along this continuum, he may find retirement from the job a blessing or a curse.

Among manual workers, especially those with jobs requiring heavy physical activity, as well as white-collar employees who are bored with their repetitive tasks, freedom from work would seem to bring far greater satisfactions than work itself. The major concern of one large group of manual workers who retired early was found to be the maintenance of a reasonable level of income, not the availability of work activity.[13] Still, the satisfaction of these workers in their retirement phase has not had adequate study. It may well be that their capacities for nonwork pursuits are more limited than they imagine prior to retirement; certainly their incomes are likely to set constraints on what they can do.

For that group of workers who make up Wilensky's "long-hours" group—generally persons with higher earnings and more stable career patterns, most often professionals and executives—the value of work is obviously high, and retiring altogether would seem to be more difficult.[14] But, again, the obvious needs to be examined carefully. To what extent do these persons retire, as opposed to merely shifting from one type of work to another? And how much value do they put on free time, which has heretofore been scarce and expensive for them? If, as has often been suggested, persons who have difficulty with retirement are those who also had problems with work, the long-hours crowd should have an easy time with their new leisure.

A recent study by a French sociologist finds that an "undervaluation of leisure, which is not geared to the way of life experienced by the majority of the retired population, dominates the outlook of gerontologists and is accompanied by an overassessment of work and of family ties."[15] The work emphasis is dying out, the author argues. Retirement is freely chosen in two-thirds of the cases in the United States, and the drive to return to work is not strong.[16] In France, moreover, unions are now demanding a reduction in retirement age from sixty-five to sixty. The author concludes that these actions represent "a growing lust for active leisure in the third age."[17]

THE VALUE OF PEOPLE IN OLD AGE   In a recent interview, Jack Weinberg, a psychiatrist, declared:

> In our value system, we believe the elderly are nonproductive, unattractive, useless, garrulous, old-fashioned. . . . When we are young, we absorb these notions on a subconscious level and when we reach that age period we have a built-in system of self-deprecation, causing the elderly themselves to shun the notion of being old. Furthermore, the young in a society that's fashion-conscious, feel that the elderly are old-fashioned, and everything in our society that's old is to be discarded.[18]

The strength of these negative views is documented in the findings of a survey conducted for the National Council on the Aging.

Both the young and the old saw old age as a period of severe loneliness, characterized by poor health, inadequate income, and numerous hardships.[19]

Yet there were wide differences between this public view of old people and the elderly's perception of their personal well-being. Some of the discrepancies are striking: 51 percent of the public (including the older people surveyed) thought of the elderly as being in poor health, but only 21 percent of the people sixty-five and over found themselves with health problems; 60 percent of the public thought old people were lonely, in contrast to the 12 percent in that age category who actually felt lonely; 62 percent classified old people's incomes as too low to live on, but only 15 percent of the aged felt they themselves had this problem; half the respondents thought crime was a very serious problem for the elderly, whereas only 23 percent thought of themselves as threatened. In each instance older people shared the public view, but exempted themselves from the stereotype.[20] Having bought the conventional wisdom on the quality of life in old age, and then having found that once old they do not fit the preconception, the elderly appear to be able to set aside the negative image for themselves but unable to change their view of old age in general.

The expectation that the quality of life in old age will be bleak helps to explain the dislike for aging. But it is difficult to understand the persistence of a view that proves to be in error; the simple expedient of excusing oneself from the stereotype is too facile. There is surely some tendency for the older person to play down his age-related problems; to want to spare children and friends any additional burdens; to want to retain a feeling of independence and competence as long as possible. In short, we may refuse to acknowledge the onset of problems that would confirm us as elderly. One would prefer not to identify with his age group when his concept of what it is like to be old leads him to view that phase of life as totally unrewarding.

A realistic appraisal of their economic status would certainly document the public's view that a large proportion of the elderly "do not have enough money to live on." Among those aged sixty-five and over, the prevalence of poverty is twice as high as it is among the young. Median income for families headed by an older person is about half that of younger families, and among older single persons (most often women) incomes are lower than for any other group in society. It is important to review some of the data on their financial status in order to bring perspective to our view of the condition of the elderly. If indeed they are deprived of resources by reason of being old, this deprivation is perhaps the clearest evidence of the negative public view of old people. How important to the non-aged is the economic well-being of the elderly in our society?

Some Economic Facts and Fallacies

Although economists insist on classifying old people as dependents, this view is not always held by others. By economic reckoning, one who is currently not a producer is dependent on the output of others. He receives a transfer of income as a result of privately made arrangements, as in the case of an annuity he has purchased; or on the basis of need, as in the case of a payment for dependent children; or as a result of a state-insured contingency, such as unemployment compensation. The fact that the person receiving the transfer may have made earlier payments in support of the program means that he provided income for earlier dependents, but does not alter his present reliance on the productivity of other workers.

In the public view, dependence usually means something quite different. One is dependent if his transfers and savings are inadequate to support himself, and he must rely on public or private charity. The notion that Social Security benefits are a right that has been earned by past contributions further removes any aura of public dependency. Whether he is economically productive or not is less important than the degree to which he is self-supporting. On the other hand, when an older person lacks the means to live in his own quarters and manage with his own resources, he is likely to be categorized as dependent. In this broader view of the term, only the very old and the very poor among the elderly are dependent.

On close examination, then, most older persons are not degraded by a status of economic dependency; people who reach the age of sixty-five are increasingly able to maintain their separate households during most of the retirement period, and are thought to be independent while doing so. The economists' terminology, of which, fortunately, most people are unaware, would seem to have little influence on society's view of the aged.

The economics of the financial support of the elderly is important, nevertheless, for the level of that support is determined primarily by legislative choice rather than in the marketplace that fixes the incomes of most non-aged. Failure to observe the low levels at which a large proportion of the elderly live, and to understand the issues involved in intergenerational transfers of income, obscures the problem of maintaining adequate living standards for older people—which may well be the most important single problem they confront.

THE ECONOMIC STATUS OF THE ELDERLY   Most older Americans do not work for pay. In 1974 slightly more than one in five men and one in twelve women aged sixty-five and over continued in the labor force. The jobs held were often part-time, in agriculture, or in self-employment. The fact that only a small proportion of the aged have earnings makes it necessary for the elderly as a group to rely primarily on Social Security benefits, private pension incomes, and their own savings through what is now a substantial retirement period: an average life expectancy at age sixty-five of 13.1 years for males and 17.2 years for females.

The income levels in older families are low, and poverty is the lot of a large proportion of the group. Median incomes for 1973, by age and sex of family head, along with the percentages of each group in poverty (according to the Social Security system's widely used index), are given in table 1.[21]

As the comparison shows, older persons have about half the incomes of the young and are far more frequently below the poverty threshold. Older single women are particularly prone to suffer extreme economic deprivation; one-third live on incomes that do not permit even a poverty-level existence. There are hardships for the middle-income aged as well. Only about half the aged couples, who tend to be somewhat younger and better off financially than single persons, could afford the "modest but adequate" standard of living described by the Bureau of Labor

TABLE 1. *Median incomes for 1973*

			Percent Poor	
	14+	65+	14+	65+
All families	$12,051	$6,426	8.8	10.5
Male head	12,965	6,458	5.5	9.4
Female head	5,797	6,149	32.2	16.8
Unrelated individuals	4,134	2,725	25.6	31.9
Male	5,657	3,087	19.8	27.1
Female	3,300	2,642	29.7	33.4

Statistics in 1973. The consumption patterns of the lower half of the aged income recipients parallel somewhat those of other low-income groups—a higher proportion of their income is spent for food and shelter than is the case for families with more comfortable levels of resources. In the case of the aged, medical costs are also high; per capita costs are almost four times the amount spent by younger persons. Public programs pay about 60 percent of the health-care costs of the elderly.

Clearly, the living standards of at least half the nation's older people are quite low. The extent to which the elderly perceive themselves as poor or nearly so is not clear, however, nor has research shown the precise differences between the living levels of old people and the living levels they observed when they were younger. Most of the present elderly, who suffered through the depression and worked in an earlier, less productive era, have had low incomes throughout their lives. The drop in money income at the time of retirement (particularly for the very old) may have been less severe than will be the case in the future. Nevertheless, the incomes of the bulk of the aged are far too low to allow any optimism as to the economic quality of life in that stage.

The persistence of these low incomes suggests that society does not find the financial needs of old people of primary importance. Other societal goals assume higher priorities, and expenditure patterns follow from the priorities established either in the marketplace (which, being highly competitive, calls for younger and more recently trained persons to replace the older workers) or in the legislatures. Since most of the retirees' income depends on congressional action, it is well to review the rationale for public policy as it affects that income, and to ask what this rationale reveals with respect to society's view of old people.

THE FUNDING OF PUBLIC TRANSFERS   Current tension over the economic status of the aged is now being highlighted by the media's expressed fear that birth rate declines will mean that the Social Security fund will eventually go broke. As the ratio of taxable wage earners to retirees declines, the taxes necessary to support retirees will grow ever more burdensome for the smaller number of workers, reducing their capacity to support themselves and their children. A reduced number of births and later a reduced labor force, the press has argued, mean that the funds for retirement benefits may have to be reduced or taxes raised, or both.[22]

The concern over future tax receipts is not an idle one. The total population of the United States has grown steadily since the passage of Social Security legislation in 1935, and the number of persons of working age has continued to provide a growing base for tax collections with which to support retirees. In addition to larger numbers of wage earners, the rate of economic growth has lifted hourly rates of pay and made it possible for both benefit levels and the range of persons receiving benefits to improve through time. It was this growth that led Paul Samuelson to speak of a "Social Security paradox"—that is, everybody got back more than he put into the retirement insurance system.

A significant slowing of the rate of population growth ultimately results, of course, in fewer persons entering the work force. In contrast to a population growth rate of 1.7 percent during the two decades following World War II, the 1965–72 rate was 1.0 percent, and the current rate is 0.7 percent. This decline in growth means that the school-age population has stopped growing; it is not expected to be any higher in 1990 than at present. But the number of working-age persons will continue to grow rapidly: from 115 million to 141 million in the fifteen-year period. Those persons born in the period of the baby boom are now swelling the labor force, and not until the last decade of the century will there be a leveling-off in the size of the working-age group. Persons aged sixty-five and over will continue to be the fastest-growing segment of the population during the next two decades. If the fertility rate were to hit 2.11, the average needed for maintaining a stable population, the proportions of the population in various age groups for selected years would be those given in table 2.

Shifts in age structure accompanying the cessation of population growth do generate certain possible adverse effects.[23] Perhaps the most important of these, as Spengler has noted, is the threat of unemployment, which, if severe or prolonged, can reduce seriously the economy's capacity to provide support for retirees as well as workers. Payroll tax receipts, the source of revenue for Social Security benefits, depend on taxable earnings. The excess of total benefits paid over payroll taxes in 1975 resulted in part from the high level of unemployment and the consequent loss of taxable wages. Deficits in tax receipts due to an increase in the ratio of beneficiaries to workers, although frequently cited as the explanation for the Social Security system's imbalance, will, in fact, not be a threat before the end of the century.

The fear that the Social Security fund will go broke reveals a failure to understand some basic features of the system. In essence, it operates on a pay-as-you-go principle, with annual tax receipts roughly equaling benefits paid out. A small fund accumulated prior to the maturation of the system, when the taxes that were being collected exceeded the relatively low aggregate benefits being paid. The ability to raise payroll (or other) taxes means that benefits can be at whatever level Congress chooses, subject only to the collection of the necessary funds.

When the population of working age declines relative to the numbers in retirement, tax rates on earnings must be raised in

TABLE 2. *Percentage of the population in various age groups*

	Population (percentage)			
	1974	1980	1990	2000
School age (0–19)	36	32	31	30
Working age	54	57	58	58
24–44	34	37	39	36
45–64	20	20	19	22
Retirement age (65+)	10	11	12	12

order to fund a given level of benefits. The effect of this change in the ratio of workers to retirees can be offset by extending worklife, or offsets may occur in the form of fewer dependent children, or higher earnings per worker. If the retirement age were to drop further (or real benefits were to be raised), however, the problem of financing these benefits could become quite critical, particularly as we reach zero population growth. Clark has estimated that the 1970 payroll tax rate will have to be increased by 50 percent by the year 2050, when stable population is reached, assuming that retirement age and age of entry to work remain constant. Noting that retirement age has been declining in recent decades, however, he speculates on the effect of a continuation of this trend. If the age of exit from work has fallen to sixty by 2050, for example, a more than threefold increase in taxes would be necessary. To the extent that age of entry is rising, the tax rate would need to be even higher.

Improving the replacement ratio (the proportion of earnings provided by benefits) above the present average of about 40 percent would also raise taxes. To raise the ratio by half—to 60 percent—would, of course, mean a 50 percent increase in tax receipts.[24] Alternatively, the higher cost of Social Security could be borne by postponing retirement at full benefits to, say, age sixty-eight. The decrease in costs would be significant even if the age were moved only to sixty-six. As Morgan has pointed out, extending worklife by one year has a triple effect: it reduces the number of years of payout, increases the taxes paid in, and increases the interest accumulation.[25]

Economic Constraints and Human Values

Raising the income levels of the elderly is not easily accomplished. Both institutional and resource constraints restrict the rate at which improvements can be made, even if the goal of higher standards of living in old age is agreed to and given some priority over other social goals.

Resources and the state of the technology set the parameters within which total output can be expanded in a given amount of time, say a year. Over a longer time, greatly improved techniques and new resources can be developed, provided sufficient capital is directed to future, rather than present, consumption. Capital shortages limit the rate of economic growth, as do shortages of natural resources. In addition, growth may be deliberately restrained in order to prevent further destruction of the environment or an upward pressure on prices. In setting societal goals, the necessary tradeoffs between growth and other objectives have to be taken into account.

Restraints on growth in output, for example, will impede the movement of families out of poverty. In the past two decades, growth has been largely responsible for this upward movement; very little redistribution of income has occurred. Choosing to honor legitimate environmental concerns, therefore, by setting lower growth targets, makes it imperative to find other solutions to the low-income problem, nationally and internationally. The only alternative we know is income redistribution. Other economic tradeoffs appear to be necessary: how much unemployment can be tolerated in order to deflate prices? When are public goods preferable to private goods? Is economic security a deterrent to productive incentive?

Institutional arrangements sometimes pose further barriers. Customary arrangements for work dictate the limits of one's contribution at some times and prevent any work at all in other life stages. Expectations of low levels of performance elicit those levels, even when adequate incentives might greatly improve output. Conventional notions as to which work is appropriate for youth, which for older people, which for minorities, have retarded job mobility and productivity.

Some of these constraints, mainly the institutional ones, can be removed as societal views shift. Some of the economic restrictions are relaxed through time, as well: the technology improves, capital can grow, and so forth. But at any stage in an economy's development, significant improvements in one sector are likely to be made only at the expense of other social objectives. Thus, it may be necessary to agree, for example, that certain living levels are intolerable and will be improved even at the expense of lowering other incomes. The range within which society evens out incomes depends ultimately on such factors as its taste for equity, the role imputed to income incentives, and reverence for tradition as opposed to thirst for change.

In the case of improving the economic well-being of the elderly, the sums of money called for are large, and they must come from tax collections, which redistribute income from one generation to another. Viewed differently, the tax mechanism can be used to apportion income more evenly through one's lifespan and also to reallocate money in favor of lower-income persons, including the elderly. Individual support for this form of income leveling varies, depending primarily, perhaps, on whether one is young or old, rich or poor. In the final analysis, the allocative decision is value-laden, for it demonstrates the society's willingness to commit scarce resources to the elderly. How much the society commits relative to what it has is a good indication of how that society views the aged—how important their needs are in relation to the needs of other age groups.

Low incomes of any group in a society can result from a lack of material resources that would permit an improvement in economic well-being. When one particular group suffers a significantly greater degree of deprivation, however, the question of resource allocation is immediately raised. Distributive arrangements may reflect an implicit decision as to the desired level of equality, or a perceived need for income differentials in order to stimulate productivity, or some compromise between what is thought to be equitable and what is thought to be efficient. A distributive system that provides greater rewards to workers than to retirees is not surprising in a free market economy; indeed, the existence of income differentials is considered a requisite for the market's operation. There is no rule that specifies how great the differences should be, however. Nor, in the case of the aged is there any rationale for lower transfers as a means of encouraging people to work. On the contrary, the pressure has been applied to induce the elderly not to work. The only justification for not raising the volume of transfers from the young and the middle aged to older people is the belief that the current distribution is fair, given the material needs of the different age groups. The question of what is fair or just lies outside the economist's realm, but not beyond those branches of knowledge spanned by the humanities.

Notes

1. United Nations, *The Aging: Trends and Policies* (New York: United Nations Department of Economic and Social Affairs, 1975), p. 11.

2. Wilbert Moore, *Man, Time, and Society* (New York: 1967), p. 4. He noted further that "loyalty or affection, too, turns out to be a universal scarcity on close examination."

3. Sigmund Freud, *Civilization and Its Discontents* (New York: W. W. Norton, 1962), p. 27.

4. See the author's "Modern Man and His Instinct of Workmanship," *American Journal of Psychiatry* 130 (1973) : 179–83.

5. Leslie Stephen, "Vacations," quoted in *Cornhill Magazine* 20 (1869), and in Eric A. Larrabee and Rolf Meyersohn, *Mass Leisure* (Glencoe, Ill.: Free Press, 1958), pp. 281–90.

6. Freud, *Civilization and Its Discontents,* p. 27.

7. B. B. Seligman, "On Work, Alienation, and Leisure," *American Journal of Economic Sociology* 24 (1965) : 337–60.

8. Ibid., p. 338.

9. Walter Kerr, *The Decline of Pleasure* (New York: Simon and Schuster, 1962), p. 39.

10. Steffan B. Linder, *The Harried Leisure Class* (New York: Columbia University Press, 1970), p. 1.

11. A. K. Davis, "Veblen on the Decline of the Protestant Ethic," *Social Forces* 22 (1944) : 284.

12. U.S. Department of Health, Education, and Welfare, *Work in America* (Washington, D.C.: U.S. Government Printing Office, 1972).

13. Richard Barfield and James Morgan, *Early Retirement* (Ann Arbor: University of Michigan Press, 1969).

14. Harold L. Wilensky, "The Uneven Distribution of Leisure," *Social Problems* 9 (1961) : 32–56.

15. Joffre Dumazedier, *Sociology of Leisure* (New York: Elsevier, 1974), p. 93.

16. For these figures, Dumazedier quotes Ethel Shanas et al., *Old People in Three Industrial Societies* (New York: Atherton Press, 1968). A recent Harris poll found approximately the same percentage of retirements to be involuntary. A slightly smaller proportion wanted to be back at work.

17. Dumazedier, *Sociology of Leisure,* p. 104.

18. Quoted in *Memo from the National Institute of Senior Centers* (Washington: National Council on the Aging, June/July 1975), p. 3.

19. *The Myth and Reality of Aging in America* (Washington: National Council on the Aging, 1975).

20. Ibid.

21. Herman B. Brotman, *Fact Sheet on the Older American Woman* (1975), p. 2.

22. This issue, summarized here, is discussed more fully in a series of papers prepared by Juanita M. Kreps, Joseph J. Spengler, R. Stanley Herren, and Robert Clark for a report to the National Science Foundation on *The Economics of a Stationary Population: Implications for the Elderly* (Washington, D.C.: National Science Foundation, 1975).

23. Spengler, "Stationary Population and Changes in Age Structure: Implications for the Economic Security of the Aged," Ibid., pp. 11–39.

24. Clark, "Age Structure Changes and Intergenerational Transfers of Income," Ibid., pp. 65–76.

25. James Morgan, "Welfare Economic Aspects of Prolongation of Life," abstract of a paper delivered at the Tenth International Congress of Gerontology, June 1975.

ERIK H. ERIKSON

REFLECTIONS ON DR. BORG'S LIFE CYCLE

I. *Wild Strawberries*

1. THE PROLOGUE   Ingmar Bergman's motion picture *Wild Strawberries* depicts an old Swedish doctor's journey by car from his place of retirement to the city of Lund. There, in the ancient cathedral, Dr. Isak Borg is to receive the highest honor of his profession, a Jubilee Doctorate marking fifty years of meritorious service. But this journey by car on marked roads through familiar territory also becomes a symbolic pilgrimage into his childhood and into his unknown self. For the doctor has had strange dreams lately. "It is as if I'm trying to say something to myself which I don't want to hear when I'm awake"—so he says during the course of the day to his daughter-in-law, Marianne, his companion on the drive, who (for reasons of her own) confronts him in their conversation with disturbing, but ultimately liberating, truths about himself and about the Borgs generally. At the end of the day, the ceremonial honor bestowed on him seems almost unreal or, at any rate, transcended by a certain simple depth of wisdom that he has gained—and by a decision through which he and his immediate family become firmly and subtly united.

I shall use Bergman's screenplay for a presentation of my concept of the life cycle and of the generational cycle, both of which I find illuminated in it. The opening scene presents a memoir which begins with the end—that is, it demonstrates how a significant moment in old age can reach through a man's unresolved adulthood to the dim beginnings of his awareness as a child.

Although I use the screenplay as a basis, I will retell it in my own words. This is already the first step in interpretation. It also allows me to select quotations from Bergman's text and to describe his imagery, both of which are apt to get lost in the cumbersome experience of non-Swedish audiences, who must read the captions and ignore the foreign dialogue as they attempt to view the picture in all its detail.

The prologue of the screenplay shows a scene depicting the old doctor jotting down the events and the reflections of that memorable day. Sitting at his massive desk, on which we see family pictures and writing utensils in faultless array, the white-haired, slightly stooped but solid old man with square, handsome, aged face introduces himself as Dr. Isak Borg, aged seventy-six, a Swede, and, of course, a Lutheran (for "a mighty fortress," in Swedish, is "an vaeldig borg"). He has outlived nine brothers and sisters and has been widowed for many years. He is the father of one married but childless son, also a doctor, who, in fact, lives and teaches at Lund. Borg says of himself in a voice both pedantic and querulous, as if somebody had accused him of something:

> "At the age of seventy-six, I feel that I'm much too old to lie to myself. But of course I can't be too sure. My complacent attitude toward my own truthfulness could be dishonesty in disguise, although I don't quite know what I might want to hide. Nevertheless, if for some reason I would have to evaluate myself, I am sure that I would do so without shame or concern for my reputation. But if I should be asked to express an opinion about someone else, I would be considerably more cautious. There is the greatest danger in passing such judgment. In all probability one is guilty of errors, exaggerations, even tremendous lies. Rather than commit such follies, I remain silent.

> As a result, I have of my own free will withdrawn almost completely from society, because one's relationship with other people consists mainly of discussing and evaluating one's neighbor's conduct. Therefore I have found myself rather alone in my old age. This is not a regret but a statement of fact. All I ask of life is to be left alone and to have the opportunity to devote myself to the few things which continue to interest me, however, superficial they may be."[1]

Incidentally, at the doctor's feet as he writes at his desk is a Great Dane bitch, to all generous appearances a recent mother.

Knowing Bergman, we realize this must be symbolic of a forth-coming major theme. In the meantime, we note in Borg's opening statement a strange half-awareness that he can maintain a certain strained integrity only by withdrawing ("of my own free will") from sociability and attending to his own restricted sphere of interests. It is fascinating how, from the beginning, Bergman the director reveals in visual and auditory hints a "classical" case of compulsive character: here, it is the old man's defensive voice and his punctilious manners that indicate the enormous amount of self-restriction he has paid for that autonomy of proud with-drawal. It is, indeed, as if in the future journey we were to be led from the compulsive "rituals" of a lonely old man, through every-day ritualizations of his culture, to a grand ritual which both seals and permits a transcendence of his overdefined professional existence.

2. MY TASK   Before I continue to record Bergman's record of Dr. Borg's self-reflections, and reflect on them, let me acknowl-edge a few unsolvable aspects of my task—and explain why I persist in it. The occasional and cryptic use of psychoanalytic jargon by Bergman's characters both acknowledges and awards off his obvious knowledge of depth psychology, Jungian and Freudian. In the foreward to the screenplays, he in fact refers to a textbook on the psychology of personality by Eino Kaila, which he says was a tremendous experience for him: "His thesis that man lives strictly according to his needs—negative and positive—was shattering to me, but terribly true. And I built on this ground."[2] It is not my intention, however, to search the reflections that have been recorded by his "hero" regarding him-self and others, encountered or remembered, for indices of what may have been conscious or unconscious to whom. As Bergman said, he "built on this ground," and a master's building has its own laws of construction and beauty. It is his art alone that per-mits him to present people of different ages in acute life crisis. These episodes typify the whole course of their lives so vividly that the viewers are sure we have "met" them, both on the screen and in ourselves. That these persons are also linked with each other in an intricate network of archetypal symbolism is intrinsic in the artist's medium. One can, of course, elect to show in all detail the

superb use of that medium and to show, say, how the director uses an intricate composition of facial expressions and postures, of landscapes and seaviews, of roads, streets, and buildings in line with a symbolism that makes the journey at the same time a pantheistic reunification with nature, a Christian pilgrimage to salvation, and, indeed, a modern self-analysis.[3] Or one could show, as I shall indicate, that what is pictured here is imbued, as well, with the inner logic of Freud's discoveries of the repressed unconscious, a logic equally indispensable for the foundation of such work. But the building itself is held together (maybe more than any other Bergman play) by a pervasive realism, a tender earthiness in all its characters, and a sometimes ironical appreciation of their existence at their age in that spot on earth in that period of cultural and historical determination. It is this that makes them prototypical for human beings in other times and places and thus existential in the most concrete sense of the word.

The psychoanalytic symbols are not indicative of the repressed unconscious, except in well-defined moments, but rather denote a potential knowledge of the dimensions of existence that dwell in our preconscious. We can gain insight into the preconscious in special moments, whether these are brought about by the "natural" crises of life, or by confrontation with a significant person, or, indeed, by fitting ceremonies. As we shall see, all three conditions coalesce in Dr. Borg's journey: old age, confrontation, ceremony. The result is one of transcendent simplicity rather than mystical rapture or intellectual reconstruction. Only the rarest rituals convey this kind of truth, but works of art are bridges to them. In this screenplay I found a representation of the wholeness of the human life cycle—stage by stage and generation by generation.

After a summary of each major scene below, I offer my terms for the psychosocial stages and crises encountered, capitalizing them to emphasize the scheme that will be systematically presented in the second part of this paper.

3. THE DREAM Over the years, my students nicknamed my course on the human life cycle "From Womb to Tomb," or "From Bust to Dust." It was to me, therefore, of some ironic significance that this screenplay opens with a view, as it were,

from tomb to womb, or more accurately, from coffin to cradle. It begins with a dream in which the doctor encounters his own corpse. This dream is the psychic background for the day's events; we will learn only later what—beside the dreamer's age—were the dream's own "causes."

In the dream memoir we see Borg briskly pursuing his "usual morning stroll" through some familiar but now, indeed, empty streets, their facades shining in the northern summer's morning light. The "silence was absolute," and his footsteps echoed rhythmically. Over a store, apparently shared by a watchmaker and an optometrist, hung a large clock by which he usually set his own watch for the exact time. Now it had no hands; and two large eyes-with-eyeglasses that hung beneath it appeared to have been bloodied. The doctor pulled out his own watch: it, too, was without hands, and when he held it to his ear, he heard his heart beat wildly. But, ah, there *was* somebody standing there in all the emptiness: a man with a felt hat, his back to Borg. On being eagerly touched, the man turned. He had "no face," and promptly collapsed. On the sidewalk there lay only a heap of clothes with liquid oozing out of them: the person was gone.

Up the empty street now came the sound of trotting hoofs as church bells began to toll. An ornate hearse appeared. As it passed, one of the wheels got stuck on a lamp post, broke off, and struck a church wall right behind the doctor. The hearse began to sway, somewhat like a cradle, with an eerie creaking sound reminiscent of a tortured birth cry. A coffin, splintered, lay on the ground, and from it a corpse reached for the doctor. It had, in fact, the doctor's face, "smiling scornfully." The dreamer awakened.

Let us see: footsteps that echo; bells that toll; a clock that ticks but does not tell time; a heart that thumps and pounds. Thus enumerated, the symbolism might seem trite. But there is the overall imagery and, of course, a sequence of convincing closeups of the old man's facial expression, ranging from outright fear to the daily dread known to all old people: when will it all suddenly stop? Then there is an inkling of a personal, a neurotic, anxiety revealed only in the imagery. The text says that the other man's, the double's, face was "empty." Yet, his appearance shows thin lips tightly drawn down and eyelids pressed hard together: tight-sphinctered, then, and caricaturing a retentive personality—holding in and keeping out. That other person, that double, collapses and spills his lifeblood in the gutter—a theme to be repeated that day in a number of wasteful and destructive "spillings."

Awakened, the dreamer, as if to ban a curse with a formula, pronounces: "My name is Isak Borg. I am still alive. I am seventy-six years old. I really feel quite well." The viewer's first impression is that the dream tries to tell the dreamer—is it "merely" because of his advancing age, or in view of the approaching "crowning" event in his life, or for some other reason?—that he must not permit his official and isolated self to beckon him into the grave. Perhaps he must still learn how to die.

At this point, I will introduce some capitalized terms for the last crisis of the Life Cycle. In my publications on the subject, I have postulated a dialectical struggle in old age between a search for Integrity and a sense of Despair and Disgust, all three, in dynamic balance, essential to a final human strength: Wisdom.[4] These terms should denote to the reader some of the qualities of Borg's inner, as well as social, discord and suggest that such qualities can be present, in some form, in any old person. If I also assume that these qualities have precursors in earlier crises throughout the life cycle, "crisis" at any age does not necessarily connote a threat of catastrophe but rather a turning point, a crucial period of increased vulnerability and heightened potential. "Cycle," in turn, conveys the double tendency of individual life to "round itself out" as a coherent experience and to form a link in the chain of generations, from which it receives, and to which it contributes, both strength and discord.

It will take Dr. Borg's whole journey (and this whole paper) to come to a closer formulation of the old-age crisis in the light of the entire course of life.

4. THE DECISION. It is three o'clock in the morning, a Swedish summer dawn, when Borg knows what he must do: he will go to Lund by car rather than, as planned, by airplane. We learn only gradually that this is, indeed, a fateful decision, for the fourteen hours required for the trip also allow for a number of half-planned, half-improvised events. But we know immediately that such

autonomy itself is utterly surprising, for in a scene both humorous and pathetic, it becomes clear that the widower lives in some antagonistic interdependence with a bosomy and possessive housekeeper named Agda. She has been with the family for forty years. She is his age, but (typically?) he refers to her as "an old woman." Awakened by Borg (his nightclothes in disarray), she can only ask, "Are you sick, Professor?" Hearing his decision, she is upset and hurt: he is destroying, she says, the most solemn day of *her* life. Whereupon he mumbles that they are not married, and she praises God for it. But she gets up, dramatically packs his clothes, and sulkily serves breakfast, anticipating with disgust that she must fly ahead alone to get things ready in Lund.

Then a houseguest appears, awakened by the old couple's bickering. She is a beautiful, clear-eyed, strong-faced young woman in a dressing gown: Marianne, his son, Evald's, wife. She has been visiting and asks whether she can accompany the doctor to Lund. Thus, truly, the scene is set for the most significant of a number of masterly encounters. For as they leave the big city and drive into the countryside, Bergman fully utilizes the alternative possibilities of the perspectives provided by the automobile. We first see the car from the air, moving with other tiny vehicles on a big traffic circle, choosing their destined exit. Then, focusing on the car's interior, we see the rest of the world move by. Both driver and passenger can look ahead at near and distant goals or inward into the sequence of their thoughts; they can steal sideward glances away from each other, or look at each other with rare, and necessarily fleeting, visual engagements. Whoever is driving can glance at the rearview mirror and see what is approaching, or perceive the faces of whoever may be in the back seat. This moving stage also permits dozing off—and dreaming! Thus, Bergman civilizes the mechanical range of the car's interior for his own storytelling purposes. Let me list the scenes that follow and then characterize some in my terms.

First, as Borg drives along dreamily (maybe thinking of his dream), he is obviously uncomfortable in the young woman's presence. Marianne, with a determination born of a yet unrevealed circumstance, decides to confront him with his discomfort: one can not help thinking of Cordelia driving Lear's despair to the surface. It all begins—as it will later end—with trivial items that betray basic attitudes. She, nervous, wants to smoke; he stops her nastily. She says the weather is nice; he predicts a storm. Suddenly, she asks him his "real" age for no "real" reason. But under the impact of his dream, he knows that she, too, wonders when he will die. Prosaically, he thinks of the money her husband owes him, pleads principle: "a bargain is a bargain." Evald certainly understands this, for they are "alike," as she, indeed, admits they are. Then the bombshell: "But he also hates you," she says. An indescribable horror appears on his face, but he keeps calm. She explains that although she has now stayed with him a month with the "idiotic idea" that he might help Evald and her, he has adamantly refused to hear about their marital trouble, suggesting that maybe she needs a quack, or a minister. He is half-amused, half-shocked to hear some of the uglier things he has said. She concludes that she does not dislike him, but "I feel sorry for you." But they both maintain the amenities—even some amusement.

The issue is joined. And the interplay (one could speak of the interlocking) between his dream and her behavior leads to surprising acts on his part. First, he, of all people, wants to tell her his dream. She is not interested. But soon there is a chance to involve her in his life: arriving at a side road, he swings the car into it, to lead her down to a house by the sea where he spent much of his childhood and youth. At this point I would like to share one of those "clinical" impressions which seem to explain why the old man and the young woman, at that time, experience one another as living in an increasingly tense polarity. If it is true (the text does not confirm it) that in Borg's dream the noise made by the broken-down hearse, swaying like a cradle, eerily reflects the crying of a newborn, then the old doctor's medical intuition may have told him that the reason for proud Marianne's seeking help from him is that she is pregnant, and that his reaction to pregnancy is, to say the least, ambivalent (see the Great Dane bitch). If this is so, the issue that is joined is Marianne's concern over harboring a new Borg and the old man's awareness that he who is close to death must yet learn to affirm life. This assumption is necessary to recognize Marianne's (and, as we shall see, her husband's) aggravated life crisis as being what I have called the psychosocial crisis of Generativity versus Stagnation.[5] For each such crisis I have postulated an emergent "virtue" that is a vital strength necessary for the life cycle as well as for the cycle of generations. Care is the strength of this second stage of adulthood. For now, acute fate, as well as life lived so far, decides whom and what one is committed to take care of in order to ensure the next generation's life and strength. But for the destructive counterpart to Care, I would nominate Rejectivity, and I suggest that it is this rejective trend which Marianne recognizes as a well-rationalized developmental defect in Dr. Borg—and a generational one in the Borgs. Marianne evinces a strong ethical determination that the future must be saved from what is dead in the Borgs' past. Similarly, Borg's old-age struggle against despair helps him comprehend that what he has become must not be all that he is and must not be all that he leaves behind. To paraphrase William James, he must find behind his relatively peaceful and yet disdainful isolation not only his "murdered self" but also his murderous one, so he may find his living and life-giving self.

5. THE STRAWBERRY PATCH   They are driving down the side road to a point where they can see the old summer house. The facade of the house first looks like the tightly closed face of the dream's alter ego: it "slept behind closed doors and drawn blinds." Marianne, in fact, calls it "a ridiculous old house" and decides to take a dip in the sea, leaving Borg to his reveries. In a dreamlike fashion, he knows where to go: to the strawberry patch. He sits down in the grass and slowly eats some strawberries "one by one," almost ritually, as if they had a consciousness-expanding power. And, indeed, he now hears somebody playing a piano, and suddenly the house appears transformed. The facade comes alive—"the sun glittered on the open windows"—and the place seems to be "bursting with life," although no one is in sight as yet.

Then, he sees his "first love," his cousin Sara, as she had been (nearly sixty years ago), a blond, "light-hearted young woman," kneeling in the patch in a "sunyellow cotton dress." She is gathering strawberries in a small basket. He calls; she does not hear. Then his elder brother, Sigfrid, appears in a college student's white cap, self-assured to the point of sassiness. He wants to make love to her, and over her weakening protests that she is engaged to Isak, he embraces her with a passionate kiss, which she returns. Then she falls weeping to the ground; the strawberries are spilled, and a red spot appears on her dress: he has, she cries, turned her into a "bad woman, at least nearly." She is a fallen woman, then, and one senses that this earthy scene, beyond its precious gaiety and its symbolic reference to defloration, points to something primeval, some garden, long forfeited by Isak.

Then, as Borg continues to "dream," a breakfast gong sounds, a flag is raised (the flag of Swedish-Norwegian unity, to be exact), and a crowd of brothers, sisters, and cousins converge on the house. The festivity is presided over by a dictatorial aunt. The center of attention is nearly deaf Uncle Aron, whose birthday it is. "The only ones missing were Father, Mother, and I," says Borg significantly. Somebody announces that Isak is out fishing with his father—"A message," Borg later notes, at which he felt "a secret and completely inexplicable happiness," wondering at the same time what he should do in this "new old world which I was suddenly given the opportunity to visit." It is impossible to describe the noisy and gay, intimate and also somewhat grating, birthday scene that follows. As old man Borg appears to watch his childhood milieu, it becomes clear that he had always felt like an isolated onlooker in that gaiety and activity, which, to a withdrawn and sensitive boy, must have seemed marked by overpopulation. There are a series of skirmishes between the authoritarian aunt and a succession of healthy, boisterous children who protest their right to be. At the end, it is Sara who takes the brunt of the impertinent vitality, for two unspeakable twin sisters in braids, who always chant in unison, announce that they saw Sara and Sigfrid kiss in the patch. Sara runs from the room and out onto the veranda. There, she tearfully confesses to her older cousin, Charlotta, how much she loves Isak, but that he (who will kiss her only in the dark) is simply too mysterious a man for her: so "enormously refined" and sensitive, so "extremely intellectual," and so moralistically aloof.

Now I will correlate the brief but obviously central scene of the spilled wild strawberries with one of the stages of life. It is that of young adulthood, with its manifold playful intimacies that must mature into a quality of Intimacy—in friendship, in erotic life, and in work. The related danger is some form of Self-Absorption and Exclusion. It is likely that when he lost Sara to Sigfrid, something in Isak turned away from women. Therefore he remained lacking in Love—the strength of this stage—but possessed of a pervasive Exclusivity. There is, again, a symbolic hint pointing to Isak's past, for in the Bible Sara was Isak's mother; and we realize that Isak had known his mother as a very young woman. Is Sara's name an allusion to the fact that she had been old when young, or that he had lost his young mother, too, to another man? The breakfast scene affirms this in the noisiest way possible, for six brothers and sisters were born during Isak's childhood; it also illustrates the ruthless politics of a large and, in summer, extended family. As the aunt calls for order, respect, and propriety, each youngster in his or her way fights for survival. It becomes painfully clear that Isak's way of autonomy had been gifted isolation—as his father's may have been. At any rate, father and son went fishing together—sharing a separation from the family.

Didactically speaking, this childhood scene would permit us, step by step, to sketch the way in which, in comparison with the others, Isak resolved his childhood crises by acquiring specialized strengths that would later serve him well in a professional career in his cultural setting. He would have to pay, however, with a compulsive self-restriction that was evident while he was still young. It is this day that his central lifelong endeavor is honored; it is this day that all the unresolved crises are faced.

We almost forgot Uncle Aron: he is a man in his second childhood, prepared for *his* special day by some secret libation—also witnessed and announced by the twins. He is serenaded lustily, as Isak will be later in the day, although Aron is nearly deaf: these familial ritualizations prepare us for the more ironic aspects of the coming ceremony. Maybe being like Uncle Aron could save one much existential trouble—and some bad dreams?

6. PASSENGERS   As Isak Borg, overwhelmed by his reveries, sits by the patch and slowly comes to with a feeling of emptiness and sadness, a real, blond, and tanned young girl appears suddenly, as if jumping down from a tree, awakens him fully. Obviously a

member of Sweden's contemporary *jeunesse dorée*, she is dressed in shorts and is sucking on an unlit pipe. "Is this your shack?" she inquires, and presently asks whether the "jalopy" by the house is his. Instead of being shocked, however, he is amused, for the girl looks like a reborn Sara (and is played by the same actress, now with a pageboy haircut). And her name *is* Sara. She is on her way to Italy, and she would like a ride to the other coast. He agrees, and in his benign mood tells the returning Marianne that he has offered the young girl a ride. As they approach the car, it turns out that two strapping young men are part of the bargain: they are going to Italy with Sara. But Borg seems ready to accommodate them all. In fact, a strange bond exists between him and little Sara, who, now an apparition in his rearview mirror, adds a dimension of rejuvenation to the day. What is their stage? The three young people represent contemporary youth in search of something worthy of their incipient Fidelity as they are working on defining their Identity: one of the boys wants to become a doctor and plays the atheistic rationalist; the other intends to be a minister and defends God's existence. Both, however, when driven to defense or offense, display a naive Cynicism, which is the natural contrary to adolescent Fidelity. They both love Sara— or so says Sara, who, appropriately sitting between them, announces to Borg with a charming mixture of cynicism and sincerity that she is playing them against each other, while remaining a virgin. Currently, they are hitchhiking to Italy, where young northerners of that day expected the southern sun to dissolve their Identity Confusion.

There is an implicit scheme in this sequence—a scheme by which Borg encounters, as he now seems almost driven to do, his past selves and counterplayers. We have "located" his acute crisis in the conflicts natural to old age and Marianne's in those of the center of adulthood; and we have suggested that in his opening dream he reached back to that unfulfilled stage in himself. We will find that in each subsequent encounter he faces individuals who personify earlier stages of life as the young portray the identity crisis) and help him to return to the corresponding stage of his own life through some reverie or dream.

Borg, watching Sara in the rearview mirror, seems relaxed, almost meditative. But suddenly utter fear forces his whole attention forward: he sees a black car approaching on the wrong side of the road. He swerves his car safely off the road, while the other car overturns into a ditch (one is reminded of the broken-down hearse). After a moment of shock, they see—mysteriously unharmed—a middle-aged couple, who, it appears, have been quarreling and continue to do so. The man, the doctor notes, is limping, but he explains that he has been "crippled for years," and (so he claims his wife says) not only physically. As they, too, become passengers in the Borgs' car (occupying the folding seats), they continue their habitual reciprocal harangue, aggravated by the "death scare." The man, Alman, grants that his wife's scorn may be good psychotherapy for her, while she announces that he is a Catholic who probably perceives the accident to be God's punishment. Thus, the two ministering professions continue as an ideological double theme, full of sarcasm and obscure dread. The husband even accuses his wife, apparently an unsuccessful actress, of playing at having cancer: "She has her hysterics and I have my Catholicism." Suddenly, the wife hits the husband in the face; Marianne, who is now driving, stops the car and quietly orders the couple to get out "for the Children's sake" (born and unborn, one senses). And so, Borg records, they "quickly drove away from this strange marriage."

It will have occurred to the viewer that the full car contained a complete representation of the precariousness of adulthood, from the young people in the back seat who are on the way to the land where they hope to find their adult identities as well as each other, to the couple who have just about lost each other and themselves, to the old man and the young woman who are beginning to find each other in the attempt to prevent a forfeiture of an overdefined adulthood. Here, Marianne is the heroine; in her now-dominant determination to care, she does not hesitate to squelch the antics of the two self-absorbed and antagonistic adults. For if the simplest moral rule is not to do to another what you would not wish to have done to you, the ethical rule of adulthood is to do to others what will help them, even as it helps you, to grow.

As the car continues without the participants in the "strange marriage"—which one suspects seems foreign to Borg only because he had not as yet faced the strangeness of that part of his own adult past—he and all the others seem emptied and exhausted, as if they, as well as the car, need refueling.

7. MIDDAY   What grace had saved Borg for the transformations symbolized by that one day's journey? Sara, we now know, had been and still is with him. And for all his self-absorption, he apparently had been a good doctor. The gas station where they now stop is in the center of southern Sweden, where Borg had practiced for fifteen years before he became a researcher and professor in the city. The big, blond gas-station owner recognizes him. After all, the doctor had delivered him and all his brothers. He called his wife ("she beamed like a big strawberry in her red dress") and suggested that they name their coming baby (a boy, of course) Isak. (Will Isak, then, be a godfather to his clientele, yet not a grandfather in his own family?) Payment for the gas is refused: "There are some things that can never be paid back." And Isak, with a tragic glance, suddenly thinks aloud: "Perhaps I should have remained here." He should have stayed in touch, then, at least with those to whom he could offer competent and truly needed service—as a member of one of those mediating professions that earn a kind of social and existential exemption. Yet, a pitiless awareness may be telling him how much love one can receive—from patients and students—for what one also does for honor and for money. How many old people, maybe without knowing it, mourn for just that period of their lives?

There follows, again, an idyllic scene: a midday meal on a terrace overlooking Lake Vaettern. Over the table, they now face each other, and with the help of some consciousness-expanding wine, Isak and Marianne become part of a midsummer celebration. Anders, the future pastor, suddenly recites a religious poem. Victor, the scientific rationalist, protests: they had sworn to each other that they would not discuss God. He advocates looking biological death "straight in the eye." Finally, Victor asks the doctor's opinion. But Borg has been musing; and as Marianne lights his cigar for him (him, who had refused to let her smoke her cigarette), Isak, instead of answering, recites a poem: "Where is the friend I seek everywhere?/Dawn is the time of loneliness and care . . ./When twilight comes . . ." He asks Anders for help, but it is Marianne who continues: "When twilight comes,

I am still yearning." And as Sara, moved to tears ("for no reason at all"), says: "You're religious, aren't you, Professor," Isak continues: "I see His trace of glory and power,/ In an ear of grain and the fragrance of a flower," and Marianne concludes: "In every sign and breath of air./ His love is there."

The poem, the setting, the tone, seem to confirm the sense in which every human being's Integrity may be said to be religious (whether explicitly or not). Each person engages in an inner search for, and a wish to communicate with, that mysterious, that Ultimate Other: for there can be no "I" without an "Other," and no "We" without a shared "Other." That, in fact, is the first revelation of the life cycle, when the maternal person's eyes shiningly recognize us even as we begin to recognize her. It is also the hope of old age, according to St. Paul's promise.

This poem, no doubt, will accompany Borg to the end of this day. But first, he must encounter life's earliest Other, who, as human fate dictates, makes the origins of Hope a variably discordant matter. After a long silence, Isak arises abruptly and announces that he will visit his old mother, who lives nearby. Marianne wants to come along. She takes his arm; he pats her hand. From the sunny lakeside, they walk to a house surrounded by a wall "as tall as a man." Inside, his mother, in a black dress with lace cap, looks up sharply from an "incongruous desk." Her estranged living becomes apparent as she, having accepted his embrace, asks with a suspicious glance whether Marianne is his wife and, if so, would she leave the room, for "she has hurt us too much." Introduced, she learns that Marianne has no children, and announces that she has had ten; all are dead now except for Isak. None of the twenty grandchildren ever visit her, except Evald. And she has fifteen great-grandchildren whom she has never seen. "I am tiresome, of course . . . and I have another fault. I don't die." They are waiting for her money. She asks to have a large box full of toys brought to her, saying she had "tried to think which of you owned that." She lifts out toys, one after the other, names the owners, chats about them. And then, painfully echoing Isak's opening monologue at his desk, she concludes: "It doesn't pay much to talk. Isn't it cold in here?" and looking at the darkening sky in the window, "I've always felt chilly . . . mostly in the stomach." She lefts a last item from the box: her father's old gold watch. Drumbeats in the background: the dial is handless! Isak recalls his dream, and hearse, and "my dead self." His mother concludes with one warming memory: how little Sara always cradled her cousin Sigbritt's infant boy. Now he is going to be fifty years old! She wants to give the watch to him: "It can probably be repaired?" (Again: was the mother once motherly like this Sara?)

While kissing her goodbye, Isak notes that his mother's face is "very cold but unbelievably soft and full of sharp little lines." Marianne, who has watched all this with silent horror, curtsies, and once outside against takes Isak's arm. Isak is now "filled with gratitude toward this quiet, independent girl with her naked, observant eyes." Perhaps he feels that Evald, although his son and his mother's grandson, in marrying Marianne may have reversed the fate symbolized by his mother's father's watch, which had mysteriously entered the dream that had started him on this journey. It may have been this hope that gave Isak the courage to confront himself in yet another, more deeply "humiliating," dream.

8. THE LAST EXAMINATION As Marianne takes the wheel (is she in charge now?), all are resting, the boys in sullenness over another dispute, little Sara bored with them both. Isak sleeps and dreams profusely. Astonished at his productivity when he writes it all down later, he includes a defensive note about his lack of enthusiasm for the psychoanalytic theory of dreams "as the fulfillment of desires in a negative or positive direction." He also wonders whether this new twilight experience of memories and dreams is a sign of senility, or even a "harbinger of approaching death." In abstracting the extraordinary dream sequence here, I can only continue to point to that motivation in old age miraculously understood by the middle-aged playwright. That is, one must experience and, in fact, affirm total Despair in order to gain an integrated sense of one's life. Perhaps the life cycle, seen as a whole, is a revelation. (And dreams are not merely "self-revealing"?)

Back at the strawberry patch, in a continuation of the morning's reverie, Isak encounters the original Sara of his youth, who, with pitying tears, holds a mirror to his face, forcing him to see himself "old and ugly in the sinking twilight." Is Sara also another Other—his own female Self. For she says that she has been unintentionally cruel by not exposing him to himself. She now announces that she will marry his brother: "It's all a game." He smiles, an unforgettable smile that seems to hurt his whole face. And she says sharply that he, a professor emeritus, ought to know why it hurts, but she is sure he does not. She throws the mirror away.

Sigbritt's little boy is crying. She must hurry to him. "Don't leave me," begs Isak. She says she does not understand him, for he stammers. But it doesn't "really matter," anyway.

The day becomes utterly fateful and threatening in a darkening twilight. Black birds are screeching like furies. With tears streaming down her face, Sara, up in the arbor, cradles the little boy with lullaby words: "Soon it will be another day." The child calms down, but Isak wants to scream "till my lungs are bloody."

The wind dies, and the house again looks festive. Sara plays the piano; Sigfrid listens. They sit down to a candlelit dinner, celebrating "some kind of event." Isak watches through the glass door, pressing his hand against the frame, where there is a nail. It pierces his hand, like one of the stigmata. As if this identification with Christ the Crucified seemed too self-indulgent a gesture, the scene and the moonlight now turn cold and cruel. Mr. Alman appears, stiffly polite, and insists that the professor come into the house, which has turned into some kind of laboratory. Taken into the very lecture room where he used to give his polyclinical examinations, he now must take an examination before a silently hostile audience, which includes the young passengers. Asked to inspect a specimen, he can only see his own eye mirrored in the microscope. Asked to read a mysterious formula on the blackboard which tells of a doctor's first duty, he cannot decipher it. Alman intones calmly, politely: *"A doctor's first duty is to ask forgiveness."* Yes, of course, he knew that, laughs Isak, reduced to wincing despair. Alman persists: *"You are guilty of guilt."* (Is that sin?) Now the old man, typically, claims infirmity: a bad heart! Another judgment: *"There is nothing concerning your heart in my papers."* Finally, Isak is to diagnose a woman patient. She looks like Mrs. Alman (and one is reminded of the implied parallel between the Almans' marriage and his own). His diagnosis: "She is dead." The patient laughs wildly. A third judgment: *"He does not know when a woman is alive."* The inquisitor summarizes his guilt as "indifference, selfishness, lack of consideration." He stands so accused by his wife, Borg now learns, and he must confront her. But she has been dead for years? Come, demands the inquisitor.

He leads him out into a primeval forest. The moon is shining "like a dead eye." The ground, covered with decaying leaves, is swampy and porous underfoot and filled with snakes. They now stand by a charred ladder leaning against a burned-out hut. In a clearing, Isak sees Karin, his wife, a strong, sensual woman, being seduced by a disgusting, but virile, man; and she "received the man between her open knees." The inquisitor states the exact date: "Tuesday, May 1, 1917." May Day. Isak now has seen, but has not heard, the worst. For as the lovers then sit and talk, the woman predicts what Isak will say when she confesses. He will feel sorry for her, like "God himself," and say with a sickening nobility, "You shouldn't ask forgiveness from me. I have nothing to forgive." (But he will not think of asking for forgiveness.)

The inquisitor has the last word, mocking any attempt to gain superiority from self-revelation. "Everything has been dissected. A surgical masterpiece." The penalty? "Of course, loneliness." "Is there no grace?" asked the dreamer. But the other claims not to know.

Fleetingly, Isak appeals to Sara, who once more materializes. "If only you had stayed with me. . . . Wait for me." He wants to cry like a child, but he cannot. That escape is gone, too.

The message of the dream seems clear: Isak, who has learned how to study, to heal, and to preserve life, has not been alive to a woman's (or to his own) feelings, and so he has had to watch the women in his life, although they loved him, turn to other men. He has learned, to paraphrase Freud's formula for adulthood, to work but *not* to love. Here, in fact, a psychoanalytic interpretation seems inescapable, for why does he once more turn to Sara, who, again, personifies the young mother. "If only you had stayed with me"? We must assert an infantile trauma behind these scenes of seduction with which he has unconsciously colluded during his adult life. It is what Freud has called the Primal Scene, the child's observation or imagination of parental lovemaking, which makes an Oedipus out of the boy and alienates him from his own Id—the snaky swamp—as well as from the betraying parents. What does the charred ladder mean? Is it an existential or a sexual symbol? Could it not represent the stages of life, here marred by what was burned out on each?

9. NEW LIFE   As Borg wakes up, he finds that the car has stopped and that he is alone with Marianne. The "children" are in the woods. He tells her what he thinks his dreams are trying to reveal to him: that he is dead, although he is alive. Her gaze darkens, and she, again perceiving a generational threat, says that Evald had used the same words. "About me?" says Isak, "Yes, I can believe that." But she counters: "No, about himself." A man of thirty-eight! Isak now begs to be told "everything."

So Marianne describes a haunting talk with Evald—the very talk that made her come to see whether Isak might be of help. She had taken Evald for a ride to the sea. Parked there, she had told him that she was pregnant. From her words it is clear that neither Evald nor she had tried much to prevent this. She intends to have the child. Evald had reacted as if trapped. He walked out into the rain, and as she followed him he refused to agree to any development that would force him "to exist another day longer than I want to" or be responsible for a new human being. He referred to himself as an unwanted child, conceived in a marriage that was hell—and could he even be sure he was Borg's son? At the end, he cursed her "damned need to live, to exist and create life." Listening silently, Isak can only ask Marianne whether she does not wish to smoke.

She now sums up what we have learned of Isak's mother, of himself, and of his son as "more frightening than death itself." Not even the person she "loves more than anyone else" can take this child from her. Isak suddenly feels "shaken as never before." Maybe he realizes what his first dream had tried to tell him. "Can I help you?" he asks.

Thus, in small matters and in small but significant gestures, some measure of Care is restored. But the power of Rejectivity (from generation to generation) has been revealed. For if our generative concerns are held together by a world image which dictates what we consider relevant for the generational succession

of our own "kind," we are also (more or less consciously) possessed and obsessed by prejudices and convictions which exclude
vigorously and even viciously some "other kinds" as weak or bad,
foreign or inimical. In fact, such enmity often exists in relation to
our closest neighbors—geographic, ideological, conceptual—who
may share many of our generative concerns but differ in some
minutiae which can suddenly loom devastatingly large. It can
also exist within one's family or be turned against one's own
children, especially where conflicting generative concerns make
them suddenly appear as outsiders or worse. While there can be
no generativity without rejectivity, human survival demands that
rejectivity be counteracted by faith or by insight. What Freud has
called the narcissism of small differences, often expressed in hidden or displaced rejections, can also be projected on an overdefined otherness. This may adhere to the largest issues and collective antagonisms of mankind, whether these antagonisms are
territorial and invite periodic warfare, or credal and deny salvation to the infidels. So we are prepared to see the stage expand
from the private and the inner lives of a few individual Swedes to
an ancient cathedral rich with symbols and crowded with
uniforms.

10. THE CELEBRATION Now the great Jubilee must be lived
through. The "children" come running, bringing him, with
"friendly, mocking eyes," large bouquets of wildflowers, bowing
and chanting that he is so wise and venerable and has, no doubt,
learned all prescriptions by heart. A few hours later they arrive
at Evald's house in Lund, greeted by Agda, who is breathless
from all the preparations, while they, she is sure, had a "relaxing
and convenient" drive. Evald, handsome in tails, asks whether
Marianne wants to go to a hotel, but she says gaily that she will
stay "for another night" and she intends to go to the state
dinner with him. Borg, with Agda's help, dresses in his best.

The festivities? In his notes, Borg describes them thus:

Trumpet fanfares, bells ringing, field-cannon salutes, masses
of people, the giant procession from the university to the
cathedral, the white-dressed garland girls, royalty, old age,
wisdom, beautiful music, stately Latin sentences which echoed

off the huge vaults. The students and their girls, women in bright, magnificent dresses. . . ."[6]

Truly a crowning ritual for all he was: a doctor, a teacher, a Swede, a Lutheran, a patriot, a venerable old man. But this strange, symbolic rite now seems as "meaningless as a passing dream." Nevertheless, he marches along, upright and obedient, waving to little Sara. The preliminary ceremony in the cathedral (with its gothic niches, its saints, its crucifix) is endless, and Borg and his two old cojubilants suffer the specific discomforts of old men in sitting it out. Finally, he stands high up to be topped by the famous Lund-doctor's hat. The archetypal comparison with a crown of jewels or of thorns may seem inescapable. But Borg, as he stands there, looks above and beyond the scene and begins "to see a remarkable causality in this chain of unexpected, entangled events." The English caption says something of "an extraordinary logic." Whatever the words, they seem to connote a revelatory sensation of grand simplicity.

In view of the trumpets, the bells, and the cannons in this populous final event, we must pause and change our theoretical tune as well. For Borg is no longer one of a small circle of mutually significant persons containable in an automobile, but one in a row of black-robed men solemnly marching to honor the "immortals" of their own kind. We must recognize in such ceremonies a heritage both of triumph and of danger for human adulthood—the triumph and the danger which wisdom here transcends. No doubt, this noisy and playful Swedish version of a crowning ceremony is one of the most benign in human history, and one can well see Dag Hammarskjold in that place—in fact, he is buried in that cathedral. Yet in its combination of religious, military, national, and academic symbols, it is perhaps meant to remind us that mankind, so far, has been divided into what I call "pseudospecies": national, ideological, or religious bodies that consider their own kind the model image of mankind as intended in their version of creation and history. For its survival they are ready to kill as well as to die. Such shared identity, narrower or broader, in combination with superior accomplishments, seems to be necessary for that joint sense of the reality of reality which permits adults in their middle years to be defended against the absolute fact of death—and thus permits the full application, between adolescence and senescence, of matured energies and gifts to what the Hindus call "the maintenance of the world." But this means that adulthood is always imprisoned in the pseudo-species (we see this, of course, more clearly in foreigners than in ourselves) and thus has remained a pseudoadulthood, falling short of the potential of an all-human maturity. At the same time, we must acknowledge a universal goal in mankind which has, over the millenia, led to larger and larger units of more inclusive identity. Marx, it seems, believed in a historical trend toward such maturation by expanding unification. He spoke of history as an *Entstehungsakt*—a word that implies an evolving all-human adulthood. He could not foresee, perhaps, that mankind, when faced with this ultimate possibility, would also invent ultimate weapons for the defense of nations and ideologies and their empires and markets.

By "pseudo" I do not mean to emphasize conscious deception but the human tendency to create symbols, artifacts, and appearances, ideologies and world images, in a grandiose effort to make one's own kind a spectacular and unique sight in the universe and in history. It is a prime human dilemma that pseudospeciation can bring out the best in loyalty and cooperation, heroism and inventiveness, while committing different human "kinds" to a history of reciprocal enmity and destruction on an increasingly species-wide scale. Therefore, we have every reason to study what this moving picture reveals, namely, how large-scale adult commitments are perpared in the "politics" of small differences in everyday life and in each successive life stage. And we must learn to differentiate between the way in which such tendencies as Exclusivity and Rejectivity aggravate the *moralistic destructiveness* of public and private morals; and how virtues such as Love and Care, in turn, contribute to an insightful and universal *ethic*.

As we recognize the contraries which arise in every individual as the necessary correlates of human strength, we ought to consider the special function which the more inclusive visions of the great religions and ideologies have had in daily life. This function is to counteract the divisive potential arising in each stage of human growth. Such "sinful" tendencies as exclusivity or rejectivity thus were counteracted, say, in the Christian world view by the universal concepts of Agape and Caritas. The subtle sarcasm, however, that pervades the ceremonial scenes of our moving picture serves to point to the ritualisms which in an idolistic and formalistic fashion soon encompass any innovative world image—ritualisms which for a while may serve some conservational purpose but are apt sooner or later to neglect the vital interplay of historical change and individual life cycles.

In the meantime, we may grant a certain character type of Swedish doctor and professor, and so, obviously, an affluent member of the middle class, a moment of integrity which expresses the destiny of the old anywhere personal and social conditions favor an integrative revelation offered in the structure of existence. Where such conditions are lacking, whether because of poverty or affluence, because of laissez faire or autocracy, our critique and our protest must gain purpose and direction from the study of the resulting misery. It is the merit of *Wild Strawberries*, as of any other great drama, that it implicitly contains a social critique: one may consider only the suggestions of possessiveness and feudalism (see the high walls around Mother Borg's lonely house) in Isak's and his son's isolation.

11. THE EVENING   Dr. Borg's moment of revelation is followed by restrained, and therefore all the more universal, signs that the "remarkable causality" the old doctor had envisioned at the height of the ceremony is already working in those close to him. Borg does not attend the banquet: for him, the day is over. He takes a cab home and finds Agda (who in the cathedral had watched him with possessive pride) making his bed and arranging his things just the way he likes them. In this quiet after the storm, he tries to make peace with her. He even apologizes for his behavior that morning, which now seems long ago. She asks him once more whether he is ill. He asks dreamily, in words that must, indeed, alarm her, whether it is really so unusual for him "to ask forgiveness"? He even offers her the mutual use of the more familiar "du" (equivalent to addressing one by his first name in English), but she "begs to be excused from all intimacies" and departs, pointedly leaving her door slightly ajar. She is, perhaps, still hoping for *her* ceremony. But all this impresses one as being their normal relationship, with added friendship.

Then Isak hears a youthful duet, accompanied by a guitar, in the garden. Lifting the blinds, he sees "the children" serenading him. Sara announces that they have gotten a ride all the way to Hamburg (with a deaconess). Finally, little Sara, supported by the garden wall, lifts up her eyes to his inclined face and says with playful feminine intuition: "Goodbye, Father Isak. Do you know that it is really you I love, today, tomorrow, and forever?" Then they are gone.

He hears whispering voices in the foyer: Evald and Marianne. Evald comes to say goodnight. Marianne, it appears, has lost a heel, so she *had* to come home before the dance. Isak asks him to sit down. What is going to happen with them?

Evald: I have asked her to remain with me.
Isak: And how will it . . . I mean . . .
Evald: I can't be without her.
Isak: You mean you can't live alone?
Evald: I can't be without *her*. That's what I mean.
Isak: I understand.
Evald: It will be as she wants.[7]

Then Isak finds himself mentioning the loan. Evald protests that he will pay it back. Isak: "I did not mean that." Evald insists. But at least the "debt" is now a question of money only.

Marianne appears, dressed in rustling white. She asks whether he likes her shoes. In some of the longest such shots, they fully face each other, exchanging thanks and saying, "I like you."

The couple leaves. Isak hears his heart bump and his old watch tick. The tower clock strikes eleven. It begins to rain. Preparing for sleep, he wanders back once more to the strawberry patch. It is summer. Everybody is there. Sara runs toward him, calling him "darling" and telling him that there are no strawberries left. The aunt wants him to find his father. Isak says: "I have already searched for him, but I cannot find either Father or Mother." But she takes him by the hand. Down by the beach "on the other side of the dark water," he sees "a gentleman" fishing, and further up the bank, his mother, in bright summer dress, reading. Isak cannot make himself heard. But his father waves and his mother nods, both smiling in recognition. A truly primal scene.

He tries to shout, but his cries "did not reach their destination." Yet, he felt "rather light-hearted."

Borg has arrived at the beginning: his first childhood. We could now, as usual in our work, reconstruct the stages of life from the first Hope up the entire ladder of development strengths which old Borg, as any old person, has lived by—or has now learned to mourn. How childlike or how childish his second childhood will be—that remains open.

II. *Notes on a Conception of the Human Life Cycle*

I would like to amplify and systematize the brief formulations of the stages of life that I have so far used only as annotations to Bergman's scenes. I will use these scenes, in turn, as a way of illustrating a conception of the human life cycle to be presented in the form of a checkered chart (see page 61). For if I set down once more the principles that guided me in formulating a succession of life stages, it is in order to reflect on the nature of a total conception. The following notes illustrate the fact that any conception of the whole course, or of any phase, of life, while it may owe its structure and terminology to the sophisticated methods of a given period and field, is apt to inherit some emotional and ideological complications of a primitive nature.

1. The ceremony just described amply attests to the survival of certain basic qualities common to all adult world views. In my Jefferson Lectures, I have outlined some of the simplest spatial and temporal aspects of the sense of being grown-up, which are circumscribed by the manner in which different languages speak of adulthood.[8] The family of words related to the designation "adult" attests (to consider the Latin origins) to a state of having matured (*alescere, adolescere*) both in height and in stature and of having reached the stage of one who now nourishes (*alere*) what he bears and produces. But this means that what has developed in stages must now fit into the structure of an integrated world view which permits the vulnerabilities of human childhood to be turned into generational strengths. To be grown-*up*, in any language and vision, has a quality of standing tall, proudly, and

yet so precariously that there is a universal need to attest and to protest that one knows where one stands and that one has some status in the center of a new or, at any rate, forever renewed human type. One could go through *Wild Strawberries* and describe Dr. Borg's positions and changing points of view from the first dream, when, full of dread, he looks at the other self that lies in his coffin and attempts to drag him down, to the last moment in the cathedral, when, his head held high, he is crowned with a special top hat but gazes even higher toward a clarifying light. The ceremony further illustrates the collective need of human adults, between the complex process of having been "brought up" and a certain terminal "decline," to affirm ceremonially with whom they have grown up and whose standing in the world they now share—whether they symbolize this by marching in formation, as in the ceremony just witnessed, or, alternatively, by sitting in rows watching others march and perform. Under other cultural conditions, of course, the celebrants may link arms and dance vigorously; or, again, they may bow or kneel together or, indeed, prostrate themselves—and all this in order to confirm what they together stand for or against in the name of high principles personified by those they call "great." And the greatest, more often than not, are those rare persons who have questioned the *status quo* and have become immortal by creating a new one.

In the pursuit of the basic dimensions of a given world image, one could now proceed from the central fact of the upright existence of the human mind-organism to the periphery of its sensory, muscular, and locomotor reach (vastly augmented as they all are now by tools, instruments, and machinery), where it meets with others in affiliative and cooperative, erotic and antagonistic, interplay. Asked for a definition of what is human, a Navajo medicine man recently said, indicating the figure of a cross, that a person was most human where the (vertical) connection between the ground of creation and the Great Spirit met the (horizontal) one between the individual and all other human beings.

These are some of the simplest spatial-temporal aspects that form the perspectives of given visions of adulthood, whether they are represented in mythical, ideological, or, indeed, colloquial terms. In turn, these are enveloped in world moods such as those associated with any space-time conception of human existence, whether the dominant configuration is that of steps from birth up to maturity and down to decay, perhaps indicating some historical and technological progress; or that of a straight line from birth to death and beyond, whether up to salvation or down to damnation; or, indeed, that of a series of rebirths absorbing the individual and generational cycles in larger cycles of rebirths—and an eventual transcendence. We are thus prepared for the magic power of religious and ideological world visions. They, in turn, variously emphasize, between the highest Reason discernible and the "dumb" creatureliness shared with all creation, various core areas of physical existence and efficacy: head, mind, foresight (*"sapientissimus"* is one of the declamations we hear when Dr. Borg receives his hat); the bread of inspiration and the ritualized intake of food and drink, the passions of the temperaments and the loyalty of the heart, or the potency of the genitals and generosity of the womb that serve erotic and procreative union, are sublimated for higher endeavors, or left below to be avoided.

2. Formulated world views also contain, within larger and even eternal temporal perspectives, images of the course of life, or, at any rate, of ideal and evil adulthood, with varying perspectives on the preceding period of growing up toward this middle estate and the final period of decline and dying. The rare emphasis that the gospels place on the relation of lasting childlikeness to the coming Kingdom must be seen as a prophetic countervoice to the ancient attitude toward the child as one who, if it survives at all, must be fashioned into the adult mold. For all world views must come to terms with the irreversible ambiguities and contradictions arising from the fact that the human species (besides other extreme specializations) must undergo a protracted period in which to grow up and to grow into given specifications. Other species "know" where they belong, and their instinctual energies are tuned to their instinctive patterns of living. Human instinctuality employs a drive-equipment of loves and hates that must be ready for a variety of social settings in which to learn the intricacies of technology and custom. Therefore it is char-

acterized by a conflict-ridden dialectic of excessive drive-energy and stringent inhibition, of anarchic license and fateful repression and self-restriction. It is, again, the world religions that have striven to provide an all-inclusive world view for the containment of such human extremes as self-seeking vanity and self-abnegating humility, ruthless power-seeking and loving surrender, a search for beliefs worth dying and killing for, and a wish to empathize and understand. As I have put it in my Jefferson Lectures, there seem to be two poles to human endeavor: (1) the felt necessity to "survive and kill," where both the territorial survival and the cultural identity of human subspecies seem to depend on the defensive or offensive exclusion of (all) others; and (2) the precept "die and become," where, on the contrary, ascetic self-denial to the point of self-sacrifice appears to be the only means of becoming more inclusively human. We know how empires and creeds alternately counterpoint and reconcile or refute and exclude the belief systems that emerge from the dreadful human dilemma of reconciling a need for generational renewal in a "real" Here and Now with the certainty of individual death.

One must begin with such fundamentals if one wishes to understand the necessity for adults to arrive at some formula of adulthood and to gain some objective perspective on its precursors. Thus, one of the few grand divisions of life into stages—namely, the Hindu *asramas*—postulates a middle range of "householding" in the service of the "maintenance of the world."[9] This is preceded by a well-defined age of apprenticeship and followed by a transcendence of the individual life cycle and an entry into a cycle of rebirths. This scheme, however, has little to say about the stages of childhood. And in Shakespeare's seven ages there is, between the mewling infant and the sighing lover, only the whining schoolboy. We must consider why it took enlightened humanistic and scientific mankind so long to acknowledge and to chart the existence of developmental stages. No doubt there has been a deep-seated adult resistance (first discovered and explained by Freud) not only to the remembrance of one's own childhood, but also to the recognition in children of developmental potentials which may upset the adult conviction of occupying a safe and sanctioned place in the universe. Only a century of the child has made us study childhood and youth, not only as the precursors of adulthood as it was and is, but also as the potential for what adulthood may become.

3. As we pursue our specialized conceptions of the cycle of life, matters of overall orientation intrude, either in the ambiguities and contradictions of the material or in controversies over our choice of formulations. Questions arise when I, as a psychoanalyst, describe a psychosocial scene that consists of an interplay between antithetical qualities, from which emerges, under favorable conditions, a new "virtue" or vital strength. Do I arrive at this theory on the basis of clinical interpretation? Am I pursuing a humanist ideal with moralistic or aesthetic demands impossible to live up to in daily life? Is my view period- and class-bound, and does it suggest conformity to the requirements of a given social milieu or, on the contrary, indulgence in self-actualization? Do the overprivileged abide by such a scheme, and can the underprivileged afford it, if they want it? And, more personally, are the strivings conscious or unconscious?

Such questions are, of course, legitimate, and we have reason to pose them, whatever our method, for they may open up neglected aspects of the matter. But we must also recognize in them the (often cyclic) recurrence of attempts to resolve in some dogmatic manner the ambiguities and contradictions adhering to adulthood itself. Even methodical and trained persons when faced with the question of adult values tend to revive the totalistic tendencies of youth, whether they reassert or disavow their former stance. What is at stake here are matters of professional identity and of belief systems couched in theory. Then, there are the pervasive trends of the times. For example, critical references to my scheme omit the list of "negatives" (Isolation, Stagnation, Despair). Therefore I appear—to some for better and to others for worse—to postulate a series of ideal accomplishments (Love, Care, Wisdom) as desirable "achievements" for which the proper prescriptions should and must be found.

Here, I will briefly restate the origin of my formulations in the history of my field. Many of us who have worked not only clinically but also in child guidance and in the developmental study of children have recognized that it is our generation's task to demonstrate the complementarity between the so-called genetic point of view in psychoanalysis and a developmental one. The genetic approach reconstructs the way emotional disturbances are rooted in early traumatic events which tend to exert a regressive pull on the present. It also opens the "prehistoric" part of the human life cycle, and the unconscious dynamics of human conflict, to systematic inspection. The developmental approach, in turn, is based on the direct observation of children: following the genetic leads, we realize the developmental potentials of all stages of life. In childhood we see the actual trauma; in maturity we see the behavioral consequences of such disturbances. Furthermore, in developing or contributing to an inclusive human psychology, psychoanalysis cannot shirk the task of accounting not only for the way the individual ego holds the life cycle together, but also for the laws which connect generational cycles with individual ones—and the social process with both. My terms reflect this original task even as the first formulation of psychosocial stages is grounded in Freud's postulation of the psychosexual stages in childhood and their relationship to the psychopathological syndromes at all ages. In my extension of the principle of stages to adulthood and old age, the dystonic aspect of each stage remains related to the potential for a major class of disorders. I have abstained from viewing Dr. Borg as a case, although Bergman's remarkable clinical intuition would make it quite feasible to describe in his hero some core disturbances that might have made him (given some adverse psychogenic factors) somebody's client—a status the professor so grimly abhors. If—to speak in diagnostic terms—his compulsive character in old age borders on the depressive and paranoid, it obviously has its "classical" origins in the anal-urethral stage of libido development, with its retentive-eliminative mode emphases and the resulting over-fastidiousness and strict adherence to mutually exclusive categories in matters of value. Yet, if we let our observations indicate what could go wrong in each stage, we can also note what can go right, and we can determine what kept such a man together all those years for his crowning day.

But what, some will ask, justifies the introduction into a developmental scheme of such old-fashioned terms as Wisdom or Hope? And what could be their relationship to the unconscious conflicts that Freud has demonstrated to be central to human development? Can hope, for example, be unconscious? The answer is that hope is a prime adaptive ego quality, pervading conscious and yet emerging in and re-emerging from the dynamic interplay of conscious and unconscious forces. Whether somebody judges himself, or is judged by others, to be full of hope, and whether or not he is motivated to make the most if it by occasional or persistent display, are matters of personality and of social role. Another is the pervasive, though not necessarily always visible, and most contagious rudimentary quality of hopefulness, which (as its loss in the deepest regression indicates) emerges from the earliest experiences of abandonment as well as of closeness and which, throughout life, must rely on the power of unconscious processes as well as one some confirmation by fate—and by faith.

4. We realize that Dr. Borg's initial statement of his old-age conditions admirably describes a state of mind governed by a struggle for Integrity *versus* a sense of Despair and Disgust. Out of this conflict a certain Wisdom may emerge under favorable personal and cultural conditions. We do not, however, postulate the achievement of a victory of Integrity over Despair and Disgust, but simply a dynamic balance in Integrity's favor. "Versus" is an interesting little word because it can mean a reciprocal antagonism carried further, as in "vice versa." Developmentally, it suggests a dialectic dynamic because the final strength postulated could not emerge without either of the contending qualities; yet, to ensure growth, the syntonic, the one more intent on adaptation, must absorb the dystonic. If Hope is the first and fundamental human strength, emerging from Primal Trust versus Primal Mistrust, it is clear that the human infant must experience a goodly measure of mistrust in order to learn to trust discerningly, and that there would be neither conviction nor efficacy in an overall hopefulness without a (conscious and unconscious) struggle with the temptation to succumb to hopelessness. Dr. Borg's initial condition illustrates how unconvincing a sense of integrity can be if it does not remain answerable to some existential despair and some disgust with the repetitiveness of human pretenses—including, of course, one's own. In speaking here of various "senses of," however, we refer only to their more

conscious aspects, while Integrity, like all the other strengths, obviously must have foundations deep in the preconscious and the unconscious, even as Despair and Disgust emerge only as the latest expression of the fear, anxiety, and dread that have pervaded previous stages. Despair tells us that the time is too short, if not altogether too late, for alternative roads to Integrity; this is why the elderly try to "doctor" their memories. Rationalized bitterness and disgust can mask that despair which in severe psychopathology aggravates a senile syndrome of depression, hypochondria, and paranoiac hate. Whatever chance man has to transcend the limitations of his self seems to depend on his full (if often tragic) engagement in the one and only life cycle permitted to him. By the same token, a civilization and its belief systems can be measured by the meaning they give to the full cycle of life, for such meaning (or lack of it) cannot fail to reach into the beginnings of future generations.

All this was assumed when I came to the formulation that *Wisdom,* in whatever way it may be expressed, *is the detached and yet active concern with life itself in the face of death itself, and that it maintains and conveys the integrity of experience in spite of the Disdain over human failing and the Dread of ultimate nonbeing.* It will prove easiest, with the help of our movie, to illustrate the diagrammatic scheme for the cycle of life if we immediately counterpoint this last stage to the first one.[10] I have postulated that the first and most basic human strength of Hope emerges from the conflict between Primal Trust and Primal Mistrust. Here, the formulation goes: *Hope is the enduring belief in the attainability of primal wishes, in spite of the dark urges and rages which mark the beginnings of existence and leave a lasting residue of threatening Estrangement.* Hope, then, is the ontogenetic basis of what in adulthood becomes faith; it is nourished in childhood by the parental faith which pervades patterns of care.

If I now distribute the stages of life and the life crises in a diagram, Hope "belongs" in the lower left corner and Wisdom in the upper right, while the horizontal and the vertical meet in the upper left. All the earlier conflicts can thus be seen to reach into, and to be renewed on, the level of the last, as they are on

	1	2	3	4	5	6	7	8	
H								Integrity vs. Despair, Disgust. WISDOM	Old Age
G							Generativity vs. Self-absorption. CARE		Maturity
F						Intimacy vs. Isolation. LOVE			Young Adulthood
E					Identity vs. Identity Confusion. FIDELITY				Adolescence
D				Industry vs. Inferiority. COMPE-TENCE					School Age
C			Initiative vs. Guilt. PURPOSE						Play Age
B		Autonomy vs. Shame, Doubt. WILL							Early Childhood
A	Trust vs. Mistrust. HOPE								Infancy

each level in between—but always renewed in terms of the conflict which dominates that level. In A8, then, Primal Trust and Wisdom meet, and so do Primal Mistrust and Despair. But here another problem of theory enters that easily becomes one of ideology: are we saying that the need for a faith is "nothing but" a lifelong fixation on primal trust, childlike in the beginning and illusional at the end? Or that primal trust is "simply" the ontogenetic foundation of a capacity for some faith, necessary both for terminal peace and for the renewal of life from generation to generation?

5. The movie, as we saw, links the contemporary cast of individuals who appear in the course of Borg's journey with the important figures of his early years, and thus it gives us a chance to populate the empty boxes on the top line of the chart.

Following is the *epigenetic* principle which alone justifies the use of such a chart:

a. Each combination of primal qualities has its stage of ascendance, when physical, cognitive, emotional, and social developments permit its coming to a crisis. These stages of ascendance constitute the diagonal.

b. Each such stage has its precursors (below the diagonal), which must now be brought up (vertically) to "their" maturational crisis.

c. Each such crisis (as already stated) must at the advent of succeeding crises (above the diagonal) be brought up to the new level of the then-dominant conflict.

In Borg's case, we see how his own terminal conflicts revive his earlier ones, as personified by the younger persons who confront him (in fact or in fantasy) on his journey. To enter what we already know on the top line from right to left, his own ruefully unresolved crisis of Generativity versus Stagnation (H8) is renewed by his confrontation with Marianne, who herself is undergoing this same crisis in its age-specific form (H7) and forces her husband Evald to face it on his level. Borg's unresolved Intimacy Crisis (H6) was re-encountered, as personified in the "accidental" couple, the Almans, and relived in his reveries and dreams.

These are the adult stages proper. They emerge when a person is ready to commit the strengths which have matured earlier to the "maintenance of the world" in historical space and time. They now must merge in the qualities of Love and Care. Love matures through the crisis of Intimacy versus Isolation; it establishes a mutuality with new individuals in wider affiliations, thus transcending the *exclusivity* of earlier dependencies. Care, in turn, is the concrete concern for what has been generated by love, necessity, or accident, thus counteracting the Rejectivity that resists the commitment to such obligation.

Nobody in this cast, however, or, indeed, in life, is neatly "located" in one stage; rather, all persons oscillate between at least two stages and move more definitively into a higher one only when an even further step begins to determine the interplay: thus, if Borg, in the last stage that can be formulated as developmental, is in a renewed struggle with the two earlier ones, he is so in the face of death or, at any rate, senility; and if Marianne's struggle for generativity is still weighed down by that for intimacy, she is also alarmed at her—and especially her husband's—increasing age and threatening ossification.

Moving further left on the chart and thus to the contemporary representatives of earlier stages of life, we encounter the triad of young people. The young men, as we saw, are still in the midst of the struggle for Identity and certainly in the grips of some Identity Confusion, which they are trying to resolve by pointing up (and underscoring with blows) each other's inconsistencies. Little Sara, however, will not let them forget the approaching stage when being "in love" must mature into Love and when "intimacies" must amount to a capacity for Intimacy. What still remains of Borg's Identity Crisis (H5) comes to the fore in the declamations of the midday meal and in a playful, even impulsive, yielding to feelings and notions which might have become an important part of his identity had they not been finally subdued by the loss of Sara, who is, as first loves usually are, both the female Other and the feminine Self—that is, the Self which such a man considers too feminine to acknowledge. To continue our formulations: *Fidelity is the ability to sustain loyalties freely pledged in spite of the inevitable contradictions and confusions of value systems.* It is the cornerstone of identity, and receives inspiration from confirming ideologies and affirming companions.

6. The consideration of the eight squares in the chart's upper right corner reminds us of another pervasive misunderstanding. For theoretical, as well as clinical, historical, and autobiographical reasons, Identity terms have been emphasized in my writings and have subsequently been widely accepted or rejected on the basis of the assumption that in my scheme Identity was the teleological aim and end of growing up.[11] The Identity Crisis is definitely pivotal; but Dr. Borg's case illustrates poignantly what happens when Identity, because of some earlier partial arrests, and especially because of a retreat from Intimacy, is overdefined in terms of occupation and civic role. The "achievement" of an overformulated identity, then, may sacrifice a measure of Identity Confusion salutary for some playful variability in later choices.

In this connection, it must be emphasized that all the psychosocial strengths associated with our scheme postulate an active *adaptation* rather than a passive *adjustment*—that is, they change the environment even as they make selective use of its opportunities. Thus, the "maintenance of the world" could not be effected by servitude and compliance; it means rather a continuous reciprocal facilitation of social and psychological development. Where such facilitation has become impossible, radical changes occur in social mores and institutions. It is for this reason that study of the life cycle leads to that of biography and history and of social and economic conditions. The implication here is that if individuals do not find in daily ritualizations, as well as in the rituals of a society, the affirmation and confirmation suggested here, both individual and generational cycles will show symptoms of pathology that point to specific needs for social change. We can, at any rate, recognize in Victor, Anders, and little Sara some readiness for ideological controversies that could, in principle, involve them in a turbulent moratorium or in some ideological movement of varying revolutionary or reactionary potentials. The actual social involvements of our young ideologists seem as yet open, even as they watch with a mixture of awe and mockery how the older generation goes about honoring itself. As for Marianne, I can imagine her taking an active role in communal life after her encounter with the mixture of professional service and generational isolation presented by her two doctors.

7. Regarding the human life cycle and the places of adulthood and old age in it, no conception would be sufficient without reference to the *relativity* of three cycles.

a. All the emergent strengths are necessary to complete the *individual cycle*, although, as we saw, no such cycle can escape variable emphases on the inhibiting and isolating qualities of human development which foster fear and anxiety.

b. Any fulfillment of the individual life cycle is not only a matter of finding terminal clarity but is also responsible for and contributes to continuous solutions to the ongoing *cycle of generations*.

c. The generational cycle is vital to the maintenance of evolving *social structures*, which must facilitate the emergence of the life stages or else suffer a social and political pathology.[12]

According to the retrospective logic of this article, we conclude with some formulations concerning the stages of childhood. As Dr. Borg, on his journey, crosses the Swedish countryside (and moves further left on our chart), he encounters his erstwhile patients, who represent his most satisfying personal involvement in the "maintenance of the world" at a time when his sexual and familial intimacy was slowly going bankrupt. His patients had provided the renewal in his adult life of the strengths he had developed throughout his childhood and youth: the strengths of Purposefulness and of Competence, which also came to occupy the center of his Fidelity.

These are the corresponding formulations: Rudimentary *Purposefulness is the courage to imagine playfully and to pursue energetically goals, uninhibited by the defeat of infantile fantasies, by the guilt they aroused, and by the punishment they elicited.* It invests ideals of action, and is derived from the example of the childhood milieu. *Competence, in turn, is the free exercise of dexterity and intelligence in the completion of tasks, unimpaired by infantile inferiority.* It is the basis for cooperative participation in technologies, and relies on the logic of tools and skills. Competence emerges from the infantile struggle of Industry versus Inferiority, and Purpose from that of Initiative versus Guilt; and these original conflicts are faced in the doctor's reveries and dreams. His examination dream, as we saw, confronts him with the fact that his competence in professional life has permitted him to become insensitive to a basic feeling of inadequacy (here expressed in his failure to recognize when a woman, and, by implication, he himself, is "dead" or "alive") and to bypass his deep-seated sense of being "guilty of guilt."

The vivid reverie of his childhood milieu leads to an even earlier stage in childhood (B2), in which a person's Will receives lasting characteristics as it emerges from the conflict between the sense of Autonomy and the sense of Shame—which, like Guilt, is ingrained in the human make-up and is used by all cultures to impose special choices and restrictions on a child's development. As we saw, the great childhood scene illustrates with vital humor how all the children and young people learn to stand up to the demanding and scolding aunt who represents the potentially cruel, moralistic side of such a milieu. The implication is, in accord with psychopathology and characterology, that Isak more than any of the other children submitted to his milieu's moralism to an extent that restricted his spontaneity and playfulness. This made him, in fact, the compulsive character that he became.

When Sara, who had by then assumed the role of the young maternal person, leads Isak to the shore where he and his parents exchange smiles of recognition—if now at the safe distance of terminal resignation—she seems to restore the trust of the first stage. Without this trust Isak could not have become what he is and could not have dreamt as he did.

As I indicated in the first part of this paper, a good story does not need a chart to come alive. In the second part I have shown that a chart, especially one with so many empty boxes, can use a good story.

Notes

1. Ingmar Bergman, *Four Screenplays* (New York: Simon and Schuster, 1960).

2. Ibid., p. 21. Eino Kaila's *Persoonallisuus* appeared in 1934 (Helsinki) and was first published in Swedish in 1935 (*Personlighetens psykologi Helsinfors*, 4th edition, 1946).

3. This has been done admirably, for example, by Diane M. Bordon

and Louis H. Leiter in *Wild Strawberries: A Textbook of Aesthetic Criticism* (California Syllabus, Oakland, 1975).

4. Erik H. Erikson, *Childhood and Society*, 2d ed. (New York: Norton, 1963); *Identity, Youth and Crisis* (New York: Norton, 1968); Erik H. Erickson, "The Human Life Cycle" in *International Encyclopedia of the Social Sciences*, s.v. 'Life Cycle."

5. I will discuss the terms as well as the "versus" later on.

6. Bergman, *Four Screenplays*, p. 278.

7. Ibid., p. 283.

8. Erik H. Erikson, *Dimensions of a New Identity*, Jefferson Lectures, 1973 (New York: Norton, 1974).

9. Sudhir, Kakar, "The Human Life Cycle: The Traditional Hindu View and the Psychology of Erik Erikson," *Philosophy East and West*, 18, 3 July 1968.

10. The following formulations are adjusted from the *Encyclopedia of Social Sciences*.

11. Erik H. Erikson, "Autobiographic Notes on the Identity Crisis," *Daedalus* 99 (1970): 730–759. Revised in *Life History and the Historical Moment* (New York: Norton, 1975). For obvious reasons, I have called these stages *psychosocial*. I should add, however, that Generativity has instinctual roots in *psychosexual* development as it continues into adulthood. Psychoanalysis, paradoxically, has tended to separate procreativity from sexuality and even from genital instinctuality, although every genital act climatically involves the procreative organs and their experiential correlates.

Note within a note: the new *biosocial* point of view makes it plausible that pseudospeciation may also have a biological root, namely, in instinctive social acts which propagate and defend common genes. The term "generativity" could include such a meaning, provided it is understood that in man all "instinctive" patterns become enmeshed in instinctual drives. Thus, the "altruistic" sacrifices made for one's genes extend in man to acts of war for one's "kind" and against those deemed inimical to it on the basis of cultural and historical divisions. In turn, the world religions have attempted to counteract exclusivity and rejectivity by advocating sacrificial ideologies transcending genealogical vanity and the elitist identities based on it. I have dealt with this subject in my book *Gandhi's Truth*.

12. Elsewhere, in an account of everyday ritualization throughout human life, I have begun to explore how each stage is and remains related to an essential component of any total social structure—the conflict of the first stage (Primal Trust versus Primal Mistrust) as renewed throughout life, to belief systems, that of the second (Autonomy versus Shame and Doubt) to law, etc. See Erikson, "The Ontogeny of Ritualisation in Man," in *Philosophical Transactions of the Royal Society of London*, series B, no. 772, 251 (1966): 506–88.

ROBERT KASTENBAUM

EXIT AND EXISTENCE: SOCIETY'S UNWRITTEN SCRIPT FOR OLD AGE AND DEATH

The timekeeper mentality of our society does not permit us either to enter or to exit without proper registration. It is not enough simply to have a certificate of birth: this document must also specify the day and the hour of our coming forth. Similarly, the death certificate records our passing from society with a nice, if often arbitrary, concern for time. Custom also dictates that of all the available information about our lives, it is the dates of birth and of death that must adorn our grave markers.

Fascination with temporality may seem misplaced when the topic is death or aging. These are among the universals of human experience. What does it matter if the calendar registers A.D. 948, 1894, or 1984? Old is old and dead is dead.

And yet the historical time frame may be critical to our understanding of what aging and death mean, perhaps even what aging and death *are*. The universal may be mutable as well. This paper explores some continuities and changes in society's relation to aging and death. Nevertheless, it presents the view not of a historian with a definite notion of the situation that existed in the past, but of a psychologist who is attempting to look ahead and understand how things may be in the future. It is entirely possible that our future relation to aging and death will be strongly influenced by what we do with the options that remain in our hands today.

The Past in Portraiture

In the portrait gallery of the mind, our society often envisions an elder of distinguished countenance. Certain characteristics are invariant: the elder is male, venerated by his society, and prepared to answer the summons of death out of the ripeness and wisdom of a long life well lived. Women, shifty-eyed used-camel dealers, and senile wrecks need not apply for the job. The past must be as reassuring to us as the present is not.

Given stringent conditions, we can, in fact, retain this portrait. Select a person who in youth had strength, intelligence, and a knack for survival. Place him in a traditional, relatively static society. Make sure that neither unkind fate nor ruthless competition does him out of his steadily increasing share of the power base. Pray that he keeps his faculties. Bless him with progeny who in turn successfully reproduce their kind. Such a man may indeed be ready to sit for the noble portrait. He is wise, functional, valued, important.

The history of aging and death, however, cannot be limited to so fine a focus. A sick, confused, penniless, childless old woman shunted into a third-class nursing home also has legitimate claim upon our sympathy. It is extremely doubtful, however, that she would have fared much better in the same society that yielded our grand old sage.

Here, then, are a few generalizations about death and aging in the past that appear consistent with the current state of knowledge in gerontology and related fields.

1. *There has been a definite bias in favor of males in most of the cultural traditions that flow into our own.*[1] A schoolchild with a retentive mind can recite the lifespans of Methuselah and a dozen other biblical patriarchs. What *learned* person can do the same for matriarchs? The Scriptures also tell us that King David took the young virgin Abishag to bed, presumably to inhale her breath and thus restore something of his own lost youth. This strategy continued to find advocates down through the centuries. But where do we find old women encouraged by society to take virgin males into their beds? Rabelais conjures up such scenes in his generous imagination, but historically documented instances of such encouragement are difficult to find.[2]

Alongside the portrait of the dignified patriarch, social history is inclined to display the crone, the hag, the witch. The "weird sisters" who forecast Macbeth's rise and fall and the frightful female who flies a broomstick through the dark Halloween skies had many less dramatic counterparts in real life. An aging woman without secure social connections had almost everything to fear, especially neglect. But as Slater has observed, the older woman's actual lack of power frequently promoted other people's fantasies of her mysterious and destructive propensities.[3] She might even accept the imputation of great malevolent powers in preference to seeing herself as completely helpless, vulnerable, and uninteresting. A person might prefer being in league with the devil to being in no league at all. The old woman as witch is but an extreme point on a cultural continuum of dysvalue for the aging female.

There have been important exceptions to this generalization. However, as we shall see, the development of conditions favorable to the aging woman still requires a special advocacy beyond a basic commitment to gerontology and geriatrics.

2. *Respect and solicitude for the aged have been selectively, not universally, bestowed.* It is true that some cultures have been especially eloquent in their advocacy of affection and concern for the aged. Social gerontologists today, however, question some of the implications that have been drawn from this expression of concern. Lipman, for example, distinguishes between true respect for the aged and the kind of "ritualistic deference" that maintains courtesy in superficial transactions but does not preclude neglect or ridicule behind the elder's back.[4] Generally, it has been the healthy, well-connected, well-liked person whose status has remained intact or even been enhanced through advanced age. The lifelong derelict, the unpopular individual, the person seriously debilitated in body or mind, could not expect much from his culture simply because he had grown old. Even societies apparently committed to care of the aged made distinctions according to merit.

Furthermore, the fact that a particular culture has had to reiterate its affection and concern could itself be taken to mean that care of the aged was an ideal, rather than a common practice. In the Scriptures, the child is taught to honor father and mother; the righteous person is rewarded with long life. Yet a plea reaches out across the centuries: "Cast me not off in the time of old age; forsake me not when my strength faileth."[5] Are we to believe the good intentions and teachings of a culture, or the anxiety of its elders? We should probably look at both.

Specific characteristics of the culture also operated either to promote or to discourage solicitude toward the aged. Simmons has found that the elderly most often retained status and power in slowly changing, authoritarian cultures.[6] In these, the elders often controlled much of the property and had other vested sources of power that reinforced their importance. Rosow has added that these also tended to be cultures in which most transactions between individual persons took place face to face, among people who had clearly determined relationships to each other and who saw each other regularly.[7] The position of the aged has generally been more precarious when these conditions have not existed. Societies with limited specialization in jobs also tended to favor old people. There was usually some constructive activity for their hands to perform, freeing more vigorous people for tasks appropriate to the young.

Furthermore, the society's general value system affected the well-being of the aged. For example, the highly developed family life and social organization of the Egyptians, combined with their discoveries in health care and their religious values, provided a favorable environment for the elderly. It was not so much that the elderly were singled out for special attention as that the family and community network embodied a total-care system.[8] On the other hand, the Hellenic Greeks have left us magnificent reminders of their cultural achievements; yet they embraced a value system which regarded old age as "the most evil of things."[9]

It is, then, far from accurate to maintain that the attainment of old age ensured respect and solicitude in cultures prior to our own. The past was not necessarily simpler or less varied than the present.

3. *Dying at an early age was common; living to a ripe old age was not.* Reaching the status of an elder was a rarity in most societies prior to our own. Dublin has estimated the average life expectancy in various periods in history.[10] His figures indicate that our ancestors in the prehistoric period usually were in their graves by age eighteen, with only rare survivors into the third

decade and beyond. Even in the great civilizations of Greece and Rome, life expectancy had increased only three or four years beyond that of prehistory, if statistical estimates are accurate. By this time, however, a scattering of true elders had appeared on the scene. Longevity seems to have increased approximately 50 percent between Roman times and the Middle Ages. Yet, as Hendrik and Hendrik point out, the available information is strongly biased toward the more fortunate members of society, the aristocracy and the upper class.[11] The average life expectancy in the Western world still remained near thirty-five years at the time of the American Revolution.

Perhaps a double perspective is needed here. A person born into an affluent family who had already survived the hazards of the first two decades of life had at least a fair chance to live for several decades more, perhaps into advanced old age. But the infant born into a peasant or lower-class household was in immediate jeopardy from infectious disease, malnutrition, and accident. The infant-mortality rate was so high that census takers rarely bothered to tally children under two years of age. Warfare and other forms of violence also took a large toll on the young. The prospects for reaching maturity, then, were uncertain for most infants, while socially favored individuals who had successfully navigated the hazards of childhood and young adulthood did have an opportunity to experience a full lifespan. We sometimes forget, however, that it was not only the very young who were vulnerable to the epidemic and endemic diseases that have afflicted human beings throughout history. As the adult moved into the later decades, he or she again became exceptionally vulnerable. In the preindustrial era, it was not uncommon for an infant and an elder to be on their deathbeds at the same time—and, of course, in the same household.

Although mortality rates were especially high for the young and the old, we should not forget that by current standards the risk of death was high at every age. This meant that one did not automatically associate death with old age, although one might, in a particular society, associate the old with the *dead*, and the old ones of the society might have a special link or a special "in" with the ancestors and, on this basis, enjoy special status.

At least two other points are worth considering in this connection. First, we should differentiate between chronological age and functional status. A person who was not "old" by modern standards might take on elder status in his or her community because of *relative* seniority. He was an "old-timer" because almost everyone else was so young. In addition, he had been given elder status because the community *needed* a certain minimal number of people in that role. If we hear, then, that elders "had it made" in a particular society, we might be carried away with images of doddering nonagenarians receiving tender loving care, when in reality many of the "elders" had counted only forty or fifty birthdays.

There is a further implication in this regard: how well could a person function at a particular chronological age? We do not have dependable answers to this question for various times and places; only in recent years has strong evidence begun to emerge in our own society. Yet it is likely that two conflicting forces have been at work in many cultures. On the one hand, the rigors and hazards of life may have caused much wear and tear on the individual, so that by age fifty, for example, accumulated injuries and impairments had resulted in a degree of debilitation greater than that experienced by a relatively pampered seventy-five-year-old in the United States today. On the other hand, greater selectivity in survival would mean that those who did reach an advanced age were the hardy, resourceful people, better able to avoid or overcome adversity. On this view, the fifty-year-old serf or tribesman may have enjoyed better functional status in some important respects than a like-aged civil-service employee today who lives a sedentary existence, propped up by a wide variety of medical services within a relatively protective environment. Without trying to answer here a question that requires much further study, I would simply suggest that functional aging—in both individual and socially relative senses—probably has varied much in past cultures, and may distinguish many past cultures from our own. And should we care to define age in terms of distance from death instead of distance from birth, further differences between the past and the present must be acknowledged.

The second point concerns the older generation's investment in the future. Religious faith might comfort the elder as he contemplates the inevitable exit from this existence. But needs, motives, and responsibilities continue to strive for expression. An aging father reminds his vigorous son that we may "attain to a kind of immortality, and in the course of this transitory life perpetuate our name and seed, which is done by a progeny issued from us in the lawful bonds of matrimony." The elder presses his command forward: "I shall not account myself wholly to die, but to pass from one place to another, considering that, in and by thee, I continue in my visible image living in the world." It is clearly the grown son's responsibility to seed future generations, guaranteeing an unbroken sequence stretching back to Adam and ahead to the Last Judgment. The elder already has taken pleasure in seeing "my bald old age reflourish in thy youth," but the real test is in the future.[12] Junior must maintain his own reputation and do his part to bridge the chasm of death with another birth.

This letter from Gargantua to Pantagruel expresses something of the bond between father and son and, as the letter shows, between the father and *his* progenitor. But it also conveys the significance of what might be called the family soul, or perhaps the name soul. The waning generation seeks to preserve something of supreme value. It can do this only in the person of the generation it has seeded. The body dies, but before it does the proud and fond father should be assured that the name soul has transcended the death of the individual and will also bridge the next chasm that awaits son as well as father. (We see again the masculine bias here: the name soul most often is propagated by the male succession, with females as the necessary auxiliary agency.) After countless generations, the treasured name soul will be gathered up into deity, the safe homecoming. With such a philosophy and kinship network flourishing, the old man was more likely to be able to look squarely at his own death without flinching.

4. *We have always had mixed feelings about aging and death.* In a particular culture, one pole of the ambivalence or the other might be the more evident. The Greeks, as we have noted, raged at old age and death, while the Chinese and some other Asian peoples have worshiped ancestors and honored the dead. Yet ambivalence existed in both of these societies, and in all others that we know anything about. What are the general sources of this ambivalence? The following seem especially important.

First, we must credit our ancestors with astute powers of observation. There is no doubt that miseries and infirmities associated with advanced age were clearly noted by past societies. Descriptions in vivid clinical detail exist. Although a particular society may have found a place in its value and caring systems for old people, this did not mean that anyone sought a condition of progressive decrepitude, or preferred to interact closely with those so afflicted.

Second, in addition to being physically distressed, the aged have often been seen as unpleasant, undesirable characters. The ridiculous old person has long been a stock theatrical figure. Pope Innocent III carried on Aristotle's and Horace's earlier blasts against the aged when he labeled them "easily provoked, stingy . . . sullen and quarrelsome, quick to talk, slow to hear, but not slow in wrath, praising former times, despising the moderns, censuring the present, commending the past."[13] Shakespeare and other Elizabethans continued the catalogue of the personal and social failings of old people. When Swift introduced the infinitely miserable and misery-inducing Struldbrugs, we had perhaps the most compelling image of people condemned to perpetual aging. There was no love, glory, majesty, or satisfaction for these people whom fate had denied the ultimate release of death. This recalled the ancient myth of Tithonus, a goddess's mortal lover who, by her intercession, was granted eternal life—but regrettably not eternal youth.

Third, these sometimes unpleasant and unproductive old people have been competing with all other members of society for resources for survival. Who should be given that last bowl of rice, the child or the ancient? This dilemma was not invented in modern times. No matter how the problem was resolved, we must suspect that the tension and emotional pressures were there. Balancing one life against another cannot have been an easy matter, even when relatively clear cultural guidelines were available. The mother might consent to infanticide in order to preserve an elder—but are we to imagine that this decision was made without pangs of sorrow? The elderly person might take the initiative to self-destruct when this was expected by society—but are we to suppose that this was invariably an action unmarked by fear, anger, or regret?

We, as cultural outsiders, tend to assume that those on the inside of such alien cultures actually experience no more or less than their guidelines seem to advertise. We have been quick to assume that people in cultures different from our own possess simpler, less sensitive emotions, or can take decisive actions without being troubled by alternatives. I personally find this attitude questionable and self-serving. The fact that old people often have had to compete for scarce resources with other members of society can only have heightened tension and increased ambivalence. The notion of the old man slipping off gently into that good night appears to make it that much easier to withhold the affection, and thus the material and social resources, that could have helped him to remain a while longer.

Finally, the most obvious point of all: in the opinion of many people over the centuries, there was not really much choice between old age and death. Aging itself has been seen at times as part of the process of dying.[14] Gruman has shown that the revolt of the spirit against both aging and death has led indirectly to many advances in science, in hygiene, and even in the exploration of the planet Earth.[15] While reaching a good old age has been a common hope, being old has rarely been anyone's ambition. "I'd rather be young," said the greybeard of ancient Egypt as he studied "The Book for Transforming an Old Man into a Youth of Twenty."[16] There seems to have been no market for "The Book for Transforming a Youth of Twenty into an Old Man."

Best of all is youth. A good old age runs a distant second, historically, in the affections of humankind. I suspect, however, that a universal retrospective survey of attitudes toward the choice between death and a bad old age would result in a preference for an honorable demise. The young or middle-aged person obviously cannot know what kind of old age lies in his or her future—or even *whether* he or she will reach old age. It is the uncertainty itself that must be reckoned with. Under conditions of subjective uncertainty, a person may assume either the better or the worse, or may suffer so much from the uncertainty itself that a premature closure of the issue is forced. A life hurled about recklessly can sometimes be traced to a person's insecurity about what may happen in the future.

A further word about the other (that is, positive) side of the

ambivalence is in order. If *all* aged people suffered or were in-
sufferable, then the choice of death would be an easier one for
most people in most situations. Yet the nomad of biblical times
could see as well as we can today that there are appreciable
individual differences in what old people are like and how well
they fare. With luck, he or she might have a good old age.

Furthermore, death itself has also been painted in various
shades of hope and dread. Death is release, or it is reward. It is
unrelenting horror, or it is nothing at all. Perhaps death is just
not very different from the life one has already known.[17] So a
person is ambivalent, not only toward advanced age, but also
toward death. The conflicting movements of the spirit in a particular historical epoch have depended greatly upon the interrelated ambivalences toward old age and death, which are part
of a larger constellation of approach-avoidance maneuvers for
which I have elsewhere proposed the concept of *omnivalence*.[18]

Not So Very Long Ago

Average life expectancy increased impressively throughout the
1800s but took a truly spectacular leap ahead during the early
decades of the twentieth century. In technologically advanced
nations like our own, approximately two full decades were added
to the average life expectancy; it has already been noted that
this was the length of the *entire* life expectancy in Greek and
Roman times.

Recent increases in life expectancy have been less spectacular.
However, the resulting shifts in population structure and in the
phenomena we associate with death are still with us. There are
more old people alive at this moment—whether we calculate in
absolute numbers or in proportion of population—than ever before. Furthermore, the experts predict that this trend will extend
into the next few decades at least. About a hundred years ago,
this nation included an estimated 1.2 million people aged sixty-
five and older, or less than 3 percent of the total population. By
the turn of the century, there were 3.1 million Americans in this
age range, accounting for 4.1 percent of the population. Today
there are more than 20 million elders, who represent about 10.3

percent of the population. It is estimated that by the end of this century there will be approximately 29 million elders in the United States.[19] The *percentage* of elders in our population at that time will depend upon the interaction of various trends, but it appears that approximately one person in five living in the year 2000 will have passed his or her sixty-fifth birthday.

We can easily identify some of the corollaries and consequences of this shift, although in doing so we will be forced to neglect many other changes in life style that have influenced our current attitudes toward old age and death.

1. *More adults have living parents and grandparents than ever before in history.* This means, for example, that a sixty-year-old is not necessarily the family's ranking elder. It also means that the emotional bonds between parent and child may persist through each one's later decades. The sixty-year-old retains certain expectations and conflicts involving Momma and Poppa and at the same time represents the parent and grandparent to younger generations. Both phenomenological and intergenerational life have the potential for becoming extraordinarily complex. It has been found that a person in the postreproductive phase of life is less likely to dream of or imagine a dead parent than were earlier generations; instead, such persons' visitations and interactions remain a part of the tissue of everyday life.

2. *Although more elders are surviving longer than ever before, the association between old age and death has become stronger.* This is a paradoxical development in one sense: the fact that more people live to an advanced age might be thought to further weaken the association between old age and mortality. But it is also evident that *fewer* people are dying at an *early* age. We hear a parent explaining a death to a young child on the basis that Granny was "very old." By implication, Mommy and Daddy and the child will not die until they are also "very old," an incredibly long time from now. This is just one manifestation of the strong link between aging and death which has seized our thinking. Death? See Old Age. Old Age? See Death.

3. *We have become enthusiastic about preventive care and acute-treatment techniques; however, most deaths actually result from long-term deterioration and invasive processes.* Breakthroughs in public health and medicine in the past have helped

many people to survive into old age. But our society's priorities remain fixed on the dramatic cure, the wondrous elixir, and the surgeon's astonishing virtuosity. Continuous, systematic care for the person who is old today and will be one day older tomorrow has not captured our imagination. In this way, we tend to abandon those who have reached a state of need and peril just *because* our models of preventive care and acute treatment have proved effective. Convert this octogenarian into a child again, and we will inoculate him against life-threatening disease and stand ready to hurl every weapon in our medical arsenal against any prospect of his untimely death. But careers are not made, nor are programs funded, on the premise of converting an old man of eighty into an old man of eighty-one.

4. *Emphasis is shifting from acute to anticipatory grief.* The trajectory from life to death seems to be extending into a longer, perhaps more gentle, slope. While it is true that sudden, unexpected deaths still occur, it is increasingly common for a long life to fade off into death, providing much opportunity in advance for the family to adjust to the impending loss. I do not intend to minimize the impact of the actual death itself or to assert that all people do in fact anticipate bereavement even when the elderly person has been ill for a long time. However, when a person dies in his seventies or eighties today, there is probably less acute grief on the part of society than was the case for a modal death in past generations. And if the elder previously has been "disengaged"—removed from the mainstream of family and community life—the social significance of the death is likely to be even further reduced.[20]

5. *Being old is not special anymore.* It is not only that the novelty of having many elderly people around is starting to wear off; it is also that more and different kinds of people are surviving into advanced years. If the phenomenon of "survival of the fittest" ever existed in this regard, it was more likely to have been found in the past than in the present. In the past, a person had to be especially strong, able, and fortunate to survive past life's first prime; now a person has to be unusually vulnerable and unfortunate to perish young. There is probably still a tendency for the more competent to survive longer, but not to such a striking degree as in the past.[21] Yesterday's old person, then, had a higher

probability of earning respect both on his or her own distinctive merits and as an exemplar of a rare resource. Today's old person has a greater probability of being just about the same as everybody else in society, adding or subtracting differences attributable to life styles characteristic of a particular generation.

6. *Demands upon social resources are shifting from young to old dependents.* In general, young and middle-aged adults carry the burden of supporting not only themselves but also those who cannot function successfully on their own. Until recently, our society clearly owed most of its obligations to the young and immature. Public-health and educational programs and much of our national life style reflect this orientation. The dollar we do not spend on ourselves is likely to be spent on our children.

The balance is now shifting. The "postmature" make up an increasingly large proportion of economically- and physically-dependent people in our society. It seems we have not yet recognized the scope and significance that this shifting balance will have, especially if zero population growth prevails. Shanas and Hauser warn that "a rugged individualism philosophy [with regard to] the aged will be increasingly inapplicable in the face of their increased numbers and their continuing needs. Zero population growth will make a welfare society for the elderly inevitable. . . . ['Welfare society'] is not a pejorative phrase nor a form of undesirable socialism. It appears to be a rational response to changes in population structure and to technological advances." Whether or not one cares to accept this view completely, the facts suggest that traditional attitudes toward care of the young and the old will soon be called into question as it is perceived that these attitudes no longer reflect social reality.

How It Will Be From Now on: A Scenario

Although the background sketched in here is selective and simplified, enough salient features have been described for us to be able to construct a scenario for the future. This projection is organized with reference to the way society has been answering the following question: what value is there in being an old, dying, or dead person?

It is useful to introduce one further concept: "the death system." This term refers to the functional network through which a society comes to terms with death, including people, places, objects, and symbols.[23] Some of these components are identified primarily, and permanently, by their role in the death system—for example, the funeral director, cemetery, death certificate; other components may be recruited into the system as the occasion demands. The death system performs several vital functions: predictions and warnings of the possibility of death and actions intended to prevent it; care of the dying or otherwise doomed person; physical disposition of the corpse; consolation and reintegration of survivors and the establishment of an orientation toward or relationship with the dead. Explanations and rationalizations of death are part of the system. Those actions which have the effect of bringing about death are as much a part of the system as the components of prediction and prevention. Certain aspects of the society's economic function and structure are, of course, part of the death system. How much money do you suppose changes hands in our society each year for death-related reasons? The answer to this question would include much if not all of the national defense budget; "life" insurance premiums, payments, and commissions; floral offerings; the pet-food industry; newspaper income from death notices; and so on.

These functions can be discerned in all societies; relative emphasis varies, however, from one society to another, or within the same society in different periods. The relative proportions of children, adults, and elderly adults at a given time will be a factor; but so will the prevailing system of religious beliefs and practices or a cycle of good or poor harvests.

The scenario for the future that suggests itself for our own society is based on the assumption that certain current trends will become dominant while other already entrenched attitudes and practices will continue. It is important to emphasize that this present-tense description represents one view of the way things *might* be. One approach to this scenario can be obtained by working backward from death itself.

1. There is no point in being dead. This view has now been made palpable by the systematic conversion of burial grounds to other, more utilitarian, purposes. Except for those relatively few

cemeteries now designated as historical sites, the burial ground has virtually disappeared from the landscape. Again, with few exceptions, the recently deceased are not commemorated by conspicuous, space-wasting monuments. This practice had been losing much of its vitality for decades, anyway, as suggested by the increasing standardization of tombstone inscriptions. Other kinds of memorial practices have also been reduced to a minimum that a previous generation might not have thought possible. Traffic is no longer held up by the slow-moving cortege of limousines and mourners. Busy people no longer miss a day's work to stand in the wind or rain while a deceased colleague is lowered into the earth. Efficiency and common sense have at last prevailed. Our death system's gradually lessened interest in relating to or utilizing the dead, a phenomenon observed by a few in previous years, has moved from the mental-emotional sphere to the physical and official change of visible practices associated with disposal of the dead and with remembrance.[24] Naturally, services are available for those deviant and troubled individuals whose functioning is impaired by unresolved feelings about a dead person. According to the latest clinical and scientific reports, systematic desensitization to bereavement as a routine activity of the behavior modifiers has had reasonably consistent success.

2. There is little point in dying. In fact, as compared with the previous generation or two, there is relatively little "dying" per se. One reason for the diminished significance of dying, of course, has been the perfection of an integrated, computerized system for (1) determining a person's level of viability; (2) evaluating availability and cost of alternative treatment and maintenance procedures; and (3) resolving the problems of terminal care and body disposal. The United States Public Health Service operates the Super-Euthanasiac Computer, into which all relevant data are constantly programmed. When the computer detects and validates a critical configuration of disability, prognosis, and cost estimate, a quick and painless termination is accomplished— including selection of the appropriate body-disposal route. It is no wonder that the president of the American Medical Association has expressed unstinting approval of this technique. The need to make life-and-death decisions that began to weigh so heavily upon medical personnel in the 1960s and 1970s has now been

almost entirely eliminated. Moreover, the unacceptable expense of maintaining incurable and unproductive citizens has been sharply reduced (although it must be admitted that the cost of the new computer system has been considerably higher than anticipated). Some observers were surprised, however, when the Pope herself expressed strong approval. Few could quarrel, however, with her assertion that the new system would promote favorable reallocation of scarce resources for safeguarding the lives of those who still had a chance. The development of the Church's own Vaticaniac Computer Program to guide determinations of viability of Catholic patients based on applicable tenets of their religion no doubt had something to do with the acceptability of the system as a whole.

Another reason for the reduced significance of dying and of being a dying person is more psychosocial than technological. Dying retained some importance as long as there was any point at all in being dead. Now that the status of the dead has become so attenuated, little significance need be attributed to the preparatory phase. The "exit" phase of existence has become relatively unimportant and vestigial. It is not a critical part of the transition from one social status to another; there is little significance that dying can borrow from its destination. "I am not going to be anything to anybody when I am dead; therefore, as I approach dead-status through the process of dying, my value progressively diminishes." Much of the individual's social value is depleted, then, before the moment of death arrives.

3. There is no point in being old. This is in part a function of the reverse sequence we have been describing. Society has no use for the dead, and therefore little use for the dying. For many years, being old has meant a general reduction in social value for reasons not directly associated with death. However, with the shift in mortality peaks from early to late in the lifespan, and with other socioeconomic and attitudinal changes, a more specific association has also been strengthened between *advanced* age and death. Now when a person is recognized as "old," this status initiates a trajectory of dysvalue that moves inevitably through dying- and dead-status. "I am an old person, which means that before long I will be a dying person; therefore, as I approach dying-status through the aging process, my value progressively

diminishes." Old, dying, and dead are stations of life still differ-entiated by our society, but collectively they represent an essentially trivial postscript to authentic existence as a person in society.

This situation was anticipated by the low priority which society gave for many years to the care of the aged. Moreover, the growing trend for the aged to die in an institutional setting, coupled with the usual way in which institutions responded to the dying and the dead, provided a firm model for progressive dysvaluation.[25] Aged residents were likely to observe that the dying were isolated, and the dead removed quickly. Implicit were the messages that "Nobody has died," and "Dying and being dead are nothing." These messages registered with the impact that "Nobody has been alive," and "I *will have been* nothing when I *become* nothing." So thoroughly were the aged dying and dead ejected from the scene that the fact that they had ever been alive (and perhaps valuable) seemed entirely inconsistent. With this sort of rehearsal for their own deaths, the institutionalized aged saw their present existence drained of value.

Today, the transitions from old to dying to dead are better managed. Much of the ambiguity has been eliminated, along with the accompanying tension and occasional guilt on the part of care-givers and family as well as the aged themselves. Only a few of the factors contributing to this change can be cited here.

One important development was the change in official recognition of the start of old age, from sixty-five to seventy.[26] Although gerontologists argued, with good evidence, that even seventy is "too young to be old" for many people today, a compromise at seventy prevailed. In retrospect, the identification of official old age with the biblical specification of "threescore and ten" seems to have proved fortuitous. People in their sixties now receive a full share of benefits and privileges. The slide of value-into-dysvalue throughout the seventh decade of life has been sharply reduced. Other factors in the change include the development of more flexible retirement plans, the cultivation of multiple careers, and the increased prominence of women in the work force.

Perhaps the single most important factor, however, has been the great success of the voluntary-termination plan. Once surrounded by prohibitions and negative emotions, suicide has become, under certain circumstances, an action with great positive value. This trend was anticipated some years ago. It was shown that the implicit preferences of most Americans regarding the "ideal" way to die included the following characteristics: (1) an identifiable and rational cause; (2) some element of control; (3) an acceptable physical setting; (4) occurrence at the right time; (5) little or no suffering or experiencing; (6) rapid onset; (7) consistency with the individual's distinctive or most valued style of life. It was predicted that all of these characteristics could most dependably be invoked by suicide.[27] The suicide would, of course, have to meet certain pragmatic and moral criteria, which were also discussed in some detail.

Apparently, two major factors in the success of the voluntary-termination plan were the decades-long subjection of the aged to low-priority status and the rapid diminution of the value of the dying and the dead in our death system. People simply incorporated these cultural orientations into their own attitude structures, and when they had themselves grown old, they began to act upon the implicit commands.

The well-achieved suicide (to use the old-fashioned expression) bestows upon the old person's exit a value that it can attain in no other way. Instead of fading into a prolonged phase of senescence and dysvalue, the man or woman on the brink of old age now can elect a self-termination mode that consolidates and validates his or her existence up to that point. A good citizen, having lived a good life, no longer faces the prospect of a retroactively spoiled identity because of unnecessary aging and dying.

An Alternative Scenario

It is possible to accept the background facts and trends that generated the above scenario and yet arrive at a different one. This requires the recognition of several other trends and options that have not yet been mentioned.

"THE ROAD DOESN'T END HERE ANYMORE" The county historical society almost lost in its campaign to preserve the street in its old form as a designated reminder of how things used to be. Little could be said in favor of the structures themselves. The aesthetic appeal was virtually nil, and somehow the "bad vibrations" seemed to cling to the walls. Yet enough people appreciated the moral and educational value of preserving the row of "nursing homes" and "funeral homes" to allow the historical society to keep this relic of the not-so-distant past before contemporary eyes.

Surprisingly, the street has proved to be a popular if sobering attraction. "So this was the end of the road," a visitor may say, shaking his head as though to clear away disbelief. "You have to wonder how people felt when they turned down this street. It must have been like leaving life behind, entering a kind of slaughterhouse district, but with most of the bleeding *inside*, in the heart. How could people let the road end that way?"

The street of nursing homes and funeral homes—peculiar remnants of the past—certainly is out of place now. Old age and death once were considered the end of the road, almost functionally equivalent in many people's minds. This inaccurate assumption no longer burdens society. Advances in scientific knowledge have contributed to the change: increasingly, it has been recognized that many of the so-called inevitable changes "caused" by the aging process can in fact be attributed more accurately to a variety of specific factors. Each new rank of chronologically old men and women reaches a particular age checkpoint in better health and with greater functional capacity than the preceding one. There was no single "breakthrough"; instead, health maintenance throughout the lifespan has steadily improved. The physical impairment and vulnerability to chronic disease that were fostered by sedentary, careless, and unmonitored life styles have been sharply reduced. Sixty-five-year-olds are more physically active today than many forty-year-olds of a few generations back. Good nutritional habits carefully cultivated in the early years of life are now paying good dividends in the later decades. Specific changes, such as the enrichment of beer with vitamins, have helped to preserve the functioning of memory and the overall integrity of personality among people who in the past might have suffered deterioration not much past midlife.

The overall change, however, has occurred in the minds both

of the elders themselves and of the allied health professionals. Suffering, impairment, and disease are no longer considered especially "natural" in old age. More can be done to prevent problems and to correct or compensate for them when they do occur.

Gerontologists from a variety of disciplines have helped to clarify the distinction between growing old and becoming ill. A core of processes remains that could be characterized as "normal aging," although even this core is still subject to continuing review and experimentation.

In similar fashion, a clearer distinction has been recognized between growing old and "getting stale." As developmental psychologists finally enlarged their horizons to encompass the whole lifespan and to establish appropriate ways of assessing behavior and experience from infancy through old age, it became evident that individual patterns are at least as significant as age-related changes. There was no escaping the conclusion that some men and women have "staled out" by their forties or fifties—or even their twenties or thirties—while others show few, if any, of the stereotypical age changes after they have passed their seventieth, eightieth, or ninetieth birthday. Circumstantial evidence has long suggested the importance of individual patterns; now, abundant research supports this view in detail.

In both biomedical and psychosocial terms, then, the assumption of a close link between old age and deterioration—and therefore between old age and death—has been shown to be faulty. While it is still true that some chronologically old people are physically ill and impaired, and some very limited in their ability to experience and adapt to their environments (not necessarily the same persons in both cases) such difficulties and illnesses no longer *define* old age. In addition to the greater national commitment to the maintenance of physical health throughout life, there is now more encouragement of continuing personal growth. Recreation, for example, has become more re-creational for many people; education is now a lifelong process for a greater number; and self-development groups have survived the fad stage to become an effective and respected part of the cultural milieu. While, of course, some people continue to reach the end of the road early in life; this is no longer the expected pattern. Chronological age simply does not have much to do with the quality of one's life. As old age (in the once-traditional chronological sense of the term) has been liberated from its association with the end of health and mental vigor, so the association with dying and death has been reduced to more realistic dimensions. People still die old if they do not die young, but they are not surrounded by clouds of gloom and dysvalue while they still walk the earth.

Many other changes have contributed to the revised image and reality of old age. Reaching a particular age (and remember when that was as young as sixty-five!) once meant a virtually complete exit from the social scene. The individual stepped (or was pushed) across a single threshold and from that point on was little more than an occasional offstage voice. Now, of course, fewer of the exits are controlled by chronology. Mandatory retirement did not tremble and fall with an overwhelming crash after a fierce struggle; it just gradually passed away.

More flexible ideas of what constitutes a working life have made the single-career pattern just one among several. The framework of young adult to elderly retiree has altered just as the nine-to-five workday has given way to more flexible arrangements. Now, people move into and out of occupations in a variety of patterns, taking a year out here for re-education, six months there for community service, and so on. The availability of a large number of vigorous, skilled elders who are interested in part-time or temporary employment has proved extremely helpful to many industries and government agencies. The "average" person now may have, in effect, "retired" several times before reaching age sixty-five and yet, in another sense, not have retired at all. The ever-changing flow of workers of various ages and degrees of development of their capacities has made age-based mandatory retirement anachronistic—and eliminated one of the main symbols of exit from social participation.

The great improvement in the status of women has also been very important. The woman of today must have an informed sense of history in order to recognize that once her life might have been considered over when the last child had left the "nest," or when she became a widow (as often happened to women in earlier generations before the longevity of males improved). Today's woman, fully competent in the management of her life outside as well as inside the home, brings many skills, achievements, and interests to the later years of her life. She is seldom faced with a confusing and unfamiliar world of financial management, for example, or frustrated by other problems that someone else would have looked after in the past. She is resourceful and successful throughout her life and has no reason to be otherwise as she reaches any particular chronological-age mark.

Both men and women, of course, have found the toppling of assumptions and prohibitions regarding sexual intimacy in later life to be a truly liberating development. In the past, physical death seemed almost an afterthought for some people when they had already exited (in society's view) from the life of labor and the life of love. Now, better general health has contributed to the general maintenance of sexual tone in elders; but the change in attitudes has also been very important. The overall maturation of public opinion in relation to many aspects of human development shows some of its most favorable results in relation to old age and intimacy. There was a period in which the existence of only two "kinds" of women was generally acknowledged: "good women," and those who enjoyed sex. Then, as women achieved sociopolitical equality with men, sexual liberation followed, sometimes accompanied by new problems for some men. It took some time for many men to adjust to women who were at least their equals in all spheres, and there *were* some "casualties" along the way. Now, however, adults share sexual intimacy at all points of the life span.

In general, men and women, now able to function well physically, maintain and develop personality strengths, participate fully in the work and productivity of society according to their individual interests, and remain sexually active, seldom regard any chronological age as the end of the kind of lives they have made for themselves. Those who choose, or are forced, to leave a particular domain in which they have functioned successfully can open other doors to a rewarding life. The humanization and individualization of technology has provided many more possibilities for maintaining control after such functions as muscular strength, mobility, reaction time, and sensory acuity have been impaired. In other words, a person is not necessarily rendered powerless and isolated just because a particular physical function has become less dependable. This ability to compensate for age-related deficits has, in turn, greatly reduced passive yearning for death, as well as active suicide, among older adults.

In essence, society has come to realize that within its power is the ability to develop alternative "scripts" for the whole human lifespan. The *programmed impetus* given to each person as birthright may run its course around mid-life, if not before: the "job specifications" written into the genes have completed their schedules.[28] For many centuries there was no concerted effort on the part of society to augment this partial script for a human life; few people survived long enough to require it. Now, however, a variety of alternative paths exists for the second half of life, and the variety is constantly increasing. Development through old age is almost as enthusiastically demanded and expected—and applauded and enjoyed—as development through the childhood years.

Society places greater value on the *completed person*.[29] Although a child of ten may be, in one sense, all that he or she can be, true fulfillment of human possibilities is now seen as requiring a long life in which knowledge increases and is enriched over the years. The young are fresh and daring; middle-aged people (the term now applies to a much longer space of life) would please Aristotle with their balancing of the novel and the familiar, the necessary and the possible; elders integrate all the qualities of previous years with a cultivated sense of perspective.

THE EXIT FROM EXISTENCE *Being old* has shifted to a positive value. Yet dying and death have not been banished from the human condition, nor have they continued to operate secretly and to bizarre effect under the lugubrious apparatus of massive denial. Compared with the situation in the past, in fact, dying and death are much more out in the open today. This is due, in part, to the increased value placed upon *life* in old age. As a number of keen observers have remarked over the centuries, the person who has lived well and fully does appear more at ease with mortality.

But part of the new attitude is a result of a greater appreciation of dying, death, *and the dead* per se. When the old death system was functioning at its peak, the elderly progressed on a sort of assembly line from old age through dying to death and oblivion.[30] It is perhaps easier to understand this progression in reverse. For a time, honoring and memorializing the dead became a greatly attenuated process. Funeral processions, the use of cemetery space, and most forms of integrating the dead psychologically into the lives of individual survivors and the culture were under attack and erosion. In effect, the dead seemed to have no role in the symbolic life of society, with a few notable exceptions.

The nonutility of the dead was a phenomenon which then worked ahead in time. It made the dying person more of a threat, annoyance, or burden than a gathering place for social values and concern. There was no point in "being dead," hence little point in being a person who would soon be forgotten. This part of the process often was exemplified in congregate facilities for the care of the aged. The nonutility of the dying person worked forward in time to strip value from the old person. The elder would die, and the dead would blow away like the wind with its debris. Little wonder that many aging men and women, taking their cues from mandatory retirement, the death of a spouse, or some other major change in their lives, would disassociate from themselves just as society was pulling away from them.

Today, the aged have been liberated in both directions. In life, there is no longer an age-determined exitus from full participation and status. On the side of death, society has regained its sense of history and continuity. We no longer feel so lost, shift our feet, and avoid eye contact at leave-taking rituals. Death is not seen as a failure by the individual or the health professions. Thoughts and feelings toward the dead are accepted as a vital thread of continuity that symbolizes our existence as members of the human race rather than as solitary individuals. The neutral, objective-functional abandonment of the dead once in vogue has yielded to a more intuitive relationship, one that gives the present generation more in common with ancestors across the centuries than with those of just a few years ago. In caring about the dead and the dying, those who have barely started to approach their own elder years are already preparing the way for a personal sense of continued value throughout all the bright days and deep nights of life's seasons.

Notes

1. R. Kastenbaum and B. Ross, "Historical Perspectives on Care of the Aged," in *Modern Perspectives in the Psychiatry of Old Age*, ed. J. G. Howells (New York: Brunner/Mazel, 1975), pp. 421–48.

2. François Rabelais, *Gargantua and Pantagruel*, trans. Sir Thomas Urquhart and Peter Mottux, Great Books of the Western World, vol. 24 (Chicago: Encyclopaedia Britannica, 1952).

3. P. E. Slater, "Cross-cultural Views of the Aged," in *New Thoughts on Old Age*, ed. R. Kastenbaum (New York: Springer, 1964), pp. 229–36.

4. A. Lipman, "Prestige of the Aged in Portugal: Realistic Appraisal and Ritualistic Deference," *Aging and Human Development* 1 (1970): 127–36.

5. Psalm 71:9.

6. L. Simmons, "Aging in Preindustrial Societies," in *Handbook of Social Gerontology*, ed. C. Tibbitts (Chicago: University of Chicago Press, 1960), pp. 62–91.

7. I. Rosow, *Social Integration of the Aged* (New York: Free Press, 1967).

8. F. D. Zeman, "Old Age in Ancient Egypt: A Contribution to the History of Geriatrics," *Journal of Mount Sinai Hospital* 8 (1942): 1161–65.

9. B. E. Richardson, *Old Age among the Ancient Greeks* (Baltimore: Johns Hopkins Press, 1933).

10. L. I. Dublin, *Factbook on Man* (New York: Macmillan, 1965).

11. J. Hendrik and C. Hendrik, "The Good Old Days: What Was Old Age Really Like?" *International Journal of Aging and Human Development* 8 (1978): 139–150.

12. Rabelais, *Gargantua*, p. 81.

13. G. R. Coffman, "Old Age from Horace to Chaucer. Some Literary Affinities and Adventures of an Idea," *Speculum* 9 (1934): 249–77.

14. J. Taylor, *The Art of Holy Dying* (1651; reprint ed., New York: Arno Press, 1976).

15. G. R. Gruman, "A History of Ideas about the Prolongation of Life," *Transactions of the American Philosophical Society* 56 (1966): 1–97 (reprint ed., New York: Arno Press, 1976).

16. Ibid.

17. R. Kastenbaum, "Is Death a Life Crisis?" in *Lifespan Developmental Psychology: Normative Crises and Interventions*, ed. D. Natan and L. Ginsberg (New York: Academic Press, 1976), pp. 19–50.

18. R. Kastenbaum, "Should We Have Mixed Feelings about Our Ambivalences toward the Aged?" *Journal of Geriatric Psychiatry* 7 (1974): 94–107.

19. E. Shanas and P. M. Hauser, "Zero Population Growth and the Family Life of Old People," *Journal of Social Issues* 30 (1974): 79–92.

20. E. Cumming and W. E. Henry, *Growing Old* (New York: Basic Books, 1961); B. G. Glaser, "The Social Loss of Dying Aged Patients," *Gerontologist* 6 (1966): 77–80.

21. K. F. Reigel and R. M. Reigel, "Development, Drop, and Death," *Developmental Psychology* 6 (1972): 306–19.

22. Shanas and Hauser, "Zero Population Growth," p. 91.

23. R. Kastenbaum and R. B. Aisenberg, *The Psychology of Death* (New York: Springer Publishing Company, 1972); R. Kastenbaum, *Death, Society, and Human Experience* (St. Louis: C. V. Mosby Company, 1977).

24. Kastenbaum and Aisenberg, *Psychology of Death*; R. Blauner, "Death and Social Structure," *Psychiatry* 29 (1966): 378–94; R. Kastenbaum, "Two-way Traffic on the River Styx" (Paper presented at the annual meeting of American Psychological Association, 1969); R. Fulton, private communication.

25. E.g., R. Kastenbaum and S. E. Candy, "The 4% Fallacy: A Methodological and Empirical Critique of Use of Population Statistics in Gerontology," *Aging and Human Development* 4 (1973): 15–22.

26. This was a futuristic proposition when presented at the conference; it is now becoming the law of the land.

27. R. Kastenbaum, "Suicide as the Preferred Way of Death," in *Progress in Suicidology*, ed. E. S. Schneidman (New York: Grune & Stratton, 1976), pp. 425–43.

28. R. Kastenbaum, "Theories of Human Aging—The Search for a Conceptual Framework," *Journal of Social Issues* 21 (1965): 13–36.

29. R. Kastenbaum, "Time, Death, and Ritual in Old Age," in *The Study of Time*, ed. J. T. Fraser (New York, Heidelberg, Berlin: Springer-Verlag, 1975), 2: 20–38.

30. R. Kastenbaum, *Death, Society, and Human Experience*.

2 AGING AND DEATH IN THE PAST

ATTITUDES AND BEHAVIOR

PETER LASLETT

THE TRADITIONAL ENGLISH FAMILY AND THE AGED IN OUR SOCIETY

The historical experience of the English-speaking Western European peoples enters into our own social perceptions of aging in ways which are only now beginning to be appreciated. Historical sociology offers one way of examining societal development and aging, that is, by raising the question of how the process of aging and the position of the aged have changed over time. Such an approach involves insisting that in order to understand ourselves at all individually and socially, we must place ourselves in contrast to our past and attempt to formulate that contrast as accurately as possible. We must, therefore, guard against two frequent misuses of historical experience. The first is the compensatory practice of seeking in the past only those qualities which make up for the deficiencies and dissatisfactions which are painfully obvious in the present: utilizing the past selectively, that is, drawing upon it in order to justify a proposed change in our contemporary world by an appeal to a vanished situation which, in fact, may be entirely irrelevant to our own. The second tendency might be described as the "world we have lost" syndrome, in which the deficiencies of the present are measured by the destruction of an idealized society which is presumed to have existed at some period in the past.[1] These two tendencies are of particular importance to the topic of the aged, whose position in our view of the past has hitherto been almost entirely a matter of compensation and of legitimation. This has been inevitable, since so very little has thus far been discovered about the history of aging. Considerations of this kind are particularly relevant in a symposium on human values. Human values, however we try to define them, all share to some extent the quality of pastness.

They do so for what may seem at first sight a rather trivial reason, but one which on reflection turns out to be more impressive. For a habit, an attitude, a criterion, has to be permanent, or at least deep-rooted in time and experience, if it is to be considered a value. A value may be worth respecting and cherishing if it is widely distributed among the cultures of the world: this was the opinion of the philosophers of natural law, from the Stoics and Cicero down to Grotius and Locke. They sought to show that respect for the aged was and always had been a universal human attribute. But a value may be even more effective for a given society if it is felt to be a peculiar distinguishing feature of that society's past, one not shared by other peoples. The way to find out whether such an attribute is truly a characteristic of one's belief system is, of course, to discover how far back it goes in the records of one's own people. If distant reaches of time come into question, then Revelation may be invoked, as it is by the Jewish people in appealing to the Scriptures, and so by European Christendom as well. This means that our association of pastness with cultural values requires specifically historical criticism.

The full-scale historical-sociological account of aging and the family cannot be attempted here, but I can indicate the pitfalls of such research and what some of the preliminary evidence from past investigations suggests about the social view of aging in the family. The discoveries of contemporary gerontology with respect to the aged and the family in the United States and other highly developed countries present the inquirer with a paradox. On the one hand there is the widespread conviction, often vociferously expounded by the aged themselves, that aging is a family matter, that it is the support of the family which the aged require and feel that they have lost, and that this refers specifically to a family circle to live in. On the other hand there is the insistence by the aged that independence is an important value for them, and that dependence, even on children or grandchildren or more distant kin, is inconsistent with that value. A particularly sharp contradiction comes about when residence within a family circle not one's own is in question (where "own" means the family one has himself created), even if it is residence in the family of a married child. An aged widower, for example, may prefer lodging with a more distant relative or even with a landlady.

The implications of this paradox to the researcher on the aged and the family are extensive. When a researcher discovers, for example, the composition of family groups in the past, he cannot interpret this information in one way only. It is not necessarily true, that a society—a village community or a country—which had, for instance, a high proportion of the aged residing with their married children was a society which treated the aged in the humane way (and by "humane" I mean the way in which the aged themselves would wish to be treated). Coresidence with their married children may have been forced upon the elderly against their wishes. Nor does it follow from the presence of a large number of solitary or lodging widowed persons that the elderly were being neglected. This mode of life may have been the choice of the aged themselves, and therefore we cannot simply conclude that they were rejected by their families.

Second, a whole series of facts and circumstances have to be recovered before we can appreciate the meaning of the familial situation of the aged. Although I have hinted that, given reasonably adequate records, it is relatively easy to determine family composition in the past, it should be clear that digging out even these facts requires some ingenuity and pains. The facts which are still needed in order to interpret discoveries about the composition of the household in the past pose a higher order of difficulty altogether. They include the following:

1. The characteristics of the life cycle of the individual and those of the family cycle of domestic groups which were present in that society and persisted within it over time. This entails the determination of the age at which children generally left home; the age at which the parents retired, if they lived long enough; the frequency with which children returned, unmarried and married, to look after aged parents.

2. The residential and migratory habits of individuals and households. We need to know whether children set up households to live near their parents, or whether parents moved, or tried to move, within easy reach of children or other relatives when they grew old.

3. The extent of recognition of kinship and the strength of

kinship bonds—that is to say, their value as a resource for nurturance and welfare, and their reliability as a possible support for the aged. It is also necessary to determine attitudes toward the old in general, within the family and in society at large. Above all, it is essential to determine the influence of social and political policy. Did it, for example, encourage familial coresidence for the dependent elderly, or did it provide institutions for them? Did it respect the desire of the aged to live independently, where such a desire existed? Did it insist on the welfare obligations of the kin to the aged, and then see that these obligations were fulfilled, either by coresidence or by financial support for independent living?

On all three of the above topics, little is yet known even from the English file, at least if we concentrate, as I have done so far, on traditional, preindustrial English society before 1800. Yet much more may be discovered from the painstaking and rigorous use of straightforward, traditionally "humanistic" methods of inquiry: for instance the exploitation of U.S. census records, together with the voluminous ancillary evidence which seems to be so plentiful in the United States.

Our third major point regarding the implications of the paradoxical discoveries of gerontology requires us to insist that advanced numerical and mathematical techniques of inquiry and analysis must be applied if we are to understand at all definitely the issues of aging in relation to human values and social experience. I would like to illustrate this by asking the following question about table 1. Does it suggest a change of values in the social view of aging in England to find indications that the proportion of married men over sixty-five living as heads of households containing their own unmarried children was in preindustrial times almost twice that of today? The figures in the table certainly suggest that far more older men now suffer the ordeal of the "empty nest" than did in traditional times.

The answer to such a question certainly involves our general paradox, because we have to decide whether older married men necessarily want their children at home now, and whether they did so in the past. It is also important to discover, if we can, whether the children themselves wished to stay at home after their parents had become old. But we cannot avoid asking how

TABLE 1. *Household position by sex and marital status of persons aged sixty-five and over in five English places before 1800 compared with Britain in the 1960 S*

	Chilvers Coton 1684		Lichfield 1695		Stoke-on-Trent 1701		Corfe Castle 1790		Ardleigh 1796		Total		Percentages		Britain, 1960s percentages	
	Men	Women	Men	Women	Men	Women	Men	Women	Men	Women	Men	Women	Men	Women	Men	Women
Married persons																
Living with:																
spouse and unmarried children	3	2	8	6	12	2	7	2	5	4	35	16	46	37	24	24
spouse and married children	1	0	3	0	1	1	0	1	0	0	5	2	7	5	5	1
spouse only	5	2	8	5	4	3	11	9	3	2	31	21	41	49	67	68
others	0	0	1	2	0	1	2	0	2	1	5	4	7	9	4	7
Widowed, etc., persons																
Living with:																
unmarried children	1	0	3	14	5	8	4	1	0	1	13	24	23	20	18	20
married children	0	2	1	10	3	13	2	7	2	2	8	34	14	28	23	17
others	1	1	9	16	5	8	7	11	5	5	27	41	48	34	22	18
Living alone	0	1	1	10	4	8	3	4	0	0	8	23	14	19	37	45

common it was for old men to have surviving unmarried children and to be able to live with them, then compared with now. This is a problem in comparative historical demography, and it is not a straightforward one. Demands for information about the number of brothers or sisters or cousins or uncles or aunts or kin of any kind people may have had in the past—the preindustrial past or the recent past—also impose complex requirements. Similarly, we find difficulties with questions about the number of people who have such relatives now or will have them in the future (a trend toward zero population growth, for instance, might affect calculations).

These more ambitious quests for information offer a challenge to demographers, statisticians, mathematicians, and molders of social processes generally. Microsimulation by computer of family structure and kinship connections in relation to demographic variation is being developed to get preliminary results of this kind.[2] The great advantage of microsimulation is that it provides some idea of the limits of variation in such matters as childlessness under given demographic conditions, and it frees us from confinement to means and proportions, which affect the crude figures in table 1 and the other tables that follow.[3]

The final aim of such an exercise is to reach a point at which we could not only determine the proportions of the aged found to be in various residential situations in preindustrial times, but also predict how these proportions would change given the different demographic trends which are characteristic of English society today (much lower birth rates and death rates, a somewhat lower age at marriage, and a higher proportion of persons marrying). These outcomes would then be compared with the actual residential situations of aged persons in contemporary English society. Only after this had been done could we ascertain whether the two societies—England before and England after industrialization—differed in the social value they attached to aged persons (insofar as that value can be determined from evidence of this kind). To make an even more conclusive decision, it would also be necessary to carry out a parallel economic exercise, and find out whether people (as individuals, or as "the state") spent as much money then as now, in relative terms, in support of the aged. We would attempt to discover, for example, if coresidence was commoner in earlier times because it was cheaper. It would, no doubt, be necessary as part of such an exercise to calculate or estimate the earning power of older people in the past; this in itself would be a valuable addition to our knowledge.

In spite of the lack of answers to the above economic question, there does exist a body of knowledge, extracted from English records about the aged in relation to the family group, which suggests further research opportunities. This first crude attempt to find out whether our contemporary family treats the aged differently from the family in the preindustrial past suggests the following generalizations.

1. The "Western"—specifically the English, the Anglo-American, the Anglo-Saxon—familial policy with respect to the aged may indeed have been based on the premise of preserving the greatest possible independence for them.

2. In practice this has meant ensuring that as many persons as possible were placed at the head of their own domestic unit at marriage and kept there; that once formed, this household was conserved as far as possible under the direction of its founders—ideally until their deaths. This point can be illustrated by a rough statistic from table 3: 83 percent of all males and 78 percent of all females—that is, 80 percent of all persons of sixty years and above—in England before 1800 were heading their own households.

3. This implies, in turn, that the aged did not often have their married children living with them (only about 5 percent at sixty and above), nor did they often go to live in the households of their married children (figures are negligible for married persons over sixty but rise to 28 percent for widows over the age of sixty-five). These crude proportions from table 1 and table 2 indicate that the multigenerational household has not been the usual expedient for the support of the aged for as far back as English records go.[4]

4. Nevertheless, of those for whom it was impossible to provide an independent household because there were no surviving *unmarried* children, a significant but unknown proportion were accommodated in the households of their *married* children. Of the remainder, some seem to have lived with more distant relatives, although we simply do not know how many. More, however,

TABLE 2. *Household position of persons aged sixty and over in five English places before 1800*

	Males		Females		Both	
Married Persons	Num-ber	Per-centage	Num-ber	Per-centage	Num-ber	Per-centage
Having in their households spouses and						
their unmarried children	87	51	57	43	144	48
their married children	8	5	6	5	14	5
their grandchildren	12	7	10	7	22	7
their relatives } attached lodgers }	12	7	8	6	20	7
servants	7	4	9	7	16	5
no person other than spouse	44	26	39	29	83	27
Living in the households of						
their unmarried children	0	0	1		1	
their married children	0	0	1		1	
their relatives including grandchildren others in unclear relationship Living as lodgers	1	1	0	3	1	1
Living in institutions	0	0	1		1	
subtotals	171	101	132	100	303	100
Nonmarried Persons Having in their households						
their unmarried children	34	32	49	26	83	28
their married children	5	5	9	5	14	5
their grandchildren	2	2	3	2	5	2
their relatives or other } persons attached lodgers }	8	7	23	12	31	11
servants only	7	6	5	3	12	4
Living in the households of						
their unmarried children	0	0	0	0	0	0
their married children	2	2	21	11	23	8
their relatives including grandchildren	2	2	5	3	7	2
others in unclear relationship } Living as lodgers }	26	24	25	14	51	17
Living in institutions	16	15	16	9	32	11
Living as solitaries	5	5	29	16	34	12
	107	100	185	100	292	100

TABLE 3. *Percentage of persons aged sixty and over in six English places before 1800 heading households or living otherwise*

	Married		Nonmarried		All Males	All Females	Both Sexes
	Males	Females	Males	Females			
Heads, or spouses of heads	100	98	57	64	83	78	80
In households headed by							
their children	0	2	2	11	1	9	6
other persons	0	0	24	16	10	8	9
Lodging	0	0					
In institutions	0	0	15	9	6	5	5
Totals	100	100	100	100	100	100	100
Percentage living							
alone					4	11	8
with servants					2	2	2
entirely solitary					2	9	

seem to have lived as lodgers or in various types of inmate status, sometimes at the expense of the village or the Poor Law authorities generally. There remained a minority who lived alone, and a few in institutions. Independent living for the aged thus seems to have been the rule—a rule which could be set aside for urgent welfare reasons, but which could also go so far as to leave people as solitaries, a position occupied by 19 percent of widows over sixty-five. This rule, as far as we know, was a rule of social and political authority, of Poor Law administrators and of magistrates, as well as of individuals.

5. The conspicuous differences between the familial position of the old today and that in the preindustrial past are as follows (see table 1).

Notes to table 2

Married children include their own spouses and children if present; where *grandchildren* are specified alone, their parents (the children of the old people) are absent. *Nonmarried* means widowed for the most part, but includes some whose spouses were temporarily absent and all never-married persons. Servants and lodgers are relevant only when named, and may be present elsewhere without affecting classification.

Note: Data from Ealing, 1599; Chilvers Coton, 1684; Stoke-on-Trent, 1701; Corfe Castle, 1790; Ardleigh, 1796.

a. More than double the proportion of the widowed over sixty live alone today, and more than half again as many married persons live with their spouses only.

b. Fewer—not much more than half of the married men and about two-thirds of the married women—now live with their unmarried children. This is not true of the widowed, however, who are not less likely in the 1970s to have family circles of their own than in traditional English society.

c. About the same proportion of the married elderly now live with their married children. Perhaps more widowers do so and fewer widows. Other possible contrasts (for example, proportions in institutions or with relatives and not with children) are not yet known and are impossible to work out without more evidence, even at this crude level of estimation.

6. We cannot judge how much these differences are due to behavioral or attitudinal changes (children abandoning their parents, parents insisting on independence), and how much to demographic changes (people living longer, having fewer children, marrying earlier). We shall not be able to make this judgment until we have determined what the effects of demographic changes have in fact been. Such questions as what values are, what they were, and how they have changed with respect to aging and the family depend on technical advances and, above all, on more work.

7. These first-recovered data from England suggest that the principles of policy for the familial treatment of the aged were, and are, implied by household-formation rules and the welfare functions of kinship. The household-formation rules comprised conventions regarding age at marriage, remarriage, postmarital residence of children, and the residential situation of the aged. It might be possible to bring all these conventions under the heading of the English (or Anglo-Saxon, or even "Western") familial system. This is a system which we have begun to distinguish from other familial systems which have also endured over time. "Our" system, as far as we can yet describe it, requires the following behavior of those who deal with the aged.

a. Children are (and were) expected: to seek independence, and to leave home when independence is available; not to reside with parents after marriage, except perhaps for a few months, and then usually for lack of other accommodation; to support aged parents by means other than bringing them into their own homes—except occasionally, when parents are of use in the home and are willing to give up residential independence in exchange for nurture, or in circumstances of exceptional need.

b. Parents are (and were) expected to behave reciprocally: that is, not to require children to remain in residence after marriage; not to seek membership in the families of their children; to preserve independence, where necessary and socially acceptable, by remarriage, or perhaps by coresidence with their own siblings or even other kin; to be resigned to solitary or institutional living if finally required, or to live as lodgers.

c. Other aged persons are (and were) expected to respect the same conventions: that is, not to seek to apply what might be called the extended-family-household solution to the residential difficulties imposed by age. If without immediate kin, they are expected to seek out other persons to live with. These others would sometimes be more distantly related persons who are in the same situation. This slight tendency of unmarried elderly kin to coreside seems to be the main, or perhaps the only, function of the extended-kin network with respect to the aged, and it is probably subordinate to the function of friendship.

d. Political and social authorities are (and were) expected to dispense welfare in such a way as to underwrite the system: that is, to support the independent households of the aged rather than impose communal or nonfamilial living, or perhaps to insist that children, though not other relatives, care for their aged parents.

It must be stressed that these are impressions mainly derived from wisps of evidence about the composition of past coresidential domestic groups, supported by what we are beginning to ascertain from such sources as manorial records, Poor Law records, and, of course, literary evidence. Insofar as they are to be regarded as *rules*, they express probabilities, not certainties. Counterprinciples can in fact be seen to have had some sway. Political policy, and the social values regarding treatment of the aged, may have changed in the past in England, and then perhaps changed back again. It should be emphasized, above all, that it is hazardous to proceed from little knowledge, or even fairly full knowledge, about the family as a coresident group to conclusions about the family as a kinship system. Here, then, more information, a more satisfactory model, more work, are urgently needed.

8. The expectations which this English system placed upon individuals with respect to matters other than coresidence remain largely unknown for traditional English society. We as yet know far too little, for example, about how common it was for parents to move to live near their children or other kin; how often children at the time of marriage, or by movement afterwards, ensured that they would be close to aged parents; how often children out of affection or duty, or by parental compulsion, postponed marriage for the welfare of aged parents, or even stayed unmarried. We are not yet able to distinguish between sons and daughters in these respects. We do not know, and we cannot estimate, how much money or goods and services passed from children to aged or destitute parents; or how these transferred incomes varied from class to class, by sex of the child, by geographical proximity of parents to child, and so on. We are quite unsure to what extent parents had useful roles in the households of their own married children at a time before industrial childminding became important.[5]

9. There are signs of a counterpolicy, continuing over the period of the Great Industrial Revolution and into the twentieth century, which denied to the aged poor the familial independence maintained by those who were not poor, and institutionalized them in nonfamilial situations. This was accomplished by the establishment of the workhouses, which flourished from the 1750s to the 1930s, and which tended to break up families and to separate the sexes. These buildings and their organization were in sharp contrast to the earlier almshouses, which provided cells for individuals and family groups, and communal arrangements only for food and worship. Though this Poor Law treatment of social casualties is well documented, we know very little specifically about the concept of the aged which was held by Poor Law and workhouse administrators. We cannot yet tell whether it is justifiable to think of a change of value intervening in the early nineteenth century, persisting with respect to this one feature— a very important feature of social policy—and being superseded at the end of the Second World War in England by a return to

the older traditional attitude. Such an interpretation seems possible, but it cannot yet be proven.

It is important, however, when judging this first installment of English evidence, to bear in mind that it may not be applicable to other national situations, such as that of the United States. Americans are not wholly English in culture, or in ideological or biological descent. We must ask, therefore, what historical file to consult in relation to American values on such issues as aging. If family origins are Russian or Russian Jewish or Serbian or Latvian or Chinese or Japanese, for example, we must decide to what extent the above data and conclusions are relevant to these family origins or to contemporary American culture. Even if the family groups we are examining are of mainly WASP descent, their social experience is of a multiplex society with a polyglot historical background. It is a problem, therefore, in the historical sociology of societies like the United States, how far the ideology of the present citizenship separates an individual or group from his or its biological ancestry, and substitutes the historical background of individuals with quite different biological origins. This question is typical of the interesting issues raised by the study of a subject like aging over a long period of time.

Although we still know very little about the familial positions of the aged in non-English cultures, we do know enough to say that there is, and has been, a great variation from the English model. In fact, this variation is, and has been, greater than the variation in domestic structure itself. In addition, such variation is, and has been, wide even within Western Europe, but apparently very much greater *outside* England than *within* it. We can also suggest that the variation has been the outcome of a combination of behavioral elements such as residential choices at marriage, and particularly conventions regarding remarriage. There are a number of examples of local variations in the pattern of residence of the aged. For instance, in a Belgian village in the eighteenth century, there were practically no widowed persons living alone; remarriage had apparently eliminated them. One might conclude that Belgium encouraged, either as policy or within its social mores, remarriage. On the other hand, in a German village a few decades later, there were no solitary widows, but all lived in extended families of their children; this suggests either that remarriage was not encouraged, that there were not enough unmarried males, or that family ties were closer in the German village at the time than they had been in the Belgian. Another instance: in a Hungarian village of the same period, most elderly people were heading the households of their married children, while in Japan in preindustrial times, elderly people often lived as subordinates, not heads, in the homes of their unmarried children. The one case suggests a patriarchial society; the other suggests an unwanted social responsibility of the single and unburdened child.

All of the foregoing examples make explicit the observation that there was no single common position for the aged in traditional preindustrial societies. Where, does this leave Americans' traditional values with respect to the elderly, especially with respect to the elderly and the family? Does it lend any support to a federal or a state administrator who insists upon imposing policy on what is here called "extended-family" care of elderly kin? I realize that in putting this further challenge before American scholars, I am asking them to get to work on investigating—and conceptualizing—problems a long way from aging. These include problems of cultural continuity, for example; and of the relation of political to cultural consciousness; and of the relevance of cultures which we regard as alien to our own, bound as we are by our own historical traditions. The consideration of aging thus inevitably leads to the reassessment of the whole structure of societies over time. There is much to do.[6]

A conclusion to this ragged and wide-ranging set of considerations is the inevitable recognition that the present position of the elderly in all advanced industrial societies is quite possibly unique. Such a recognition calls for initiation and creation, rather than for further consultation with and recovery of the past. For if we return to what has been said about the possibility of a constant value system in relation to very diverse demographic conditions, we shall have to conclude that the aged in our society are too numerous to allow any appeal to traditional human values in our own past—or in that of any other nation or civilization—to be of use. There are too few children born, and they leave home too early in their parents' life cycle, and the parents live too long, to allow every American and Briton to have a family circle of his own offspring to live with when he is old. In this sense, then, because of changed demographic conditions, the traditional English, or Western, solution to the problem of providing familial surroundings for the aged is now excluded.

Elsewhere in the world the relation of the past to the present with respect to aging is different, as has been shown. The "English" pattern, which apparently gave as many of the aged as possible a family of their own to live in, seems not to have existed outside English-speaking countries to the same extent and with the same consistency. In Russia, the extended-family solution for the residence of older people seems likely, from the little we know, to have been much more common, though conceivably never as consistently applied as the "English" policy was in England. Nevertheless, the descendants of the Russian and Eastern European peasantry are faced with an entirely novel situation just as we are, even if its historical background is different. Therefore, there is no single solution to this highly complex problem.

One answer that might be offered in the United States is continuing or renewed education for the elderly. Although ethnic and traditional biological backgrounds vary widely, there is one commonality: the highly educated are generally the best fitted to face old age. Statistics show that they live longer and are better able to adapt to loneliness and disability. The coming generations of elderly people will inevitably reach old age with a much higher level of education. The innovation that I suggest, rather than drawing on "the world we have lost," relies heavily on the university curriculum—which should be reordered, based on the proportions of the population that will take part and on the time of life at which various elements that make up higher education should be pursued. Perhaps instruction in the humanities and the plastic arts should be confined, to a large extent, to elderly persons going back to university studies as they retire from their jobs, whereas advanced scientific and technical instruction should be given to young people who are about to begin their careers, in a society where earning a living is now so much a technical matter. Perhaps, moreover, most of the instruction should take place in the home, where the elderly are far more likely to be living— and living by choice—than are the young persons whom we now think of as students. This development might take as a model the British Open University, which has begun to perfect methods that could be used to teach the elderly what they can and would wish to know of intellectual and aesthetic culture, and to teach them where they live. If we are asked who would have to undertake the teaching of the aged, the answer is that historians, classicists, literary scholars, archeologists, and exponents of the plastic and performing arts are those to whom we must look.

When we consider the situation of the aged as they now are, as compared with their situation in earlier times, we must be struck by the peculiar ethical situation in which the contemporary intellectual finds himself. It can be said that in no known period before our own has the highly educated minority had greater responsibility for a definable social group than we do today for the great proportion of older people among our contemporaries.

Notes

1. Peter Laslett, *The World We Have Lost* (London: Methuen, 1966; 2d ed., New York: Scribner's, 1971).

2. Mimeographed papers by SOCSIM Project, prepared by the department of Anthropology at the University of California at Berkeley in collaboration with the Cambridge Group for the History of Population and Social Structure, 1974.

3. Peter Laslett, "Societal Development and Aging," in *Handbook of Aging and the Social Sciences*, ed. Robert H. Binstock and Ethel Shanas (New York: Van Nostrand Reinhold Co., 1976), pp. 87–116. A related essay, using the same file of data and the same tables, is Peter Laslett, "The History of Aging and the Aged," chap. 5 of *Family Life and Illicit Love in Earlier Generations* (Cambridge: Cambridge University Press, 1977).

4. In Laslett, *Family Life and Illicit Love*, p. 185 n. 6, reference is made to the outcome of a set of calculations carried out by Professor Johansen of Odense University in Denmark, contained in an unpublished paper of 1975, calculations which are not based on computer microsimulation such as we envisage. Using the excellent parish records of his country between 1741 and 1801, and drawing upon stable-population theory, Johansen is able to estimate what proportions of elderly persons had married children with whom they could have coresided (51 to 61 percent of all females 60, and 37 to 49 percent of all males sixty and over). Comparison with the detailed Danish censuses of 1787 and 1801

showed that more than half of them in fact lived apart from any married child. This proportion looks decidedly lower than those reported here for England, but in general his calculations confirm the English findings. Microsimulation of this kind cannot be easily extended to more distant kin, and for this, as well as for the estimation of variances, computer microsimulation would seem to be essential.

5. Some further detail is provided in Laslett, "Societal Development and Aging," as well as in *Family Life and Illicit Love*.

6. Work at the Cambridge Group undertaken by Richard Wall and others indicates that behavior was variable from place to place under all these heads in preindustrial England. There are indications that solitary elderly persons or married couples could usually count on the presence of some younger kinsfolk nearby, most often their married children, at least in the communities examined. There are indications, too, that most households had to contain a woman of active age, who could be a servant if not a daughter in the case of the aged, and was generally a servant in the case of the aged and privileged. This household-composition rule has yet to be tested, though it seems improbable that members of the distant kin were ever likely to be in question, and even more doubtful that common people in preindustrial times were ordinarily in contact with such kin to an extent which would enable them to share households, or join households, when mutually advantageous.

JOHN DEMOS

OLD AGE IN EARLY NEW ENGLAND

Within the past decade or so, scholars have come to appreciate the significance of age as a determinant of historical experience. At first, their interest was directed largely to childhood, then to adolescence, and now—in appropriate sequence—to the later parts of the life course. For historians, among others, old age is a time whose idea has come.[1]

The historical record of early New England includes a substantial corpus of prescriptive statements on old age—chiefly sermons and essays by leading clergymen. There is, however, a dearth of evidence directly reflecting behavior by and toward the elderly. Thus, the scholar is obliged to pursue indirect methods: for example, demographic reconstruction, the analysis of legal materials, and assorted forms of collective biography. Some important questions inevitably slip by unanswered. The most conspicuous lacunae in the present case involve the experience of New England women. Quite possibly male and female aging were significantly different, but the data seem too meager to permit even an opinion about this, let alone any solid conclusions.

It may be unfair to hold the evidence entirely to blame for such deficiencies. After all, historical evidence responds to—and, in a sense, is created by—the asking of particular questions. And in any "new field" the questions themselves are problematic. It thus seems prudent to specify in advance the questions to be asked here. First, we shall consider how old age was conceived—was thought about—in early New England. Second, we shall assess the elderly as a demographic presence: how many they were, and how they were situated in the larger population. Third, we will consider the social experience of old people: their work, their leisure, the nature of their power and prestige. The essay will close with some interpretative suggestions—and a residual agenda of questions for the future.

Rev. Cotton Mather of Boston, in publishing a treatise entitled "The Old Man's Honour," included a dedication to his elderly friend and mentor, Major John Richards. He wrote in part:

> Were there nothing else to commend my regards for you, besides the Old Age, which your out-living of three-score winters has brought you to the border of, that were enough to give you a room in my esteem, and reverence, and veneration.[2]

This passage helps to illumine two central questions pertaining to old age in early New England: its chronological definition, and its claims for attention in the culture at large. Each point merits detailed consideration.

The view of age sixty as a "border" appears in various written statements, and is implied in a different way by certain forms of legislative enactment. A clergyman noted "the considerable number of aged persons" in his congregation: "For there are many who have attained to three score, and such are everywhere accounted old men."[3] A town voted to exempt older persons from particular civic obligations, and established "60 years of age" as the official cut off point.[4] A provincial assembly set requirements of regular service in paramilitary units for all male inhabitants "between the ages of 16 and 60 years."[5]

Here, then, one finds an apparent consensus as to the beginning of old age. And yet its application in specific instances was far from precise. The requirement of military service called forth some especially revealing evidence. When a man wished to be "freed from training" (that is, with his local militia unit), he was obliged to petition the courts for a personal waiver. Thus: (1) "John Leigh, being about seventy years of age, [is] discharged from ordinary training." (2) "Robert Kinsman, being above three score years of age and having the 'seattyca', was freed from training." (3) "John Cooly, being aged, and having fits whereby he falls, is freed from training." (4) "William Lord of Salem, aged seventy-seven, [is] discharged from training, on account of age and many bodily infirmities."[6] The list of such actions could be lengthened indefinitely, but the larger point is immediately clear. The actual age invoked was often more (and occasionally less) than sixty, was sometimes omitted altogether, and was usually linked to the physical condition of the man in question. This implies a certain looseness or flexibility in the application of age norms, and—more—a functional attitude toward the process of growing old. Aging was measured, in part, by numbers, but also by the survival (or decline) of inherent capacity. The tendency of our own time is much more exclusively formal: chronology is usually the decisive consideration (for example, in retirement); biology counts for relatively little.

Cotton Mather's dedication to Major Richards spoke of "esteem, and reverence, and veneration" as appropriate attitudes toward the aged. Here, too, he expressed a widespread cultural convention. "Honour old age": so it was written in the Scriptures, and endlessly repeated in the sermon literature of early New England. There were various ways to justify this prescription. In the first place, the elderly are wiser than other persons; their "counsel" should therefore carry disproportionate weight in civil and religious affairs. Their wisdom derived, in turn, from the sheer weight of accumulated experience. When the "Pilgrim pastor," John Robinson, described the preferment due to older people, he noted in particular "their manifold advantages . . . for the getting of wisdom."[7] When the poetess Anne Bradstreet composed her verses on "The Four Ages of Life," she chose a special way of portraying the last one. She listed the numerous "private changes" and "various times of state" to which an old man of her era might bear witness, virtually defining him as a repository of experience.[8] It is not easy for us today to recapture the strength of these associations; they seem insubstantial, or simply trite. Our culture has many ways of storing experience—most obviously, in written documents. But in communities where literacy was less extensive, it was often other *people*—elderly ones—who provided a sense of contact with the past. And to the extent that the past was honored, they were honored, too.

For so-called Puritans there was a special, religious dimension to the accumulated experience of old age. The elderly were thought to have "a peculiar acquaintance with the Lord Jesus

Christel.["9] In fact, this acquaintance verged on likeness: "there is something of the image of God in age," an almost physical resemblance.[10] God, after all, "is the Ancient of Days," and when His "majesty and eternity are set forth in Scripture, it is with white hair."[11] Hence, "the fear of God and honoring the old man is commanded with the same breath and linked together in the same sentence."[12] These brief quotations, stitched together from various New England sermons, reflect an idea widely noted in studies of premodern society. Elderly persons are literally and figuratively closer than others to God. They stand, as it were, near the boundary between the natural and supernatural worlds. Indeed, they are in a special position to mediate between these worlds—which explains, in part, the preferments they customarily enjoy.[13]

To restate these prescriptive standards for dealings with the aged is to consider only one side of a highly complicated picture. Did old people, in their actual behavior, justify the confidence associated with age? Did their particular traits and tendencies inspire feelings of "esteem, and reverence, and veneration"? What was the typical predisposition of the elderly, in terms of what we now call character or personality? Such questions are also treated in the literature of early New England—and in ways that clash with the ritual exhortation to "honour old age."

Consider, for example, the opinion of William Bridge, sometime fellow of Harvard College and author of the earliest treatise on this subject published anywhere in the colonies. "Old age is a dry and barren ground," he begins. "The state of old age is a state of weakness and of much infirmity." Bridge proceeds to spell this out in great detail, separating the natural from the moral infirmities. The moral ones make an especially long list. Older people are likely to be "too drowsy and remiss in the things of God, . . . too covetous and tenacious for the things of this world, . . . too timorous and fearful, . . . too touchy, peevish, angry, and forward, . . . very unteachable . . . [since] they think they know more than others, . . . hard to be pleased, and as hard to please others, . . . full of complaints of the present times, . . . [and] full of suspicions, and very apt to surmise, suspect, and fear the worst."[14] Parts of this portrait show up in other writings from the period; the overall effect is certainly unflattering.[15]

The matter of "natural infirmities" in old age also received much attention. Cotton Mather, for one, and William Bridge, for another, catalogued the physical aspects of aging in somewhat gruesome detail. Here is a short sample.

> The sun, the light, the moon, and the stars begin to be darkened with you; that is, your parts are under a decay; your fancy, your judgment are failing you. . . . Your hands now shake and shrink, and must lean upon a staff . . . . Your thighs and legs now buckle under you . . . . Your teeth grow weak and few, and are almost all rotted out . . . . Your eyes become dim, and clouds disturb the visive powers in them. . . . You become deaf and thick of hearing. . . . You can't without some difficulty go up a pair of stairs, and are in danger of stumbling at every stone in the street. . . . Your backs are so feeble that instead of carrying anything else they can scarce bear themselves. . . .[16]

Loss, decline, decay: these were the central images. There is a note of distaste here, almost of repulsion, which betrays an important preconscious attitude.

And there is more. One feels, in the sermon literature, a sharp, even scornful quality, insofar as such literature is directed to the elderly themselves. Thus we find Cotton Mather, at the ripe age of twenty-nine, hectoring his ·older parishioners, admonishing them to repent their sins and threatening them with dreadful figures of hell. At one point Mather enumerates six particular "virtues . . . which all old men should be studious of": sobriety, gravity, temperance, orthodoxy, charity, and patience. Yet in discussing these, one by one, he emphasizes not the beauty of the virtue itself, but rather the ugliness of its associated vice. Sobriety, for example, is contrasted with drunkenness—and the terms which Mather chooses to frame the comparison express a certain relish. "For them that stagger with age, at the same time to stagger with drink; to see an old man reeling, spewing, stinking with the excesses of the tavern, 'tis too loathsome a thing to be mentioned without a very zealous detestation."[17]

Indeed, all the vices of the elderly seemed especially detestable and *visible*. One more striking image, from the essay by William Bridge, will help to make the point: "When the leaves are off the trees, we see the birds' nests in the trees and bushes. Now in our old age our leaves are off, then therefore we may see these nests of sin, and lusts in our hearts and lives, which we saw not before, and so be sensible and repent of them."[18] Among other things, in short, old age brought exposure; personal character was stripped of its protective covering, and made to seem ridiculous, even contemptible.

We cannot proceed much further in this investigation without bringing forward demographic considerations. We need to assess the actual presence of the elderly in the total population of colonial New England. How numerous was the "old" cohort in comparison with other age groups? What were the chances that individuals might survive to old age? To what degree was personal contact with elderly people a regular feature of life? Answers to these questions should permit us to decide whether there was something intrinsically "special" and exotic about old age, within the larger frame of social experience.

Among modern-day Americans, the age-group of persons sixty years old and older makes up some 15 percent of the total. We have no precisely comparable figures for early America—no figures for large populations—but assorted findings from local communities are helpful in establishing approximate trends and tendencies. There follows a brief summary of such findings, based on the study of five New England towns.

1. In 1678 all male inhabitants over the age of sixteen of Newbury, Massachusetts, were required to take an oath of allegiance to the crown; in the process their names and ages were recorded on a list which is still extant in the files of the Essex County Courts.[19] The total number of these oath-takers was 206. Twenty-eight of them were at least sixty years old; 11 were at least seventy. The entire male population of Newbury in this year (that is, including those younger than sixteen as well) can be estimated at 420. Thus, the over-sixty cohort represented about 6.7 percent of the whole. For the over-seventy category, the figure is 2.6 percent.

2. The age structure of the population of Windsor, Connecticut, has been analyzed for the years 1640 and 1686. In the former year, 1.3 percent of the settled inhabitants were found to be sixty or older; in the latter, 4.1 percent.[20]

3. Hampton, New Hampshire, has been studied by equivalent methods, and also for two different points in time. Careful recon-

stitution of Hampton families in the year 1656 yields a roster of some 356 local inhabitants. At least 14 of these people were more than sixty years old—or 4 percent of the entire list. More than two decades later (1680), the male adults resident in Hampton were "rated" for tax purposes. Their number was 126 overall; 120 of them can be assigned at least approximate ages. In addition, 90 women can be definitely associated with these men (that is, as wives or widows), and the entire population of the town (including children) can be estimated at about 525. At least 33 of the adults (22 men, 11 women) were older than sixty at this time— which translates into 6.3 percent of the total.[21]

4. Still another investigation of this type has been made of the townspeople of Wethersfield, Connecticut, as of the year 1668.[22] The results are a total population of 413, an over-sixty cohort of 9 (or 2.2 percent). If the latter figures seem small, they need to be considered in the light of a temporary demographic anomaly. The Wethersfield citizenry of 1668 included a disproportionately *large* group of persons in their fifties (26 altogether). Thus, the officially "old" cohort must, within a few years, have grown considerably.

5. There exists for the town of Bristol, Rhole Island, in 1689 an actual (and unique) census of local inhabitants.[23] An absence of reliable vital records precludes any full analysis of age groups in this case; however, approximate ages can be assigned to the 68 adult women on the list. Within the latter group only two may possibly have been as old as sixty, and even there the evidence is ambiguous. Another local census was made in Bristol nearly a century later (1774). By then, it can be shown, the over-sixty cohort had risen to 5.6 percent of the total citizenry. (See table 1.)

These somewhat scattered findings must now be sorted so as to yield a more general conclusion. In five of eight instances (Newbury, 1678; Windsor, 1686; Hampton, 1656; Hampton, 1680; Bristol, 1774), the "old cohort falls within a range of 4 to 7 percent of the total population. The remaining three cases (Wethersfield, 1668; Windsor, 1640; Bristol, 1689) all produce significantly lower results. We have seen, however, that the first was subject to a quirk in the numbers themselves, and there were special circumstances affecting the other two as well. Windsor in 1640 and Bristol in 1689 were new communities, barely re-

TABLE 1. *Age structures in New England towns:*
Seventeenth and Eighteenth centuries

Town	Year	Persons over sixty	Total population	Percentage over sixty	Total adults over twenty	Percentage over sixty
Newbury, Mass.	1678	28	420*	6.7*	206**	13.5
Windsor, Conn.	1640	—	—	1.3	—	4.1
Windsor, Conn.	1686	—	—	4.1	—	8.5
Hampton, N.H.	1656	14	356	4.0	136	10.3
Hampton, N.H.	1680	33	525*	6.3*	240	13.8
Wethersfield, Conn.	1668	9	413	2.2	174	5.3
Bristol, R.I.	1689	2 (?)	—	—	68	2.9 (?)
Bristol, R.I.	1774	—	—	5.6	—	10.6

* estimate
** over sixteen years old; elsewhere "adults" means over twenty.

Note: Newbury, Mass. (1678) includes males only.
     Bristol, R.I. (1689) includes females only.

Sources: *Records and Files of the Quarterly Courts of Essex County, Massachusetts* (Salem, Mass.: Essex Institute, 1911–1921), 7:156–57.
    Linda Auwers Bissell, "Family, Friends and Neighbors: Social Interaction in Seventeenth-Century Windsor, Connecticut" (Ph.D. diss., Brandeis University, 1973), p. 41.
    Local records, Hampton, N.H., and Wethersfield, Conn. Family reconstitution by the author.
    John Demos, "Families in Colonial Bristol, R.I.: An Exercise in Historical Demography," *William and Mary Quarterly*, third series, 25(1963):40–57.

moved from a "wilderness" state. Evidently the settlement process was an affair of young people, or at least of those not old. For some years, in such places, the age structure of inhabitants was foreshortened. Later, as the commmunities themselves aged, so, too, did their populations, with an "old" cohort gradually filling out at the farther end of the demographic spectrum. These changes belonged to a regular morphology of town growth and development.

We may therefore regard 4 to 7 percent as the likely portion of elderly people in established New England communities. Yet these findings need to be refined in one additional connection. With fertility limited only by natural constraints (for example, menopause, and the contraceptive effects of lactation) the birth rate was consistently high; hence colonial populations were everywhere skewed toward youth. Persons under twenty normally made up a majority of the whole, and the relative size of all older cohorts was diminished accordingly. Perhaps, then, we should measure the elderly in relation to other adults. In modern America the over-sixty age group is some 23 percent of the larger adult population (defined, for the moment, as all those who are at least twenty). In our five leading cases from the colonial era, the comparable figures are: 8.5 percent (Windsor, 1686); 10.3 percent (Hampton, 1656); 10.6 percent (Bristol, 1774); 13.5 percent (Newbury, 1678); 13.8 percent (Hampton, 1680). This is to say that the numerical presence of old people, among adults generally, was about half as large in colonial New England as it is now. The difference is certainly substantial, but it does not seem overwhelming.

We shall now alter our line of approach, translating our interest in age structures and "cohorts" into questions about personal expectation of life. To what extent, as individuals, did New Englanders actually survive to old age? Was this a prospect for only a very few, or was it something that many younger people might reasonably anticipate? The evidence is less full and less reliable than scholars might wish, and the currently available results show some points of difference and disagreement. Still, most signs point strongly in one general direction, with implications for the study of aging that are truly profound.

The first substantial research on "survivorship" in early New England appeared about a decade ago. Its geographical foci were the Massachusetts towns of Andover and Ipswich and the colony at Plymouth.[24] In each case local populations were scanned for information on age at death, and the results, taken together, showed a very considerable pattern of longevity. In all three settings, the majority of recorded deaths occurred among persons distinctly "old." (Indeed, at both Plymouth and Andover the most common age decade for mortality was the seventies.) Given what is known of other premodern populations, these figures seemed quite incredible—and some scholars found them literally so.

In fact, the Plymouth, Andover, and Ipswich studies displayed a number of methodological shortcomings. Particularly troublesome was the question of bias in the various sample populations: were short-lived persons less likely than others to find their way into the records? New studies were called for which would deal with this possibility more effectively; the returns are just now coming in. One recent investigation has canvassed all deponents in the quarterly courts of Middlesex County, Massachusetts, during the period 1661–1675.[25] By comparing age at the time of witnessing (usually recorded in the deposition itself) with age at death (where known), it was possible to construct a "life table" for this particular group. At birth 44.5 percent of the population might expect to live to age sixty or more, and 20.8 percent to at least seventy. Among those who survived to age twenty, the percentages rose to 54.9 and 34.6 respectively. Mean life expectation among the twenty-year-olds was an additional 40.5 years. (See table 2.)

An alternative strategy is to analyze the entire populations of particular town-communities at given points in time. These populations can, with only marginal error, be reconstructed from local censuses, tax lists, meetinghouse plans, and other town records. Once again, a process of linkage to death dates yields an approximate life table. Unfortunately, however, the deaths of some persons were not recorded; in their case, the method substitutes the latest date when they are known to have been living. (This amounts to an assumption that all such persons died in the

TABLE 2.   *Survivorship in Seventeenth-century New England*

Town/Colony	Percentage of twenty-year-olds surviving to at least age sixty
Plymouth Colony	68.0
Andover, Mass.:	
first generation (born 1640–69)	60.4
second generation (born 1670–99)	65.7
Ipswich, Mass.	71.7
Middlesex County, Mass.	54.9

Sources: John Demos, *A Little Commonwealth: Family Life in Plymouth Colony* (New York: Oxford University Press, 1970), p. 193.
Philip J. Greven, Jr., *Four Generations: Population, Land, and Family in Colonial Andover, Massachusetts* (Ithaca, N.Y.: Cornell University Press, 1970), pp. 27, 110.
Susan Norton, "Population Growth in Colonial America: A Study of Ipswich, Mass.," *Population Studies* 25 (1971):440.
Carol Shuchman, "Examining Life Expectancies in Seventeenth-Century Massachusetts" (Unpublished paper, Brandeis University, 1976).

same year that they last appeared in the records—clearly an over-estimate of mortality.) The result is a two-part construction, establishing an upper bound of survivorship (based only on known ages at death) and a lower one (based on the entire population at risk). Presumably the actual rate of survivorship lay somewhere in between.

This method has been applied, for the present study, to two local communities: Hampton, New Hampshire, in the year 1656, and Wethersfield, Connecticut, in 1668. In the case of Hampton, the chances of survival from age twenty to at least sixty were between 61 percent and 77 percent. Mean expectation of life for young people of about twenty was between forty-two and forty-seven years; for children of ten the comparable figures were forty-seven and fifty-two. (Life expectation at birth is harder to calculate, owing to irregular recording of infant deaths; however, a reasonable guess would be forty-four to fifty-two years.) The Wethersfield figures are not quite so high. Survivorship from age twenty to age sixty was between 60 and 62 percent. Life expectation at the same age averaged thirty-nine years; at age ten it was forty-four years. (See table 3 for a fuller summary of these findings.)

Taken together, these results do not markedly alter the picture of longevity drawn in the earlier studies. Additional research is surely needed—especially for larger, more commercial communities, such as Boston and Newport—but the evidence at hand is already fairly substantial. And *all* of it suggests that survival to old age was a better-than-even prospect for young people in colonial New England.

Some questions remain, finally, about actual contacts between the generations in these communities. Granted that the "old" cohort was a definite part of the larger age structure; granted, too, that survival to old age was a reasonable expectation for many of the New Englanders; we may yet wish to know how much, and in what ways, the elderly were *known* by others in the course of daily experience.

A partial answer to this question can be obtained by reconverting the age-structure percentages to numbers of individual people. If an average New England community contained some 500 inhabitants, and if the over-sixty cohort was normally in a range of 4 to 7 percent, the total of the elderly in such places

TABLE 3. *Life Expectation and Survivorship:* Hampton, N.H. (1656) and Wethersfield, Conn. (1668)

Life expectation at ages:	Hampton (males and females)			Wethersfield (males and females)		
	High	Low	Medium	High	Low	Medium
	years	years	years	years	years	years
0–5	51.6	44.0	47.8	60.3	54.0	57.2
6–15	52.5	47.1	49.8	45.9	41.2	43.6
16–25	47.0	41.9	44.5	39.3	38.3	38.8

Percentage surviving to age 60 from ages:	Percentages					
0–5	57.5	41.0	49.3	63.6	57.1	60.4
6–15	62.9	48.6	55.8	42.9	38.0	40.5
16–25	77.4	60.9	69.2	61.8	60.0	60.9

Percentage surviving to age 70 from ages:	Percentages					
0–5	40.0	25.3	32.7	50.0	39.3	44.7
6–15	51.4	36.7	44.1	26.2	22.0	24.1
16–25	58.1	43.5	50.8	26.4	22.5	24.5

Note: "High" estimates are based exclusively on persons for whom the age at death is known. "Low" estimates add to this group all other known residents of the town; in their case death is assumed to have occurred immediately following the date when they are last noted as being alive in any of the extant records. The latter procedure clearly overstates actual mortality. The "medium" estimate simply averages "high" and "low" in each instance.

The age groups for which the material is organized (see left-hand column) are meant to produce rough averages for ages 2, 10, and 20. The findings are summarized accordingly in the text.

The Wethersfield data are flawed, for the earliest ages, by incomplete recording of infant deaths. The findings for the age group 0–5 years cannot, therefore, be given much credence.

Sources: Local records and genealogies from Hampton, N.H., and Wethersfield, Conn. Family reconstitution by the author.

must have fallen between a low of about 20 and a high of about 35. The figures for smaller and larger communities are easily computed according to the same principle. This, in short, is a simple way of gauging the numerical possibilities for intergenerational contact.

However, the question should ideally be redefined so as to express specific *forms* of contact. Here one rather direct line of approach suggests itself. New Englanders of the colonial era were deeply responsive to family ties; and perhaps the family offered, at least to some of them, early and powerful experience of older people. The reference, of course, is to grandparents. It was suggested some years ago in a scholarly review that grandparents may well have been a "New England . . . invention, at least in terms of scale";[26] but we have as yet virtually no published research on the subject. The following paragraphs are intended as a modest beginning.

What can be learned about the *qualitative* aspects of the grand-parent-grandchild relationship? There is, for a start, important evidence scattered through probate records: direct bequests by elderly testators to their children's children. Examples abound: "I give and bequeathe unto my granddaughter Hubbard . . . one cow [named] Primrose." And: "As concerning my grandchild Abiel Sadler . . . I do give and bequeathe unto the said Abiel Sadler my lasts and tools belonging to my trade." And again: "I give and bequeathe unto my five grandchildren, the children of my son John Neal by Mary his now wife: viz. Jeremiah, John, Jonathan, Joseph, and Lydia Neale, fifty pounds sterling between them." Considered overall, grandchildren formed the second most important category of beneficiaries in New England wills (surpassed only by the testators' own children). The records also offer passing glimpses of the same impulse at work while the old yet lived—for example, this note in an estate inventory from 1678: "My mother in her lifetime disposed of her wearing apparel by her particular desire to her granddaughter Hannah Blaney."[27]

Moreover, it is clear that grandparents and grandchildren were sometimes involved in the exchange of personal help and services. When young children were orphaned, grandparents might be called to serve *in loco parentis*; for example, a court order: "John Cheney, sr., of Newbury, was chosen guardian to his grandchild, Abiel Chandler, aged about two years"; and also, a clause from a will: "my mind is to bequeathe my two daughters unto my dear mother-in-law Mrs. Elvin in Great Yarmouth, entreating her and my loving father Mr. Elvin, her husband, to take care of them."

Sometimes a testator would make these arrangements in advance, contingent on a subsequent remarriage by his spouse: "in case [my wife] . . . shall marry, again, then my will is that if my father William White pleases he shall have full power to take my son John home to himself, and have the sole and whole care of his education and power to dispose and order him." Occasionally such transfers occurred even when both parents were living: "Philip Fowler the elder, of Ipswich, in the presence of Joseph his son and Martha his wife, and with their full consent, adopted as his own son Philip, the son of the said Joseph and Martha."[28]

But if grandparents often cared for young children, the reverse was also true. Again the probates are a useful source. One Massachusetts resident made a special bequest to his granddaughter "because of her diligent attendance on me." Another noted a prior "covenant, or agreement, betwixt myself and my grandchild," according to which the latter was promised valuable properties in exchange "for his managing my affairs." Occasionally such arrangements drew special attention from the courts. Thus, "Capt. Thomas Topping of Brandford requested the Governor and this county court to grant an exemption from public service to his grandson, sent by the youth's father from Long Island to help him in his old age in his domestic affairs and occasions." (The court responded affirmatively, citing "defects" in the old man's "sight and hearing . . . so far that he needs constant attendance upon his person and occasions.")[29]

One final piece of evidence bearing on these cross-generational ties is a striking admonition in an essay on childrearing by Rev. John Robinson. "Grandfathers are more affectionate towards their children's children than to their immediates," wrote Robinson, "as seeing themselves further propagated in them, and by their means proceeding on to a further degree of eternity, which all desire naturally, if not in themselves, yet in their posterity. And hence it is that children brought up with their grandfathers or grandmothers seldom do well, but are usually corrupted by their too great indulgence."[30]

Unfortunately, the extant records do not support any firm calculations as to the number of children actually "brought up with their grandfathers or grandmothers"—though it cannot have been very large. What can be calculated, at least on a limited scale, is the numerical presence of grandparents and grandchildren within a single community. Once again, the demographic reconstruction of Hampton, New Hampshire, provides a test case. In 1680 the population of Hampton included approximately 290 children and "youth" under the age of nineteen. For some 200 of these there is complete information about the survival (and death) of grandparents. Over 90 percent had at least one grandparent currently alive (and, with only a few possible exceptions, resident in Hampton). For obvious reasons, the pattern was strongest with respect to very young children. Thus, no child under five years old was altogether without grandparents; indeed, a clear majority of this age group had three or four grandparents still living. But older children were affected, too: in the age group from ten to nineteen, nearly half had at least two grandparents living. These findings refer only to blood relationships; they must be revised upwards when stepgrandparents are taken into account. For example, over 80 percent of the entire sample population had at least two living grandparents of either the natural or the step variety. (See table 4.)

The same data can be used to depict sequences of developmental experience with grandparents. Of course, such experience varied markedly, depending on a child's position in the birth order. A first- or second-born child was likely to know all his grandparents in his earliest years, and to have two or three still surviving as he entered his teens. A middle child (third-, fourth-, or fifth-born) would have perhaps one grandparent less at each equivalent stage along the way. And a child born near the lower end of the birth order (below fifth) was lucky to have two living grandparents at the outset and one as he grew up. The median age, for each of these groups, at the death of the *last* surviving grandparent was approximately twenty-five (first- or second-born), twenty (third through fifth), and twelve (fifth or below).

These materials suggest, in conclusion, that grandparent-grandchild ties were (potentially) close and (relatively) widespread. Many children received exposure, in the context of family experience, to the ways and wisdom of the elderly. There was much interest and affection in this relationship, at least on the side of the grandparents; occasionally, there was coresidence and mutual dependence. Whether or not grandparenthood was "invented" in early New England, it certainly seems to have flourished there.

Our detour into demography has, at length, yielded valuable

TABLE 4. *Children and Grandparents: Percentage of Children with Living Grandparents in Hampton, N.H., 1680*

Children's Ages	Number of Living Grandparents					(N)
	0	1	2	3	4	
0– 4	0	18	28	46	9	(19)
5– 9	2	30	38	23	8	(53)
10–14	6	31	31	25	8	(53)
15–19	44	34	6	16	0	(32)

	Number of Living Grandparents and Step-Grandparents					(N)
	0	1	2	3	4	
0– 4	0	5	22	20	53	(79)
5– 9	2	11	32	17	38	(53)
10–14	6	6	36	17	36	(36)
15–19	44	13	22	13	9	(32)

Note: Sample includes 200 children, from sixty-one families. Another 86 children, from twenty-one families, were not included because of incomplete information as to the pertinent relationships.

Sources: *Documents and Records Relating to the State of New Hampshire*, ed. Nathaniel Bouton (Concord, N.H.: E. A. Jenks State Printer, 1874), 1:424.

Town Book of Hampton, 2 vols. (manuscript volumes in Town Offices, Hampton, N.H.).

Joseph Dow, *History of the Town of Hampton, New Hampshire* (Salem, Mass.: Salem Press, 1893).

Sybil Noyes, Charles Thornton Libby, and Walter Goodwin Davis, *Genealogical Dictionary of Maine and New Hampshire* (Baltimore: Genealogical Publishing Company, 1972).

results. It is evident now that old age was (1) an attribute of a small but not insignificant portion of local populations in colonial New England; (2) a life stage at which many persons would eventually arrive; and (3) a human condition which almost all, as children, observed from close-up. There was, in short, nothing intrinsically unusual about growing—or being—old.

Just as the culture at large recognized old age as a distinct time of life, so, too, were elderly people conscious of their own aging. They thought about it, and talked about it; and in various ways they acted from a particular sense of age-appropriate needs and requirements. "Old age is come upon me," wrote one man in beginning a letter to his brother. "This is a matter of great grief to us now in our old age," stated an elderly couple when obliged to testify in court about a quarrel with their daughter and son-in-law. And there were set-phrases included in various New England wills as a kind of explanatory preface: "being ancient and weak of body," or "considering my great age and the many infirmities accompanying the same," or (more grandly) "having through God's goodness lived in this world unto old age, and now finding my strength to decay [and] not knowing how near my glass is run . . ." A rare seventeenth-century diary throws indirect light on the same point: Thomas Minor of Stonington, Connecticut, began to note his birthdays only when he had reached a fairly advanced age. Minor kept his diary on a fairly regular basis from 1653 until 1684, covering the age span in his own life from forty-five to seventy-six. The first of the birthday entries was made on 23 April 1670: "I was 62 years old." The next one came in 1675; similar notations appeared thereafter on 23 April of each year.[31]

But if Thomas Minor counted the passing of his final years, numbers were not ordinarily the chief criterion of old age. As noted earlier, chronological age was imprecisely specified on various official documents (for example, those that certified release from military training); indeed, there is reason to think that many New Englanders did not know, or did not care, precisely how old they were. More important, surely, to the subjective experience of aging was the whole dimension of physical change and decline. Again, we should note the relevant phrases from the wills, which invariably coupled "age" and "infirmity." (In some cases the former is subsumed under the latter: for example, "by reason of my great age and other infirmities.")[32]

We touch here on the physiology of aging, a particularly difficult and elusive subject for historical study. Lacking any equivalent of modern geriatric data, we can reach only a few relatively simple conclusions. Demographic materials suggest that the elderly in colonial New England were not a great deal more liable to mortal illness and injury than their twentieth-century counterparts. Life expectation at age sixty appears to have been at least fifteen years; at seventy, about ten; at eighty, about five. These figures are only a little lower than the comparable ones for today.[33]

Yet there is no doubting the depth of the association between age and physical depletion in the minds of the New Englanders. "Infirmity," "deformity," "weakness," "natural decays," "ill savors," "the scent of rottenness": such terms recur throughout their writings on old age. Anne Bradstreet's poem "The Four Ages of Man" puts some especially pungent description into the mouth of a fictive representative of the elderly.

> My almond-tree [gray hairs] doth flourish now,
> And back, once straight, begins apace to bow,
> My grinders now are few, my sight doth fail,
> My skin is wrinkled, and my cheeks are pale.
> No more rejoice at music's pleasant noise,
> But do awake at the cock's clanging voice.
> I cannot scent savors of pleasant meat,
> Nor sapors find in what I drink or eat.
> My hands and arms, once strong, have lost their might.
> I cannot labor, nor can I fight.
> My comely legs, as nimble as the roe.
> Now stiff and numb, can hardly creep or go.[34]

Language such as this implies some particular element of stress and shock in physical aging as typically experienced by the New Englanders. Was morbidity, their presumed vulnerability to illness, the critical factor here? Perhaps—but the evidence is ambiguous at best. Old people in this setting certainly suffered from frequent and protracted bouts of illness; but so, too, did many others still young and vigorous. Compared with our own time, morbidity was not particularly age-specific; hence, this factor alone would not distinguish old age from the earlier phases of life.

In fact, the literary materials on old age make little reference to illness; they stress instead the loss of capacities and skills. Just here lies an important clue. We can scarcely overestimate the importance of physical exertion in premodern times: the "strong arms" and "nimble legs" of which Bradstreet wrote were directly engaged by the work of the farm, the routines of the household, travel, transport, and a host of other mundane activities. In this context "infirmity" was bound to have an intense and focused meaning. It seems likely, moreover, that physical decline was often postponed until quite late in life. Even today the pace of such changes varies markedly from one individual and one setting to another. Strength, coordination, and a relatively trim physique can be preserved long after youth has passed, by regular exertion and exercise. Conversely, physical decline can be hastened, given a more inactive and sedentary style of life. We may suppose that the former pattern best approximates the experience of the early New Englanders. If so, their subjective sense of the life course was shaped accordingly. Nowadays physical aging is typically, and often powerfully, associated with the passage from youth to middle age; here indeed lies an important part of what we call the "mid-life crisis." But centuries ago an equivalent crisis may well have marked the entrance to *old* age.

These considerations should help to explain some distinctly negative undertones in the attitudes of the elderly toward their own aging. For despite the "honor" that was prescribed as their due, few of them seem to have enjoyed being old. Increase Mather advised "aged servants of the Lord" to "comfort themselves with this consideration: God will never forsake them. They may live to be a burden to themselves and others; their nearest relations may grow weary of them; but then the Everlasting Arm will not grow weary in supporting them." Another minister, himself past sixty, urged his peers to avoid any semblance of "foolish" or "ridiculous" behavior. He particularly warned against "everything in our old age which may look as if we were loath to be thought old" (for example: "vain boasts of the faculties yet potent with us"). The same man three decades earlier had rebuked all "trifling and childish and frolicsome sort of carriage" in the elderly. "We cannot reverence you unless your grave looks, as well as your gray hairs, demand it of us."[35]

It is impossible to know how well and widely the elderly maintained their "grave looks"; there are, however, some grounds for speculation about their "gray hairs." Near the end of the seventeenth century there arose in Massachusetts a sharp controversy about what one man called "the evil fashions and practices of this age, both in apparel and [in] that general disguisement of long, ruffianlike hair."[36] Centrally at issue here was the widespread and increasing use of wigs. Rev. Nicholas Noyes of Salem sounded the tune of those who opposed the trend in a lengthy "Essay Against Periwigs." "The beauty of old men is the gray head," wrote Noyes, citing Scripture. And he continued:

The frequent sight of gray hairs is a lecture to men against levity, vanity, and youthful vagaries and lusts. . . . Others are obliged to rise up before and honor the old man, the demonstrative token of which is his gray hairs. But strangers to old men cannot so well distinguish of the age they converse with, when youthful hairs are grafted on a gray head, as is oftentimes [true] in the case of periwigs . . . and when peri-wigged men are known to be old, though they do the utmost to conceal their age, yet such levity and vanity appears in their affecting youthful shows as renders them contemptible and is in itself ridiculous.[37]

Unless the concerns of Rev. Noyes were totally removed from social reality, some elderly men preferred to appear younger than they actually were. In fact, although the symbolic importance of gray hair was every where recognized in New England society, the context of such recognition was at least occasionally pejora-tive. Here is a small but revealing instance. Two older, and locally eminent, men—Mr. Edward Woodman and Capt. William Gerrish—were arguing opposite positions before the town meet-ing at Newbury, Massachusetts. In the heat of the debate Gerrish made a slighting reference to the "gray hairs" of his adversary. The rejoinder was reported as follows: "Mr. Woodman said . . . that his gray hairs would stand where Capt. Gerrish, his bald pate, would."[38] It appears, then, that the "demonstrative token" of old age did not always elicit "honor," even from the elderly themselves.

But, most of all, old people dreaded what the young might think or say about them. "Our patience will be tried," declared Cotton Mather in his mid-sixties, "by the contempt which the base may cast upon us, and our beholding or fancying ourselves to be *lamps despised* among those who see we are going out." A generation earlier Increase Mather had composed a tract of *Solemn Advice to Young Men*, in which the following idea was central: "It is from pride that young men do not show that re-spect to their superiors, or unto aged ones, which God com-mandeth them to do. . . . Such especially whose parts and abil-ities are through age decayed: proud youth despiseth them." And elsewhere the same author wrote:

To deride aged persons because of those natural infirmities which age has brought upon them is a great sin. It may be they are become weak and childish: they that laugh at them on that account, perhaps if they should live to their age will be as childish as they. And would they be willing to be made a laughingstock by those that are younger than they?

This preoccupation with ridicule—whatever its relation to actual experience—implies a considerable insecurity in the aged themselves.[39]

There is one additional device—an ingenious creation of David Fischer's—for measuring attitudes toward aging. For all sorts of reasons and in many different settings, people misreport their age. This tendency is evident even in our own day, but it was much stronger in premodern times. Its chief manifestation in colonial New England was the practice of rounding off exact figures to a multiple of ten: twenty-nine sometimes became thirty, sixty-two might be reduced to sixty, and so forth. When these reports were grouped (for example, in a large population listing), they showed an effect now called "age heaping"—a disproportionate clustering around the aforementioned ten-year levels. Thus, five times as many people would report themselves as being fifty as would give forty-nine or fifty-one as their ages—and likewise at the comparable points across the entire age spectrum. An interesting question in the present context is the direction of this effect: did more people round-off *up* or *down*? Did they prefer to make themselves a little older, or a little younger, than they actually were? If the former was true, we may infer an "age bias," and if the latter, a "youth bias," in the population at large.[40]

The only large sample of age reports currently available for seventeenth-century New England involves some four thousand Massachusetts residents called as witnesses in trial proceedings before the Essex County Court. (Witnesses were normally required to give their age before testifying.) The critical data are the ages within two years on either side of the rounded levels (for example, 38, 39, 41, and 42 around age 40). Careful tabulation shows a preponderance of downward revision—in short, a youth bias. (See table 5.) Curiously, the pattern weakens somewhat near the end of the life cycle, and disappears altogether for people of seventy and more. (However, the sample numbers are probably too small, at the most advanced age levels, to yield results of much significance.) Taken as a whole, the material shows a personal orientation toward aging that is markedly unfavorable.

We turn now from subjective considerations—the "self" view of aging—to questions of social experience. Here, fortunately, the

TABLE 5. *Age-Heaping Ratios, Essex County, Mass.*

Age levels	Ratios	Age levels	Ratios
28–29	0.920	51–52	0.460
30	2.349	58–59	0.627
31–32	0.667	60	3.222
38–39	0.754	61–62	0.535
40	3.109	68–69	0.511
41–42	0.621	70	2.764
48–49	0.976	71–72	0.748
50	3.232		

Note: Ratio is computed by dividing the actual number of persons of a given age by the number of those reporting the age. ("Actual" numbers are determined by averaging reports for age levels within five years on either side of the given age.)

Underreporting can be expected within two years on either side of the ten-year intervals, and the material has been organized accordingly.

All data have been taken from age reports given by deponents in the Quarterly Courts of Essex County, Massachusetts, 1636–1682.

Source: *Records and Files of the Quarterly Courts of Essex County, Massachusetts* (Salem, Mass.: Essex Institute, 1911–1921).

evidence becomes more ample and varied, and conclusions can be more directly reached.

There is the important matter of domestic location: how the elderly were positioned in relation to home and family. In our own time a considerable number of people lose their homes, or find themselves living alone, as they pass into old age; the "nest" is empty or abandoned altogether. In colonial New England such conditions were rare.

For one thing, most New Englanders continued to live in their own homes even after their children had grown up and moved out to begin separate families. There was no general pattern of relocation for the elderly, in response to altered needs for space or altered resources. In fact, the issue of resources was crucial: the majority of older people were well-off compared to those in other age groups. The evidence for this conclusion derives from tax and probate records. When age is correlated with wealth— both for decedents whose estates were inventoried, and for heads of households "rated" by local tax-committees—a consistent pattern emerges. Average wealth was lowest for the age group of men in their twenties, rose strongly through the thirties and forties, reached a peak in the fifties, and declined gradually thereafter. (See table 6.) The reason for the eventual downward turn is obvious: men past sixty were deeding away property to their grown children. But if the elderly had somewhat less wealth overall than their "middle-aged" neighbors, they also had greatly lessened needs. A household in which the head was forty or fifty would normally include a number of young children, including some too young to earn their keep by contributing meaningful labor. The same household twenty years later was much reduced in size. The (by then) old man might well have no one to support beyond himself and his spouse. He might perhaps be labor-poor, but much of his property would remain intact—and this with many fewer mouths to feed.

Let us try to visualize other aspects of the same man's situation. His children, grown by now and established in their own households, were still a part of his social environment. The lure of new lands and fresh opportunities might possibly have drawn one or

TABLE 6. *Correlations of age and wealth in Colonial New England*

Age groups	Hampton, N.H., tax list (1653)	Hampton, N.H., tax list (1680)	Easthampton, R.I., tax list (1675)	Inventories, 5 towns**: 17th century	Inventories: Lyme, Conn. 1676–1776
20–29	43.7*	86.7*	41.3*	£112	£72
30–39	41.2	61.3	37.0	134	224
40–49	36.1	45.8	17.6	431	442
50–59	13.9	28.1	9.0	555	517
60–69	22.0	39.0	16.4	434	335
70–79	55.0	42.3		308	262
80–89		94.5		286	
(N)	(73)	(123)	(34)	(196)	

* Average rank, relative to all other taxpayers on complete list.
** Sample includes estate inventories for men whose age at death can be determined, from the following towns: Hampton (N.H.), Springfield (Mass.), Northampton (Mass.), Wethersfield (Conn.), Easthampton (R.I.), and Lyme (Conn.).

Sources: Local records and genealogies from the towns involved.
Family reconstitution by the author.
Jackson Turner Main, "The Economic and Social Structure of Early Lyme," in *A Lyme Miscellany*, ed. George Willauer, Jr. (Middletown, Conn.: Wesleyan University Press, 1977), p. 33.

two to distant locations, but most of them would be living near-by.[41] The details of these intrafamilial relationships remain obscure, and there are no grounds for assuming any special elements of closeness or harmony. Still, the simple fact of the children's presence within the same community was important in its own right.

To the children, moreover, were added the grandchildren. We have already considered this matter from the standpoint of the young, but we should look at it again from the farther end of the life course. Most elderly New Englanders were grandparents many times over. Two cases, drawn from the Hampton data, illustrate the common pattern. Isaac Perkins and his wife, Susannah, were born about 1610 and 1615 respectively, and were married in 1636. Together they produced twelve children, three of whom died before reaching adulthood. Of the nine children who married, eight produced children of their own. The eldest of the latter was born in the year 1660—when Isaac and Susannah were approximately fifty and forty-five. (Susannah bore her last child the year *after* the birth of her first grandchild—thus did the generations overlap.) By 1670, when Isaac had reached sixty and Susannah fifty-five, there were twelve grandchildren; a decade later there were thirty-one. When Isaac died in his mid-seventies, there were thirty-nine grandchildren; when Susannah died at eighty-four, the total had risen to fifty-six. By this time, too, great-grandchildren were starting to arrive. The experience of the Perkins' neighbors, Morris and Sarah Hobbs, can be more quickly summarized. The first of their grandchildren was born when they were about fifty and forty-five years old; thirteen more had arrived by the time Sarah died at sixty-one. Morris lived on another twenty years. At seventy he had twenty-three grandchildren; at seventy-five, thirty-six grandchildren and two great-grandchildren; and at eighty-six (the year of his death), forty-four grandchildren and seventeen great-grandchildren.

These figures seem extraordinary by the standards of our own day, but, given the arithmetic of high fertility and surprisingly long life expectation, they are plausible—indeed, virtually inevitable. Again, they establish only the statistical presence of grandchildren, but stray notations gleaned from court records hint at the qualitative dimension as well. Thus, one old man remembered dispatching his grandson "to the cowhouse . . . to scare the fowls from my hogs' meat"; another, needing spectacles to read a neighbor's will, "sent his grandchild Mary . . . to Henry Brown's and she brought a pair."[42]

While presumably enjoying their proximity to kin, elderly couples preferred to look after themselves. Thus, Gov. George Willys of Connecticut wrote, in concluding a long letter to his son about various matters of inheritance: "I will say no more; for you know, as it is a way of prudence, so it is also my judgement and shall be my practice, not so to dispose to any child but that (God preserving my estate in an ordinary course of Providence) I may have to maintain myself and not to be expecting from any of them." An Essex County farmer invoked the same principle when asked whether he might not increase the "portion" of his married son: "He answered that he had been advised to keep his estate in his own hands as long as he lived, and as they were young and lusty, they could work to get themselves necessaries."[43]

It appears that most elderly couples succeeded in remaining self-sufficient; as noted previously, they retained on average a relatively high level of wealth. Inevitably, however, there were some circumstances in which they required assistance. The most obvious and certainly the most common of these was widowhood. When a man died, his wife was placed in a position of some doubt, or even one of jeopardy. If she was still young, she might look forward to remarriage—which would automatically supply her deficiencies. But if she was elderly, her prospects that way were greatly reduced.[44] In any case, her rights to her late husband's property must be secured through appropriate action in the courts. The principle of the widow's "thirds" was long established in custom and in common law: she would have the use of a third of the family lands during her lifetime, plus full title to a third of all movable properties.[45] Often the wills of the decendents added explicit provisions for her daily maintainence. "My will is," wrote Jonathan Platt of Rowley, Massachusetts, shortly before his death, "that my two sons John and Jonathan do provide well for my beloved wife, and that they let her want nothing that is needful for herself so long as she remaineth my widow." Similarly, John Cheney of Newbury "enjoined" his son Daniel to supply his widow with "whatever necessaries . . . her age shall require during the time of her normal life."[46]

In many instances these arrangements were spelled out with extraordinary precision. Typically, the widow was guaranteed appropriate space for her lodging ("the parlor end of the house . . . with the cellar that hath lock and key to it"); access to other parts of the household ("free liberty to bake, brew, and wash, etc. in the kitchen"); a fuel supply ("firewood, ready cut for the fire, at her door"); furnishings ("the bedstead we lie on, and the bedding . . . thereunto belonging . . . and the best green rug . . . the best low chair . . . and a good cushion"); and household implements ("pots, kettles, and other vessels commonly made use of").[47] She might also be given domestic animals ("two cows, by name Reddy and Cherry, and one yearling heifer") and regular assistance in caring for them ("kept for her use by my heir, wintered and summered at his charge, and brought into the yard daily, as his own is, to be milked"); a share in the fruits of the garden ("apples, pears, and plums for her use"); and a means of travel ("a gentle horse or mare to ride to meeting or any other occasion she may have").[48] Less often— and chiefly where there was considerable wealth in the family— she would receive regular payments in money or produce ("eight pounds per year, either in wheat, barley, or indian corn"); personal service ("Maria, the little Negro girl, to be with her so long as my wife lives"); and special sustenance for mind ("the book called *The Soul's Preparation for Christ*, and that of Perkins upon the creed") or body ("her beer, as she hath now").[49]

These provisions, reflecting a broad range of probate settlements, directly involved the testator's children (and heirs) in his widow's care. Frequently, the widow herself was empowered to see to their fulfillment. Thus, one man directed that "if Nathaniel [his son] fail of anything he is to do for my wife, my will is that he shall forfeit ten pounds every year he fails"; and another left all his movable property for his wife to bequeath "to my children accordingly as she shall see cause and they deserve, in their carriage and care of her in her widow's estate."[50]

Sometimes elderly men made formal arrangements for their own care, following the death of their wives. One old farmer promised a bequest to his son-in-law on condition that the latter "be helpful towards the maintenence of him while he lived." And a second, noting his "weak body . . . and solitary condition," conveyed his entire estate to a relative who would "find and provide for me wholesome and sufficient food and raiment, lodging, attendance, washing, and other necessaries, as well in sickness and weakness of old age as in health." Similar arrangements could be made even while both spouses survived: "I bequeathe to my cousin Daniel Gott all my neat cattle and sheep and horse-carts, chains, plow, and tools . . . in consideration that he is to remove his family and come to live with me and my wife at Lynn during our lives and carry on our husbandry affairs."[51]

The care of old and infirm persons did not, of course, always require a legal document; sometimes it was managed informally—or simply developed out of familial closeness and affection. Here and there the wills afford a retrospective glimpse. "Forasmuchas my eldest son and his family hath in my extreme old age and weakness been tender and careful of me," wrote one testator, identifying the chief beneficiary of his estate. Another—a woman making "her last will . . . upon her death bed"—particularly remembered "my daughter Ann, in consideration of her staying with me in my old age and being helpful to me."[52]

When such "considerations" were not specifically acknowledged in probate documents, they might give rise to legal proceedings. The relatives, even the children, of the deceased were quite ready to put a price on their "tendance and care." When the courts settled the estate of Jeffrey Massey of Salem, Massachusetts, a son filed bills for his "charges . . . with my father and mother in the time of their age and weakness . . . both food, physick, and tendance for the space of four years." Occasionally, such claims were disputed by other family members, and witnesses were called to establish particulars. Thus, one dutiful son was described as having taken such "great trouble and care . . . with his mother that he could hardly spare time to go abroad about his business." Another had helped his aging father to frame a house, and—a witness remembered—"did almost all the work"; the father had subsequently remarked "that his son was the best friend he had."[53]

At least a few elderly New Englanders, finding themselves in need of help but without relatives living nearby, were obliged to appeal to public authority. Usually, the local meeting would supervise their care. Particular tasks and services were assigned to individual townspeople, who were subsequently reimbursed out of town funds. The financial accounts of Watertown, Massachusetts, for the year 1670 reveal the process at work in a specific case.

	£ s d
To widow Bartlett, for dieting old Bright	10-00-00
To John Bisko, for a bushel of meal to old Bright, and 7 loads of wood	01-11-06
To William Perry, for work for old Bright	00-03-03
To Michael Bairstow . . . for cloth for a coat for old Bright	01-18-06

The recipient of these charities, Goodman Henry Bright, was "old" indeed—ninety-five years old by the best available estimate. The local records of New Haven, Connecticut, show a similar involvement with a man identified only as "old Bunnill." The town voted him "maintainance" of two shillings per week (among other benefits). Eventually "the town was informed that old Bunnill is desirous to go to old England . . . where he saith he hath some friends to take care of him," and public funds were authorized to pay for his passage.[54]

The problems created by infirmity were only one part of the experience of old age. Many elderly New Englanders retained a substantial capacity for work, for public service, for ordinary forms of social intercourse. The same thing is true—even more so—of our own society; however, the context is now vastly changed.

To make such comparisons with modern conditions is to spotlight at once the issue of "retirement." Did the New Englanders retire from active pursuits as they crossed the "borders" of old age? A quick answer is likely to be negative. Almost any set of local records can be used to observe old people in the postures of their workaday world. Here are several examples, culled from the files of the Essex County courts: Edward Guppy, aged 60, "employed by Edmund Batter to mow salt water grass in the marsh"; William Nichols, aged 70, hauling grist to the local mill; Evan Morris, aged 66, working "as a retainer" at the Rowley ironworks; William Boynton, aged 68, hired by a merchant to transport "rugs and blanketing" to Boston; George Kesar, aged 67, tanning leather for his neighbors; James Brown, aged 74, still active as a glazier; Edmund Pickard, aged 60, "master of the [ship] *Hopewell*"; Wayborough Gatchell, aged 70, continuing "her services as midwife"; and—most remarkably of all—Henry Stich, aged 102, working as a "collier" at Saugus.[55]

As in everyday labor, so too in public service, did older people play substantial parts. The various governors and assistants of Plymouth Colony seem, for the most part, to have retained their offices until the end of their lives. The careers of New England clergymen were also extremely prolonged; in a sample of thirty-five, only three were terminated by causes other than death.[56] Individual cases are no less impressive. In 1700 the Hampton vital records gave special notice to the death of "Henry Green, Esq., aged about 80 years, for several years a member of the Council of New Hampshire until by age he laid down that place, but a Justice till he died which was the 5th of August." In 1669 Thomas Minor of Connecticut made the following entry in his diary: "I am by my own accounts sixty-one years old. I was by the town this year chosen to be a selectman, the town's treasurer, the town's recorder, the brander of horses, [and] by the General Court recorded the head officer of the train-band, . . . one of the four that have the charge of the militia of the whole county, and chosen and sworn commisioner and one to assist in keeping the county court."[57]

Yet the total picture is complicated, and the evidence does not run entirely in a single direction. Henry Green, after all, had "laid down" one of his offices on account of age. And there are similar indications in the careers of other public officials—such as the notorious Samuel Sewall of Massachusetts. When Sewall was sixty-five years old and long established as a magistrate, he put his name forward for the position of chief justice. The governor was evasive in his reply: he recognized Sewall's qualifications, but "did not know but that by reason of my age I had rather stay at home." Sewall "humbly thanked His Excellency" for this mark of personal consideration—and continued his quest for the position. Ten years later, though, it was Sewall himself who cited the exigencies of age: "I went to the Lieut. Governor and desired to lay down my place in the Superior Court. I was not capable to do the work, and therefore was not willing to hold the place." Thomas Munson of New Haven made a similar plea while seeking, at the age of sixty-three, to retire from his post as lieutenant in the local militia: "He said he had been an officer to the company long, and had willingly served to the best of his ability, but he finds such decays in himself, and thereby [feels himself] unfit to serve in that place and office any longer."[58]

Lieutenant Munson seems, in fact, a better case for our purposes than either Green or Sewall; as a local (not provincial) official, he more closely approximated average experience. But the study of local leadership is most usefully pursued by way of collective biography. Were selectmen, for example, often men of advanced years? Might they continue to serve until the time of their death? A modest sample of Hampton selectmen has been investigated with these questions in mind, and the results establish distinct trends in relation to age. The largest portion of the sample comprised men between the ages of fifty and fifty-nine years (32 percent); the next largest group were in their forties (27 percent). A smaller, though still considerable, number were in their sixties (18 percent); however, very few (3 percent) were seventy or more. (See table 7.)

A subsample drawn from the same material yields an even clearer picture of withdrawal from officeholding in relation to old age. The nineteen selectmen in this group all served at least three terms, and all died at ages of 70 or over. Their mean age at the time of final service was 65.8. Only one of them actually died in

TABLE 7. *Selectmen's Ages, Hampton, N.H.* (1645–1720)

Age group	Number of Selectmen	Percentage of Sample
20–29	2	1
30–39	31	19
40–49	45	27
50–59	52	32
60–69	30	18
70+	5	3

Sources: Town Book of Hampton, 2 volumes (manuscript volumes in Town Offices, Hampton, N.H.).

Joseph Dow, *History of the Town of Hampton, New Hampshire* (Salem, Mass.: Salem Press, 1893).

Sybil Noyes, Charles Thornton Libby, and Walter Goodwin Davis, *Genealogical Dictionary of Maine and New Hampshire* (Baltimore: Genealogical Publishing Company, 1972).

office, and fully 90 percent lived at least five years after retirement. Indeed, the average interval between final term and time of death was more than eleven years. (See table 8).

Thomas Minor qualifies as a "local leader" in another settlement (Stonington, Connecticut), and his diary offers a unique opportunity to study the career of an older man in detail. Minor's varied responsibilities as an officeholder in his sixty-first year

TABLE 8. *Selectmen's ages at retirement and death,*
Hampton, N.H. (1645–1720)

Age in last term as selectman		Interval between last term and death	
Age	Number	Years	Number
59 or less	2	0	1
60	1	1	
61	1	2	1
62		3	
63	2	4	
64	2	5	1
65		6	
66	1	7	3
67		8	1
68	4	9	1
69	1	10	2
70		11	1
71	1	12	1
72	3	13	1
73		14	1
74	1	15	2
75 and over		16	
Average = 65.8 years		17	3
		18 and over	
		Average = 10.3 years	

Note: The sample includes nineteen men, all of whom died at the age of 70 or older, having served at least three terms as town selectmen.

Sources: Town Book of Hampton, 2 volumes (manuscript volumes in Town Offices, Hampton, N.H.).

Joseph Dow, *History of the Town of Hampton, New Hampshire* (Salem, Mass.: Salem Press, 1893).

Sybil Noyes, Charles Thornton Libby, and Walter Goodwin Davis, *Genealogical Dictionary of Maine and New Hampshire* (Baltimore: Genealogical Publishing Company, 1972).

have already been noted. He continued to serve, in similar ways, for some while longer, and was even "employed in the country's service about the Indian War" at the age of sixty-seven. After seventy, however, the pattern seems to have changed. The diary makes no further reference to officeholding, or indeed to any other form of public responsibility.[59]

Minor's life as a private citizen is also fully chronicled; again, there is evidence of vigorous activity well into his seventh decade. Here is the record of a typical month in his sixty-sixth year.

> The third month is May and hath 31 days. Friday the first: this week I made my cart. Friday the 8: a town meeting. Monday the 11: I and my wife was at New London. Friday the 15: we pulled down the chimneys. Monday the 18 day: Thomas Park began to build. Friday 22: we shore the sheep and had home one of the manteltrees. 25: we had a town meeting. 27 Wednesday: we laid out Bay grants on the east side [of the] Poquatuck[60]

Beyond the age of seventy, Minor continued to work on his farm, to visit friends, and the like—but at a somewhat reduced pace. By this time he was receiving considerable help from others. In the spring of his seventy-third year, for example, one of his sons "took all the corn to sow and to plant, to halves for this year."[61]

One final test has been made of the effects of aging on Thomas Minor, by coding the events noted in his diary on a simple "self/other" basis. Minor's reports of his own activity (any event in which he is himself a chief agent) can then be compared with his references to the doings of others. The results, briefly summarized, show a modest lowering of the self-to-other ratio as Minor passed into his sixties, and a marked decline in his early seventies. (See table 9.) Though this measure is admittedly crude, it allows us to glimpse the deeper rhythms of aging in one particular case.

The retirement question evokes, in sum, a complex and divided answer from the New England source materials. It appears that most men past sixty voluntarily reduced their activities in work and public service. Yet nearly always this was a gradual process—a quantitative rather than a qualitative change—and rarely did it lead to complete withdrawal. There were two main categories of exceptions: those ministers and magistrates whose exalted rank

TABLE 9. *Thomas Minor (Stonington, Conn.): Activities Pattern*

Years	Minor's Age	Self	Other	Ratio
1654–1657	45–48	98	25	3.92
1658–1661	49–52	149	44	3.39
1662–1665	53–56	129	50	2.58
1666–1669	57–60	151	52	2.90
1670–1673	61–64	156	88	1.77
1674–1677	65–68	144	68	2.12
1678–1680	69–71	88	41	2.15
1681–1684	72–75	88	93	0.95

Note: The first six calendar months of each year (January–June) were coded
for references to personal activity. The numbers in the "self" column
include all activities in which Minor describes himself as a major
participant. The "other" column includes activities which Minor attri-
butes to other people in his local environment. (The following kinds
of activity are *not* included: marriages, births, deaths, sicknesses, injuries, holidays, and religious observances.)

Source: Thomas Minor, *The Diary of Thomas Minor, Stonington, Connecticut, 1653 to 1684*, ed. Sidney Miner and George D. Stanton (New
London, Conn.: Day Publishing Company, 1899).

exempted them from even a partial retirement, and those among
the ordinary folk whose "infirmities" were simply incapacitating.

We should understand, too, that the idea of retirement was not
entirely unknown to the New Englanders. The Mathers, father
and son, both remarked on its sometimes painful aspect. "It is a
very undesirable thing for a man to outlive his work," wrote
Increase, "although if God will have it so, His Holy Will must
be humbly and patiently submitted unto."[62] Cotton pursued the
same thought at greater length:

> *Old folks* often can't endure to be judged less able than ever
> they were for *public appearances*, or to be put out of *offices*.
> But good sir, be so wise as to *disappear* of your own accord,
> as soon and as far as you lawfully may. Be glad of a *dismission*
> from any *post*, that would have called for your *activities*. . . .
> Let your *quietus* gratify you. Be pleased with the *retirement*
> which you are dismissed unto.[63]

Comments like these seem to reach forward to our own time; yet
the similarities, no less than the differences, are liable to over-
statement. The germ of modern retirement was present three

centuries ago—but *only* the germ. What was then gradual, partial, and indefinite at many points has now become abrupt, total, and rigid in its specific applications. A *process* with intrinsic biological connections has become a *moment* plucked from the calendar.

There is one more aspect of social experience to which our study should make some approach. I established at the outset that the normative code of colonial New England was decidedly favorable to old age. "Honor," "respect," even "veneration," were the terms most frequently used in prescribing attitudes toward the elderly. Younger people were urged to "rise up . . . before the old man," and conduct themselves with "a bashful and modest reverence." The elderly, for their part, would "use a kind of authority and confidence in their words and carriage." But were these precepts actually followed in practice?[64]

Occasionally—*very* occasionally—some fragment of the documentary record allows us to glimpse people of different generations dealing with one another face to face. A few of these have been noted already; one more will be added now. Two residents of Scituate, Massachusetts, were arguing one summer day in 1685 about a debt for several bots of cloth. One was Nathaniel Parker, aged twenty-three, the other Edward Jenkins, aged approximately sixty-five. (The site was Jenkins' own house.) Tempers flared, and then: "Nathaniel Parker ran to Edward Jenkins and took Edward Jenkins by the collar or neckcloth that was about Edward Jenkins' neck; and Nathaniel Parker said, 'God damn me, if thou were not an old man, I would bat thy teeth down thy throat.' " Shall we count this as an expression of deference to age? Literally, yes—but, in context, no. Certainly it was not the kind of deference prescribed in the published literature on old age. Parker's comment seems, in fact, to imply *contempt* for his adversary's weakness as an "old man."[65]

The connotations, in the New England setting, of the word "old" deserve our further consideration. Again and again in local records we find elderly people mentioned in a special way: "old Bright," "old Bunnill," "old Woodward," "old Hammond." Their given names are, in effect, discounted, and age itself becomes an identifying mark. (For younger persons, the pattern of reference was consistently otherwise; in their case given name and surname appeared together.) This usage was not, moreover, a matter of indifference to the elderly themselves. Increase Mather made the point very clearly: "To treat aged persons with disrespectful or disdainful language only because of their age is a very criminal offense in the sight of God; yet how common is it to call this or the other person 'old such an one', in a way of contempt on the account of their age."[66] A list of householders in the records of Watertown, Massachusetts, includes five men designated in precisely this way. Their ages, as determined from independent evidence, ranged between sixty-seven and eighty-two. Interestingly, there are other men of equivalent age on the same list who are not called "old." The distinction was one of social rank, pure and simple. Thus, the man listed as "Simon Stone" (age seventy-two) was wealthy, a deacon of the Watertown church, and frequently a town officer; whereas "old Knapp" (age seventy-four) was a sometime carpenter of little means and no public responsibilities whatsoever. The implicitly pejorative prefix could only be applied in the latter instance.[67] Probate documents afford parallel evidence on the same matter. Testators called themselves "ancient" or "aged" (when they referred to such things at all), but never "old." It was fine to describe property that way—"old housing," "old lumber," "old cows,"—but not the *person* writing the will.[68]

So much for individual terms of reference; were there no formal—perhaps even institutional—expressions of deference to the elderly? One possibility comes immediately to mind. The inhabitants of New England towns, like people in traditional communities everywhere, came together at regular intervals to honor in a ceremonial way their deepest values and spiritual commitments. Weekly (sometimes twice-weekly) they gathered for worship in the village meetinghouse. On these occasions they reaffirmed not only the shared basis of their corporate life, but also the hierarchical arrangement of its constituent parts. Every meetinghouse was carefully "seated"—that is, all adult members of the community occupied places assigned to them in accordance with their individual status. The basic principle was: the higher the rank of the person involved, the closer his seat to the front.[69] The official criteria for making these status evaluations invariably included "age"—along with "estate" (that is, wealth), "office" (public service), "dignity of descent" (pedigree), and "pious disposition."[70] Here, then, was an unmistakable mark of the preferment deemed appropriate for older citizens.

However, we may well ask to what extent, and in what ways, this criterion of status was actually applied in conjunction with all the others. Fortunately, detailed seating plans have survived in various town archives; unfortunately, they have not as yet received much systematic attention from scholars.[71] That they deserve such attention seems indisputable, for they are virtual "sociograms" and would tell us much about seventeenth-century life. But for the moment we have only one set of results on which to base some very tentative conclusions.

The Hampton (New Hampshire) meetinghouse was seated in the early months of the year 1650.[72] The design of the building was relatively simple. The pulpit was on the north side; just below, and roughly in the middle of the floor, was a "table," where men of the highest rank were privileged to sit. The other male members of the congregation were assigned to eight benches in the west and southwest parts of the building; the women occupied comparable places directly opposite. We do not know precisely what instructions were given to the committee that took the measure of every single person named on the plan; nor could we, in any case, deal with such intangibles as "pious disposition." We can, however, investigate the importance of age and wealth relative to one another.

Predictably, age and wealth were substantially inter-correlated overall, and in many individual cases they simply cannot be distinguished. Older men (or women) who were also wealthy had a double claim on front-row seats, while those who were both young and poor invariably occupied places near the rear. In other instances, however, there were sharp status discrepancies— for example, a young and rich man, an old and poor one. What places were thought appropriate for *them*? Most such people were seated on the basis of wealth. For example, William Cole, at seventy-nine the oldest resident of the town, had one of the lowest tax-assessments; he sat on a back bench in the meetinghouse. By contrast, Thomas Ward, only thirty-one but already near the top in terms of wealth, was assigned to the front row. Cole and Ward belonged to a group of eleven particularly discrepant cases (that is, cases where rankings for age and wealth are at least three quintiles apart). In nine of these, wealth was the decisive factor for seating position; in the remaining two, there was something of a compromise. An additional group of sixteen cases, in which the age-wealth discrepancy was less (two quintiles), includes eight which favored wealth, four which favored age, and four in the compromise category. (See table 10.) In truth, the Hampton materials from 1650 are not the best imaginable for this inquiry. The town had been settled barely a decade earlier, and few of its people were truly old. The data strongly suggest that age *in general* was not an important criterion of social rank, but it might yet be shown, on other evidence, that *old* age was treated specially.

This long excursion through an extremely varied and tortuous body of source materials is now at an end; there remains, however, the question of central themes and tendencies. Here we may allow ourselves to be openly speculative. Moreover, we may look for help to the social sciences, where the study of aging has been more extensively pursued.

We are told by sociologists that the status of old people, in any culture, turns on a cluster of institutional factors. Among these the following seem especially important: (1) property ownership; (2) the possession of strategic knowledge; (3) the predominant modes and styles of economic productivity; (4) an ethos of mutual dependence (or, conversely, of "individualism"); (5) the importance of received traditions (especially religious ones); (6) the strength of family and kinship ties; (7) the range and character of community life.[73]

Measured against this checklist, the position of the elderly in colonial New England looks strong. We know, for example, that some of them (merchants, artisans, or particularly successful yeomen) controlled large amounts of property, and that old people in general were well-off in comparison to most other age groups. "Strategic knowledge" was also an acquirement of the elderly. Farming, marketing, domestic craftsmanship: these things they knew at least as well as their younger neighbors. In addition, and more important, they controlled a variety of significant information about the community's past. Much that pertained to the settlement of legal questions—boundaries, contracts, the details of ownership—was never written down, and had to be recalled in some appropriate forum by those who could bear

TABLE 10. *Hampton (N.H.) meetinghouse plan, 1650:*
status-discrepant cases

3–4 Quintiles

Name	Age (in quintiles)	Wealth (in quintiles)	Seat Row	(Section)
Brown, John	4	1*	1	(s)
Cole, Eunice	1	5*	5	(e)
Cole, William	1	5*	3	(w)
Elkins, Gershom	2	5*	3	(w)
Elkins, Mary	2	5*	4	(e)
Fuller, Frances	4	1*	1	(s)
Huggins, John	2	5*	5	(w)
Moulton, Margaret	5	2	2	(s)
Sanborn, John	5	2	2	(s)
Ward, Margaret	5	1*	2	(s)
Ward, Thomas	4	1*	1	(w)

2 Quintiles

Name	Age (in quintiles)	Wealth (in quintiles)	Seat Row	(Section)
Brown Sarah	3	1*	1	(e)
Estow, Mary	1	3*	2	(s)
Estow, William	1*	3	Table	
Green, Henry	5	3*	2	(w)
Leavitt, Thomas	4	2	2	(w)
Marston, Mary	5*	3	3	(s)
Moulton, William	4	2	2	(s)
Philbrick, Thomas	1*	3	1	(s)
Sanborn, Mary	4	2	2	(e)
Sanborn, Mary	5	3	2	(e)
Sanborn, William	5	3*	2	(s)
Sleeper, Thomas	3	5*	3	(w)
Smith, Deborah	3	5*	4	(e)
Smith, John	3	5*	4	(w)
Swain, William	1*	3	1	(s)
Taylor, Anthony	2	4*	3	(s)

Note: Ages have been computed (in some cases estimated) from vital records, genealogies, etc. Wealth was determined by averaging positions (relative to all other taxpayers) on tax lists of 1647 and 1653. Asterisk indicates factor apparently given greatest weight in seating assignment.

Sources: Town Book of Hampton, 2 volumes (manuscript volumes in Town Offices, Hampton, N.H.).

Sybil Noyes, Charles Thornton Libby, and Walter Goodwin Davis, *Genealogical Dictionary of Maine and New Hampshire* (Baltimore: Genealogical Publishing Company, 1972).

Joseph Dow, *History of the Town of Hampton, New Hampshire* (Salem, Mass.: Salem Press, 1893).

personal witness from long ago.[74] ("John Emery, sr., aged about eighty-one years, testified that about forty years ago he saw laid out to William Estow, then of Newbury, a four acre lot. . . .")[75] In a society only partially literate and without comprehensive record-keeping, the memories of old people gave them a certain advantage.

Other institutional factors can be followed in the same way— and to roughly parallel conclusions. Thus, the fact that early New England was land-rich and labor-poor enhanced the productive value even of marginal workers (such as the "aged and infirm"). The principle of reciprocity was established at the very core of the value structure: "we must be knit together in this work as one man," John Winthrop had said in a famous speech prepared en route to the New World.[76] The force of tradition was appreciated, even venerated, throughout New England society. Most people were well supplied with kinfolk, and there was a vigorous network of neighborly relationships. In sum, the position of the elderly was supported, even enhanced, by prevailing social arrangements. Certainly their power and influence compare very favorably with what obtains for their counterparts in our own time.

We may now feel that we have finally uncovered the basis in social reality for the dictum "honour old age." And yet, too, we have seen how that dictum was subject to varying interpretations—and was often directly controverted by actual behavior. To understand these somewhat paradoxical findings, it is necessary to look beyond social structure to considerations of psychological functioning. Just here there are valuable suggestions to be taken from anthropological research on the aging process in a variety of premodern cultures.[77] This research can be summarized only at the risk of gross oversimplification, but the effort is worth making nonetheless. In most, if not all, premodern settings, the elderly occupy a position of far greater social importance than is true in our culture; this is based in part on their control of valuable resources, and in part on their presumed status as "closer to God." But however powerful, they are not invariably *secure*. In some societies the elderly elicit great respect and affection; in others they are the object of deep resentment and mistrust, and live in a chronic state of fear. The difference is not based on their institutional position, which may be strong in both cases, but rather on the predominant style of affective and interpersonal life in the culture—in technical language, on a culture-specific capacity for "object relations."

In fact, older people everywhere are liable to be considered alien, different, strange; given certain preconditions, they arouse in their younger culture mates mixed feelings of awe and apprehension. In a society where interpersonal relations are more or less relaxed, where there is little subjective tension between the claims of self and others, where psychosocial conditions favor the formation of "internalized objects"—in such a society the elderly remain secure. As one scholar has written, "By keeping his 'object' status the older person avoids becoming the *stranger* . . . [who arouses] fear and revulsion."[78] Or, to put it in still another way, the older person is experienced fully as an individual being, in whom the past (what he formerly *was*) and the present (what he now *is*) are implicitly joined. But things are not always so. In other societies—where object relations are narrower, less differentiated, more narcissistic in tone—the aged (and sometimes also the very young) are distinctly at risk. Their strangeness is highlighted, and often deeply feared. No matter what their socioeconomic power and official prestige, they are vulnerable to various forms of covert, even overt, attack.

These two situations are, in fact, the opposite ends of a single spectrum. And we must now ask where on that spectrum to locate the New Englanders. The question seems impossibly large; yet the materials discussed in the preceding pages suggest at least some parts of an answer. The people of early New England had many strong and admirable qualities, but there was indeed something problematic about their "object relations." In the doings of many of them, one feels a thin edge of psychic vulnerability—a sense of self somewhat insecurely held, a view of others not fully three-dimensional. Committed always to goals of "peaceableness," they often disappointed themselves: inner and outer conflict was the actual condition of their lives. The doubt, the distress, the occasional rages which fueled such conflict are manifest all through the documentary record they have left to us.[79] Inevitably, under such conditions, there was some narrowing of their perception and understanding of others. The very qualities of "otherness" were hard for them to appreciate. Their view of the American Indians, for example, was notoriously constricted:

Indians must behave in all things like Englishmen, else they are "savages" and "beasts."[80] Even their attitudes toward their own children expressed a certain lack of empathy. They were determined, insofar as possible, to "beat down" infantile expressions of willfulness, and they insisted on confronting their young with painful reminders of sin and death.[81] This does not imply an absence of parental love, but simply an inability to credit fully the inherent childishness of childhood.

And what about the bearing of such considerations on old age? First, the elderly themselves were burdened with an especially difficult experience of their own aging. Growing old always creates some narcissistic imbalance, but for persons who are already sensitive on that count, the problems are greatly compounded. Here, then, is one way to account for the "peevish," "suspicious," and "complaining" character usually attributed to the aged in colonial New England. But we must also look at the matter in terms of what the others, the not-old, contributed. For reasons related to their own character structure, they were frequently unable to "see" the elderly in a way that embraced the full richness of human individuality.[82] To them the old person was indeed something of a stranger. Thus, they tended to stereotype him (calling him "old such an one"), to fear him (especially for his alleged "covetousness"), and indirectly to ridicule him (witness the figure of the staggering, spewing old drunkard, and the metaphor of the tree with its leaves off).

To summarize these rather diverse and crosscutting materials, we may say that the position of the elderly in early New England was sociologically advantageous, but psychologically disadvantageous. Their control of important resources seemed to command honor and respect, but not affection or sympathetic understanding. Simone de Beauvoir has written that the only sure protection for old people is "that which their children's love provides."[83] And precisely here the situation of old New Englanders was doubtful.

We have pressed about as far as our evidence will carry us— perhaps indeed a bit farther. And yet there are important questions which we have scarcely touched. As noted at the start, most of the available data concerns aging in men, but sooner or later we will need to find some parallel way of investigating the experience of women. Another major lacuna in the present treatment is the matter of attitudes toward death. In all cultures and epochs the elderly must anticipate death by one means or another, and such anticipation was expressed with great emphasis in early New England. But death is a huge subject in itself; fortunately, there are other studies which approach it more directly and at considerable length.[84]

One further issue should be confronted, if only in a speculative way. Can we say anything about our material in relation to historical change? Were the central tendencies in aging gradually altered as time and circumstance moved them along? And what was their eventual direction, seen in retrospect?

There is reason to think that the position of elderly people was improved between the middle of the seventeenth century and the middle of the eighteenth. Some of our own measures, when applied to later materials, strongly suggest as much. "Age heaping," for example, begins to show an age bias after 1700. A meeting-house plan from the year 1774 seems to give strong priority to age (as compared with wealth). Wigs were increasingly designed to make their owners look older, not younger, than was actually the case—likewise the sartorial fashions of the eighteenth century. The unfriendly undertones, so persistent in seventeenth-century literature on old age, appear to have faded thereafter.[85] It seems possible, then, that the decades immediately preceding the American Revolution were a time of maximum advantage for old people.

If so, we may well wonder *why*—and it is worth recording certain points of plausible relevance out of the present research. We have learned that life expectation for the early New Englanders was surprisingly long. Evidently, they survived to old age in numbers unequalled elsewhere in the colonies or in old England across the seas.[86] Perhaps, under these conditions, the aura of strangeness around elderly people was gradually dissipated.

Perhaps, too, there were complementary changes of inner life. This possibility is hard to explore on an empirical basis, but it does link up with reigning themes in New England historiography. Thus, the harsh lines of Calvinist belief are thought to have softened somewhat after the middle of the seventeenth century. The balance of social concern tipped away from religion toward secular experience; in terms of cultural types, the shift

was "from Puritan to Yankee."[87] There was, moreover, an ecological shift spanning roughly the same time period. The "wilderness," in which personal security and cultural integrity both
seemed at risk, gave way to a settled society with its various pro-
tections and amenities. New England character was modified
accordingly. The claims of self were now more freely acknowledged, and this, in turn, broadened the psychic space available for
experiencing others—indeed "otherness" in general.[88] The inherited social core remained intact (Anglo-Saxon, Christian,
adult, and effectively male), but people on the margins were less
vulnerable to implicit or explicit stereotyping. And old people
were particular beneficiaries.

A further consideration—no easier to specify, but probably no
less important—was the meaning of age in a society still relatively
new. The example of the "planters" seems to have gained a
deeper and deeper significance as the decades passed. These re-
doubtable men and women were the roots of the growing community. History had opened to them a uniquely creative path,
and they had followed it unswervingly. Their success in "settlement" would remain, for all their descendants, an achievement
of stunning proportions. To be sure, the effect on their immediate
descendants was problematic: the sons of the planters found it
hard to measure up. Tension built to a peak in roughly the third
quarter of the seventeenth century: the religious controversies of
that era represented, in part, a crisis in age relations.[89] The members of the settler generation were leaving "the earthly stage"
en route to their reward beyond. Their deaths occasioned special
comment in local diaries, and some notably elaborate funerals;
perhaps, too, there was a connection with the dominant religious
motif of "declension."[90] There were signs of sharpened age-con-
sciousness overall: increasingly, for example, individuals identified themselves as old.[91]

In time, of course, the "crisis" eased. Gone as a living presence,
the planters survived as the heroic figures of legend. The ambivalence they had aroused in their own children yielded to the
unqualified admiration of succeeding generations. The residue of
this process was a growing regard for age: old people were closest
to the hallowed beginnings of New England, and that alone gave
them a certain cachet. Here is Samuel Sewall, writing in his diary
in the spring of 1726: "The honored, ancient, elder Faunce . . .

kindly visited me. *Laus Deo.*" Thomas Faunce was then about eighty, and had served for many years as deacon of the first church at Plymouth. He is said to have "kept in cherished remembrance the first settlers, many of whom he well knew. He used to identify the rock on which they landed."[92] Another venerable link to the same era, Goodwife Ann Pollard, was memorialized in a famous portrait of 1721. She was then past a hundred, old enough to have come to Boston with the very earliest settlers. Indeed, she was known as a *raconteur* of that experience, and claimed to have been the first person ashore, a spry girl of ten, leading Governor Winthrop and his colleagues onto the site of what would later become New England's greatest city.[93]

When Ann Pollard was young, Charles I was king of England, and Sir Walter Raleigh had only just died; by her last years, Benjamin Franklin was already a young man. The life of the "honored, ancient, elder Faunce" ran from the old age of William Bradford to the childhood of John Adams and Thomas Jefferson. Franklin, Adams, and Jefferson would, in time, lead a political revolution and launch a new nation on its collective life course. Franklin was the most famous old man of the Revolutionary era, and, indeed, he capitalized on that fact. Adams and Jefferson, too, would be admired, even "venerated," in their old age. And yet a new "revolution in age relations," as David Fischer has called it, was coming: "young America" of the nineteenth century was less and less inclined to acknowledge the claims of age. From the ambivalent circumstances of the settlement period—the main concern of the present essay—old people's experience had moved through a long cycle of change. More cycles, more changes would follow. It was, and is, a fascinating story, which historians are only beginning to tell.

Notes

For valuable comment and criticism on an earlier draft of this essay I am grateful to: Rudolph Binion, David Hackett Fischer, David Gutmann, Nancy Roelker, and David Rothman.

1. The overall topography of the field has been recently charted in a bold and brilliant book, David Hackett Fischer, *Growing Old in America* (New York: Oxford University Press, 1977). At some variance with the

Fischer model for the United States is Peter Stearns, *Old Age in European Society* (New York: Holmes & Meier, 1976).

2. Cotton Mather, *Addresses to Old Men and Young Men and Little Children* (Boston: R. Pierce, 1690), dedication page.

3. Increase Mather, *Two Discourses* (Boston: B. Green, 1716), p. 120.

4. *Records of the Colony and Plantation of New Haven, from 1638 to 1649*, ed. Charles J. Hoadly (Hartford, Conn.: Case, Tiffany, and Company, 1857), p. 375.

5. *Records of the Colony or Jurisdiction of New Haven, from May, 1653 to the Union*, ed. Charles J. Hoadly (Hartford, Conn.: Case, Lockwood, and Company, 1858), p. 602.

6. *Records and Files of the Quarterly Courts of Essex County, Massachusetts* (Salem, Mass.: Essex Institute, 1911–1921), 1: 336, 1: 179, 1: 187, 1: 380.

7. *The Works of John Robinson*, ed. Robert Ashton (Boston: Doctrinal Tract and Book Society, 1851), 1: 253.

8. *The Works of Anne Bradstreet*, ed. Jeannine Hensley (Cambridge: Harvard University Press, 1967), pp. 61–62.

9. Cotton Mather, *Addresses*, p. 6.

10. Increase Mather, *Two Discourses*, p. 65.

11. Nicholas Noyes, "An Essay against Periwigs," in *Remarkable Providences*, ed. John Demos (New York: George Braziller, 1972), p. 215.

12. William Bridge, *A Word to the Aged* (Boston: John Foster, 1679), p. 5.

13. See, for example, David Gutmann, "The Cross-Cultural Perspective: Notes Toward a Comparative Psychology of Aging," in *Handbook of the Psychology of Aging*, ed. James E. Birren and K. Warner Schaie (New York: Van Nostrand Reinhold, 1977), pp. 302–26.

14. Bridge, *A Word*, pp. 3–4.

15. Cotton Mather, *Addresses*, pp. 37ff.

16. Ibid., p. 40.

17. Ibid., p. 37.

18. Bridge, *A Word*, p. 11.

19. *Records of the Quarterly Courts*, 7: 156–57.

20. Linda Auwers Bissell, "Family, Friends and Neighbors: Social Interaction in Seventeenth-Century Windsor, Connecticut" (Ph.D. diss., Brandeis University, 1973), p. 40.

21. The reconstitution of Hampton families in 1656 has been done by the author of this essay. The 1680 tax list is published in *Documents and Records Relating to the Province of New Hampshire*, ed. Nathaniel Benton (Concord, N.H., 1867), 1: 424.

22. Also by the author of this essay.

23. "Census of Bristol in Plymouth Colony, Now in Rhode Island,

1689," *New England Historical and Genealogical Register* 34 (1880): 404–5.

24. Philip J. Greven, Jr., *Four Generations: Population, Land, and Family in Colonial Andover, Massachusetts* (Ithaca, N.Y.: Cornell University Press, 1970); Susan L. Norton, "Population Growth in Colonial America: A Study of Ipswich, Mass.," *Population Studies* 25 (1971): 433–52; John Demos, *A Little Commonwealth: Family Life in Plymouth Colony* (New York: Oxford University Press, 1970).

25. Carol Shuchman, "Examining Life Expectancies in Seventeenth-Century Massachusetts" (unpublished paper, Brandeis University, 1976).

26. John M. Murrin, "Review Essay," *History and Theory* 11 (1972): 238.

27. *The Probate Records of Essex County, Massachusetts* (Salem, Mass.: Essex Institute, 1916–1920), 2: 61, 2: 54, 2: 50.

28. Ibid., 1: 150, 1: 76, 2: 108, 1: 132.

29. Ibid., 3: 266, 3: 11. County Court Records, New Haven County, 1, folio 153 (manuscript volume at the Connecticut State Library, Hartford, Conn.).

30. *Works of John Robinson*, 1: 246.

31. Correspondence of Thomas Leeds and William Leeds, in Demos, *Remarkable Providences*, p. 151. *Records of the Quarterly Courts*, 4: 81. *Probate Records of Essex County*, 3: 13, 3: 278, 3: 141. *The Diary of Thomas Minor, Stonington, Connecticut, 1653 to 1684*, ed. Sidney Miner and George D. Stanton (New London, Conn.: Day Publishing Company, 1899), pp. 95, 128, 135, 141, 148, 154, 160, 166, 172, 183.

32. *Probate Records of Essex County*, 2: 441.

33. Demos, *A Little Commonwealth*, p. 192; Shuchman, "Examining Life Expectancies," p. 15.

34. *Works of Anne Bradstreet*, pp. 62–63.

35. Increase Mather, *Two Discourses*, p. 105; Cotton Mather, *A Brief Essay on the Glory of Aged Piety* (Boston: S. Kneeland and T. Green, 1726), p. 27; Cotton Mather, *Addresses*, p. 37.

36. *Probate Records of Essex County*, 1: 332.

37. Noyes, "Essay against Periwigs," p. 215.

38. *Records of the Quarterly Courts*, 4: 123.

39. Cotton Mather, *A Brief Essay*, pp. 29–30; Increase Mather, *Solemn Advice to Young Men* (Boston: B. Green, 1695), p. 20; Increase Mather, *Two Discourses*, p. 99.

40. On the analysis of age heaping, see Ansley J. Coale and Melvin Zelnick, *New Estimates of Fertility and Population in the United States* (Princeton: Princeton University Press, 1963).

41. On geographic mobility in seventeenth-century New England, see Greven, *Four Generations*, chap. 2; Kenneth A. Lockridge, "The Population of Dedham, Massachusetts, 1636–1736," *Economic History Review* 19 (1966): 318–44; Bissell, "Family, Friends and Neighbors," pp. 59–71.

42. *Records of the Quarterly Courts,* 7: 356, 4: 347.

43. *Collections of the Connecticut Historical Society,* vol. 21: The Willys Papers (Hartford, Conn.: Connecticut Historical Society, 1924), p. 71; *Records of the Quarterly Courts,* 7: 269.

44. Rates of remarriage have been calculated for seventeenth-century Windsor, Connecticut. Among younger widows (those whose first marriage lasted les than ten years), the portion remarrying was 67 percent; among older ones (with a first marriage lasting at least twenty years), the comparable figure was slightly under 25 percent. See Bissell, "Family, Friends and Neighbors," p. 56. The actual numbers of widows in local populations at given points in time can be calculated from census, land, and tax records. In 1670 the Connecticut towns of Hartford, Wethersfield, and Windsor were found to contain a total of 335 heads of household; 18 of these (slightly more than 5 percent) were widows. A land-allotment list from New Haven in 1680 contained the names of 220 proprietors—25 of whom were widows (11 percent). See *Collections of the Connecticut Historical Society,* 21: 191–99; *New Haven Town Records, 1662–1684,* ed. Franklin Bowditch Dexter (New Haven, Conn.: New Haven Colony Historical Society, 1919), pp. 405–10. For an excellent discussion of widowhood in a slightly later period, see Alexander Keyssar, "Widowhood in Eighteenth-Century Massachusetts: A Problem in the History of the Family," *Perspectives in American History* 8 (1974): 83–119.

45. Richard B. Morris, *Studies in the History of American Law* (New York: Columbia University Press, 1930), chap. 3; Demos, *A Little Commonwealth,* p. 85.

46. *Probate Records of Essex County,* 3: 390; 2: 52.

47. *Probate Records of Essex County,* 3: 223; *Mayflower Descendant* 30 (1928): 101; *Probate Records of Essex County,* 2: 221, 63; *Mayflower Descendant* 2 (1900): 184–85.

48. *Probate Records of Essex County,* 1: 96; 2: 346, 263; *Mayflower Descendant* 2 (1900): 184–85.

49. *Probate Records of Essex County,* 3: 48; *Mayflower Descendant* 2 (1900): 184–85; *Probate Records of Essex County,* 2: 64, 3: 175.

50. *Probate Records of Essex County,* 2: 239; *Mayflower Descendant* 17 (1915): 34–36.

51. *Mayflower Descendant* 11 (1909): 92–93; *Probate Records of Essex County,* 3: 351, 2: 251.

52. *Mayflower Descendant* 6 (1904): 81; *Probate Records of Essex County,* 2: 171.

53. *Probate Records of Essex County,* 3: 150–51, 3: 377, 2: 144.

54. *Watertown Records,* 1 (Watertown, Mass., 1894), part one, p. 101; *New Haven Town Records, 1649–1662,* ed. Franklin Bowditch Dexter (New Haven, Conn.: New Haven Colony Historical Society, 1917), pp. 116, 208.

55. *Records of the Quarterly Courts*, 3: 276, 5: 29, 5: 396, 5: 188, 6: 77, 6: 44, 7: 326, 8: 345, 2: 97.

56. See Demos, *A Little Commonwealth*, pp. 174–75; Fischer, *Growing Old in America*, p. 45.

57. Quoted in Joseph Dow, *History of the Town of Hampton, New Hampshire* (Salem, Mass.: Salem Press Publishing and Printing Company, 1893), 2: 740; *Diary of Thomas Minor*, pp. 207–8.

58. Diary of Samuel Sewall, *Collections of the Massachusetts Historical Society*, fifth series (Boston, Mass.: Massachusetts Historical Society, 1882), 7: 168, 382; *New Haven Town Records, 1662–1684*, p. 331.

59. *Diary of Thomas Minor*, p. 133 passim.

60. Ibid., pp. 122–23.

61. Ibid., p. 165.

62. Increase Mather, *Two Discourses*, p. 134.

63. Cotton Mather, *A Brief Essay*, p. 28.

64. Noyes. "Essay Against Periwigs," p. 215; *Works of John Robinson*, p. 251.

65. Davis Scrapbooks, 3: 8 (manuscript volumes, Pilgrim Hall, Plymouth, Mass.).

66. Increase Mather, *Two Discourses*, pp. 98–99.

67. *Watertown Records*, 1, part one, p. 53.

68. See, for example, *Probate Records of Essex County*, 2: 4, 2: 229, 2: 315, 2: 345, 2: 352, 2: 426, 2: 441, 3: 13, 3: 183, 3: 187, 3: 278, 3: 329, 3: 345, 3: 375.

69. On the practice of seating the meetinghouse, see Robert J. Dinkin, "Provincial Massachusetts: A Deferential or a Democratic Society" (Ph.D. diss., Columbia University, 1968).

70. See, for example, *Watertown Records*, 1, part one, p. 47; Town Votes, Wethersfield, Conn., 1, folios 115–16 (manuscript volumes, Connecticut State Library, Hartford, Conn.).

71. See John Coolidge, "Hingham Builds a Meetinghouse," *New England Quarterly* 34 (1961): 435–61. Coolidge makes some approach to the issue of seating and social rank in Hingham, and clearly believes that older persons received favored positions. However, he does not seem to have attempted systematic comparison of the age factor with other variables, like wealth.

72. Town Book of Hampton, 1, folios 28–29 (manuscript volume, Town Offices, Hampton, N.H.).

73. See Irving Rosow, *Socialization to Old Age* (Berkeley: University of California Press, 1974), chap. 1.

74. The effect of this pattern can be measured quantitatively from legal records. Persons over sixty, we know, made up 10 percent or so of the total adult population of early New England; yet they account for some 15 percent of all witnesses in court cases in mid-seventeenth-century Massachusetts. Data compiled by the author from *Records of the Quarterly Courts*, passim.

75. *Records of the Quarterly Courts,* 7: 194.

76. John Winthrop, "A Model of Christian Charity," *Puritan Political Ideas,* ed. Edmund Morgan (New York: Bobbs-Merrill, 1965), p. 92.

77. The best summary of this viewpoint is found in Gutmann, "The Cross-Cultural Perspective," pp. 302–26.

78. Ibid., pp. 315–16.

79. See Demos, A *Little Commonwealth,* pp. 136ff; Richard L. Bushman, *From Puritan to Yankee: Character and the Social Order in Connecticut, 1690–1765* (Cambridge: Harvard University Press, 1967), pp. 20–21; Darrett B. Rutman, "The Mirror of Puritan Authority," *Puritanism and the American Experience,* ed. Michael McGiffert (Reading, Mass.: Addison-Wesley, 1969), pp. 65–79; Emory Elliott, *Power and the Pulpit in Puritan New England* (Princeton: Princeton University Press, 1975), pp. 76ff.

80. See Neal Salisbury, "Conquest of the 'Savage': Puritans, Puritan Missionaries, and Indians, 1620–1680" (Ph.D. diss., University of California at Los Angeles, 1972).

81. See Demos, *A Little Commonwealth,* pp. 134ff; Edmund Morgan, *The Puritan Family* (New York: Harper & Row, 1966), chap. 3; David E. Stannard, "Death and the Puritan Child," in *Death in America,* ed. David E. Stannard (Philadelphia: University of Pennsylvania Press, 1975), pp. 9–29.

82. This line of argument draws heavily on recent work in the clinical theory of psychoanalysis, especially the so-called psychology of the self. See the writings of Heinz Kohut: *The Analysis of the Self* (New York: International Universities Press, 1971), and *The Restoration of the Self* (New York: International Universities Press, 1977).

83. Quoted in Gutmann, "The Cross-Cultural Perspective," p. 314.

84. David E. Stannard, "Death and Dying in Puritan New England," *American Historical Review* 78 (1973): 1305–30, and *The Puritan Way of Death: A Study in Religion, Culture, and Social Change* (New York: Oxford University Press, 1977).

85. This evidence, and much more from eighteenth-century sources, is presented in Fischer, *Growing Old in America.* See pp. 39, 85–90, and passim.

86. For a summary of the comparative material, see Fischer, *Growing Old in America,* pp. 225–27.

87. See, for example, Bushman, *From Puritan to Yankee;* Kenneth A. Lockridge, *A New England Town: The First Hundred Years* (New York: W. W. Norton, 1970).

88. See Richard Brown, *Modernization: The Transformation of American Life* (New York: Hill and Wang, 1976), chap. 5; Demos, "Introduction," in *Remarkable Providences,* pp. 19–22.

89. This idea is fruitfully explored in Murrin, "Review Essay," pp. 235–40.

90. See Perry Miller, "Declension in a Bible Commonwealth," in

Nature's Nation (Cambridge: Harvard University Press, 1967), pp. 14–49.

91. Elderly people writing wills did not, before about 1660, make reference to their age; after that time they did so with growing regularity. See, for example, the wills included in *Probate Records of Essex County*, 1–3, passim.

92. Diary of Samuel Sewall, p. 376. The comment on elder Faunce's personal connections with the Pilgrim fathers is by Sewall's editor.

93. On the portrait of Ann Pollard, and her stories of arriving in Boston with the Winthrop group, see James Thomas Flexner, *First Flowers of Our Wilderness* (Boston: Houghton Mifflin, 1947), pp. 46–49.

TAMARA K. HAREVEN

THE LAST STAGE:
HISTORICAL ADULTHOOD AND OLD AGE

"To learn that one is old is a long, complex, and painful experience. Each decade the circle of the Great Fatigue narrows around us, restricting the intensity and endurance of our activities." It was probably no coincidence that G. Stanley Hall, who had developed the concept of "adolescence" as a psychosocial stage in the 1880s, offered a synthesis of "senescence" as his last creative opus in 1920, when he himself was eighty years old. While his contemporaries focused on the deterioration of old age, or sought the secrets of longevity, Hall emphasized the unique psychological processes connected with aging and their societal significance. Rather than viewing old age as a period of decline and decay, he saw it as a stage of development in which the passions of youth and the efforts of a life career had reached fruition and consolidation: "There is a certain maturity of judgment about men, things, causes and life generally, that nothing in the world but years can bring, a real wisdom that only age can teach."[1]

Interest in the meaning of aging in the early part of the twentieth century had not grown merely from idle curiosity. It was related to questions about the limits of usefulness and efficiency on the job that had arisen with industrialization and to the movement for providing social insurance for the aged. In 1874 the phychologist George Beard had already begun to ask questions about the limitations of old age: "What is the average effect of old age on the mental faculties?" "To what extent is the average responsibility of men impaired by the change that the mental faculties undergo in old age?" Analyzing the record of "human achievements," he considered at what age the "best work of the world" had been done and found that 70 percent of creative works had been achieved by age forty-five, and 80 percent by age fifty. Within this range, he identified thirty to forty-five as the optimal period of life. Although he was emphatic about the need for setting a retirement age for judges, he did not recommend any retirement age for laborers.[2] Beard's investigation represented the first attempt at a scientific inquiry into the relationship between aging and efficiency, and it set the stage for the concept of the "superannuated man" that was to come.

In the late nineteenth century, American society passed from an acceptance of aging as a natural process to a view of it as a distinct period of life characterized by decline, weakness, and obsolescence. Advanced old age, which had earlier been regarded as a manifestation of the survival of the fittest, was now denigrated as a condition of dependency and deterioration: "We are marked by time's defacing fingers with the ugliness of age."[3] Writers began to identify advancing years with physical decline and mental deterioration. Beginning in the 1860s, the popular magazines shifted the emphasis of discussion from the attainment of longevity to the medical symptoms of senescence. In 1910, I. L. Nascher, a New York physician, became the first to formulate the biological characteristics and medical needs of senescence as a life-cycle process. He drew on the work of his predecessors to conceptualize its medical treatment and thus laid the foundation for geriatrics as a medical discipline.[4]

In the beginning of the twentieth century, public concern for and interest in old age converged from various directions. In addition to physicians, psychologists, and popular writers, efficiency experts and social reformers were especially instrumental in attracting public attention to old age as a social problem. A variety of medical and psychological studies by industrial efficiency experts focused on the physical and mental limitations of old age. At the same time, social reformers began to expose the poverty and dependency suffered by many old people, as part of a general investigation of "how the other half lives," and to agitate for social security and social insurance.

Government recognition of old age evolved more gradually and began on the state level. By 1920 only ten states had instituted some form of old-age legislation; all programs were limited in scope, and most of them were declared unconstitutional by the Supreme Court. Nevertheless, agitation for old-age security continued and finally culminated in the Social Security Act of 1935. It was not until the 1940s, however, that gerontology was recognized as a new medical field, and it was even more recently that social scientists identified old age as constituting a new and pressing problem for mankind. Social definitions of age limits and public treatment through institutional reform, retirement legislation, and welfare measures represent the most recent societal recognition of this stage of life.[5]

How does one examine an age group and a stage of life when their experiences, social definitions, and public treatment change over time? How does one conceptualize "old age" and "aging" as social and cultural phenomena in relation to historical change? How does one correlate individual time and historical time; that is, synchronize individual development with historical change? Social scientists and popular writers have long been accustomed to examining categories such as class, ethnicity, and race; more recently, they have begun to use gender as a category as well. But they have been less systematic in their use of age because maintaining a distinction between an "age group" and "aging" as a process is difficult. Adolescents, for example, are an "age group." At the same time, adolescence, however bounded by sociopsychological conditions, is a process, subject to change and redefinition. Age and aging are related to biological phenomena, but the meanings of age and aging are socially and culturally determined. "Social age" is a relative concept and varies in different cultural contexts. In trying to understand the societal conditions affecting adulthood and old age, it is important to realize that the definitions of aging, as well as the social conditions and functions of every age group, have not only changed significantly over time but also varied among cultures.

Gerontological literature approaches the problems of aging from several directions: the developmental perspective has focused on biological and psychological changes conected with aging; the institutional approach has stressed socioeconomic status and the roles of old people; and the cultural perspective has concentrated on stereotypes and perceptions of the elderly. Some of these approaches have also tended to confuse the "aged" as an age group or as a social class with aging as a process.[6] Little effort has been made to integrate these views or interpret them as interrelated processes over the life course.

The emergence of "old age" as a social, cultural, and biological phenomenon can best be understood in the context of other stages of life. The social conditions of children and adolescents in a given society are related to the way adulthood is perceived in that society; and, conversely, the role and position of adults and the aged are related to the treatment of children and youths. The formidable task of investigating the synchronization of individual development with social change requires an approach that would take into account the entire life course and differing historical conditions, rather than simply concentrate on a specific age group.

The "discovery" of a new stage of life is itself a complex process. First, individuals become aware of the specific characteristics of a given stage of life as a distinct condition. This discovery is then passed on to society in popularized versions. If it appears to be associated with a major social problem, it attracts the attention of agencies of welfare and social control. Finally, it is institutionalized: legislation is passed and agencies are created to deal with its special needs and problems.

The articulation of new stages of life and their recognition in American society in the past generally came as a response to external pressures and to a fear of the disorganization which, it was thought, might otherwise ensue from societal neglect of some particular age group. In the nineteenth century, this apprehension was particularly dramatic as it was manifested in attitudes toward the treatment of children and adolescents; undisciplined and unsocialized young people were compared to the *prolétaire* of Paris and were regarded as the "dangerous classes." At that time, the elderly received comparatively little attention because they were not considered dangerous to the social order. The physical weaknesses and inevitable end associated with old age did not present an imminent danger to society and did not, therefore, evoke the anxiety produced by problems among the youth. The argument against the neglect of children was that they would grow up into dangerous, socially destructive adults. No parallel argument applied to the aged. In a society which had lost its fear of the afterlife, and in which awareness of and contact with death were not integrated into everyday life (for death no longer held a mythical power over the living), there was no reason to fear any potential revenge from the old people. Consequently, the first demonstration of organized political power on the part of the aged did not occur until the Townsend movement in the 1930s, which succeeded in forcing the federal government to institute social security.

By the late eighteenth century, however, American society had gradually begun at least to acknowledge the existence of various stages in life and to develop a corresponding series of institutions to deal with them. As we have seen, it "discovered" childhood in the first half of the nineteenth century and "invented" adolescence toward the end of it, with both concepts emerging into public consciousness as a result of social crises associated with those age groups, as old age was to emerge somewhat later.[7] However, despite the growing awareness of childhood, adolescence, and youth as preadult stages, no clear *boundaries* for adulthood in America emerged until much later, when interest in the "middle years" as a distinct segment of adult life arose out of the need to differentiate the social and psychological problems of "middle" from "old" age. The psychological, social, and cultural conditions of the past half-century have since contributed to the sharpening of the boundaries between these two stages. Several social scientists have tried to distinguish additional categories in adult life, such as the "young old" and the "old old," but it is too early to tell whether these will develop into useful concepts.[8]

It is clear, however, that in American society "old age" is now recognized as a specific period of adulthood. Unlike the other stages, it has a formal beginning—age sixty-five—at least so far as a person's working life is concerned, and it is institutionalized by a rite of passage: retirement and the commencement of social security. Since so much of adult life in American society is contingent upon work, especially for men, retirement often involves migration and changes in living arrangements.

Popular social-science literature has recently devoted a great deal of attention to the social and economic plight of older people and to their isolation as a result of urbanization and industrialization. The major developments that have been cited as explanations for these problems are demographic changes arising from increases in life expectancy in childhood and early adulthood, and, to some degree, from prolongation of life in old age due to advances in medical technology; the increasing proportion of older people in the population, resulting from the decline in fertility and increase in life expectancy; the decrease in productive roles that older people are allowed to play as the result of the shift from a rural to an industrial economy; the technological revolution; and, finally, the denigration of old age, which is thought to be explained by the "cult of youth." Without denying the importance of these explanations, problems of old age and aging in American society can be more fully understood by examining them in terms of more fundamental historical discontinuities in the life course. These changes are rooted in three interrelated areas, all of which are essential for the achievement of what Erik Erikson calls "integrity": location in historical time, worklife and productivity, and family orientation and functions. This essay will discuss briefly the historical developments in each of these aspects of adult life and their effects on the condition of old people in American society.

Location in Historical Time

Because age boundaries and criteria for adulthood vary significantly across cultures, classes, and historical periods, the meaning of adulthood cannot be defined merely in terms of a specific age span; and unlike adolescence, which represents a person's passage through puberty, it cannot be clearly defined in biological terms. Even within the same age group, the social meaning of adulthood and the functions associated with it vary among cultures and according to psychological conditions. For these reasons, it is difficult to determine to what extent and in what ways individuals have in the past perceived their entry into adulthood and transition to old age under varying historical conditions.

How did individuals pass through their life course?[9] How did they time their transitions from one role to another, and how was this timing related to their family experience and to external social conditions? In what ways did such experiences vary within the same age cohort?[10] How did these processes vary over time, and how did they differ from aging processes now? Answers to questions such as these would explain the position of individuals and age groups at different times in the past and would illuminate their interaction with contemporary conditions.

Reuben Hill has noted that in periods of rapid social change, each cohort "encounters at marriage a unique set of historical constraints and incentives which influence the timing of its crucial life decisions, making for marked generational dissimilarities in life-cycle career patterns."[11] This means that the social experience of each cohort is influenced not only by the external conditions of its own time but also by the cumulative experience of its earlier stages in life. Consequently, the position of the elderly in modern American society has been shaped in part by social and economic conditions which have combined to isolate them from family and productive life when they enter their sixties, and in part by their previous cumulative experience along their own life course. For example, individuals who reached the age of sixty in the 1890s and were still working had commenced work at an earlier age and would continue to work until the end of life, or so long as they were able. Having grown up in a period when transitions in the life course were less rigidly marked, they would have found a retirement imposed at a set age far more traumatic than would a cohort who had come of age in the early twentieth century, when both entry into and exit from the labor force were more clearly timed according to age. The response of an older cohort to changing social and economic conditions is therefore significantly different from that of a younger one because it is based on very different individual and social experiences. In trying to understand those differences, it is necessary to view both the contemporary social milieu in which the cohort reaches that age and its cumulative experience over its entire life.

In preindustrial society, demographic, social, and cultural factors combined to allow only a minimal differentiation in the stages of life. Childhood and adolescence were not regarded as distinct stages; children were considered miniature adults, gradually assuming adult roles in their early teens and entering adult life with a moratorium from adult responsibilities. Adulthood flowed into old age without institutionalized disruptions. The two major adult roles—parenthood and work—generally stretched over an entire lifetime, without an "empty nest" and compulsory retirement. In various rural societies, the insistence of older people on self-sufficiency and their continued control over family estates delayed the assumption of economic independence by their children and afforded aging parents a bargaining position for support in old age.

The integration of economic activities with family life also provided continuity in the usefulness of older people, particularly of widows, even when their capacity to work was waning. One should not, however, idealize the condition of the elderly in pre-industrial society. In his paper in this volume, "Old Age in Early New England," John Demos points out that while the elderly were venerated publicly, they were insecure in private life. Some of the symptoms of insecurity and uncertainty are reflected, for example, in contemporary wills where support for a widowed mother was made a condition for the inheritance of family estates. Nevertheless, old people experienced economic and social segregation far less frequently than they do today, and they retained their familial and economic positions until the end of their lives. If they became "dependent" because of illness or poverty, they were supported by their children or other kin or were placed by the town authorities in the households of neighbors or even strangers—but not in institutions.[12]

Under the impact of industrialization and the demographic changes of the nineteenth century, however, a gradual differentiation in age groups and specialization in functions began to emerge, although it was by no means complete by the end of that century. Discontinuities in the individual life course were still not marked, and age groups were still not completely segregated in accordance with their functions. While today parents generally complete their childrearing functions with one-third of their lives still ahead, nineteenth-century parenthood was a lifelong career: the combination of relatively late marriage, short life expectancy, and high fertility rarely allowed for an empty-nest stage. In addition, marriage was frequently broken by death of a spouse before the end of the childrearing period.[13] This pattern was more common among women because they married earlier and lived longer than men.

Whether women were widowed or not, however, the extension of motherhood over most of the life course continued to engage them in active familial roles into old age. Peter Uhlenberg has shown that what is today considered a normal life-course sequence for women—marriage, motherhood, survival with husband through parenthood, the launching of children, and widowhood— was experienced by only 44 percent of females born in 1870 who survived beyond age fifteen. The remaining 56 percent never achieved the "normal" life-course pattern, either because they died young or never married or were childless, or because their marriages were broken by the death of their husbands or by divorce.[14] As one moves into the twentieth century, the percentage of women conforming to this pattern gradually increases.

Under conditions in which the life course was compressed into a shorter and more homogeneous span, major transitions into adulthood, such as leaving school, entering into the labor force, leaving home, marrying, and having children, were not so clearly structured as they are today. Except for marriage and the formation of households, they did not even necessarily represent moves toward independent adulthood. The order in which they occurred varied significantly, rather than following a customary sequence. Children and youth shuttled back and forth from school to work, depending on the seasons, the availability of jobs, and the economic needs of the family. Departure from school did not mark a definite turning point; nor, at a time when child labor was an established practice, did entry into the labor force necessarily imply the onset of adulthood. Leaving home, a phenomenon typically associated with the commencement of adulthood today, had no such significance in the preindustrial and the early industrial periods.[15] Some children left home in their early teens to become servants or apprentices; others continued to live on the family farm and to postpone marriage and the assumption of adult responsibilities until much later. In nineteenth-century urban working-class families, sons and daughters often continued to live at home until well into their twenties and to contribute their income to the common family budget. Irish immigrant families in Massachusetts, for example, customarily kept the youngest son at home through his late twenties. Among other immigrant industrial workers in New England, the last remaining daughter was expected to stay single and continue living in the family household to care for her parents so long as they lived. When unmarried children did leave home, they often spent transitional periods as boarders or lodgers with the families of strangers, rather than set up their own households.[16]

Even marriage, which is usually regarded as an "adult" act in twentieth-century society, much less often marked the transition to autonomous adult life in the nineteenth century. In urban communities, where immigration produced both scarcity in housing and unemployment, it was difficult to set up an independent household, and newlyweds often brought their spouses to live in their parents' households for a transitional period. Even when they lived separately, they were usually nearby, often in the same neighborhood. In the early years of marriage and especially after the birth of the first child, young couples were willing to sacrifice privacy for the luxury of parental assistance and support, a willingness that increased during periods of economic crisis and depression or during a family crisis brought on by unemployment, sickness, or death.[17]

The absence of dramatic transitions to adult life allowed a more intensive interaction among different age groups within the family and the community, thus providing a greater sense of continuity and interdependence among people at various stages in the life course. But as greater differentiation in stages of life began to develop and as social and economic functions became more closely related to age, a greater segregation between age groups emerged. Child-labor laws and compulsory education to age fourteen (or sixteen) tended to segregate the young, increasingly so from around the middle of the nineteenth century. Similarly, the gradual ousting of older people from the labor force toward the end of the nineteenth century and the decline in their parental functions in the later years of life tended to disengage them from their offspring and from active social functions. Two of the most important changes affecting the elderly, therefore, were the increasing association of function with age and the formation of segregated, age-based peer groups. This segregation by age occurred first among the middle class, and was only later extended into the rest of society.

Worklife and Productivity

Beginning around the turn of the century, the growing specialization of work and the demand for industrial efficiency under the impact of advanced industrial development resulted in the imposition of age-related standards of usefulness and productivity in American society, but retirement at a standard age was an invention of the twentieth century. It represents the most drastic development in the emergence of old age as a separate stage of life. The almost universal practice of retirement at an arbitrarily determined age has imposed a uniformity which is related to age rather than to the nature of the tasks involved. By contrast, during the second half of the nineteenth century and into the early twentieth, when there was no institutionalized retirement, how "old" one was often depended on the kind of job one held, as well as on social class. Members of the working class experienced signs of advancing age earlier than white-collar workers or professionals. Industrial workers in physically demanding jobs were "old" in their middle years, while others continued to work until the end of their lives. As the system of production advanced technologically and intensified in pace, performance on the job became even more closely related to age.

Prior to the institutionalization of formal retirement, work extended over one's entire life. Although careers were frequently punctuated by long periods of unemployment, they were terminated only by severe illness or death. The nature of the employment varied, however, as men reached their forties: "The great majority of the men who do the world's work are comparatively young men," concluded an analyst of the census of 1900. Nearly half the total number of gainfully employed males in 1900 were between the ages of sixteen and thirty-four; the proportion increases to two-thirds when the category is extended to forty-four.[18] Yet 90 percent of males between the ages of fifty-five and sixty-five were still employed, a percentage not significantly different from that of employed men in their thirties and forties. By comparison, only 68.4 percent of men older than sixty-five were still working. To understand these figures, one must remember that the kind of job that was held was closely related to age. Industrial work commanded the years between twenty and forty-five; workers younger than twenty or older than forty-five were primarily employed in agriculture or in unskilled service jobs. In addition, while work careers have generally been viewed as linear progressions—either upward or downward or continuing on a relatively even keel—in reality, late-nineteenth-century work careers meandered about. Permanence on a job was rare among the majority of the working population; what we would regard today as a "disorderly" career was then often the norm.

Industrial workers experienced their first "retirement" or career change in their middle or late forties, as years of exhausting industrial labor begun at an early age began to render them "useless." (Mule spinners—skilled textile operators—for example, walked about thirty-five miles a day on the job.) Consequently, in the last third of their lives, even highly skilled workers were forced into temporary jobs in unskilled occupations, after having spent the better part of their lives in efforts to move up the ladder. "I started out as a sweeper, I worked my way up to overseer, and here I am a sweeper again," said a sixty-five-year-old former textile worker who found himself dependent on occasional jobs in the last years of his life. "The age deadline is creeping down on these men. I'd say that by forty-five, they are through," was a recurrent verdict of superintendents of major factories in "Middletown" in the 1920s.[19] One of the advocates of old-age compensation described this spreading phenomenon: "It is notorious that the insatiable factory wears out its workers with great rapidity. As it scraps its machinery, so it scraps human beings. . . . Middle age is old age, and the worn-out worker, if he has no children and if he has no savings, becomes an item in the aggregate of the unemployed."[20]

Contemplating the "industrial scrap heap" in one's middle years became one of the nightmares of industrial society. The Amoskeag Corporation, the world's largest textile manufacturer, began to lay off, rather than reassign, its slow workers beginning about 1920. When a middle-aged woman weaver protested against her dismissal, after twenty years of work, before the union's grievance committee, the management upheld the overseer's rule: "In deciding who we should keep and who we should lay off, we follow the simple rule of the 'survival of the fittest.' " This same overseer, who had risen from bobbin boy to that much-coveted position, himself ended up as a sweeper.[21]

The major transition in the worklife was, therefore, not necessarily the complete termination of a person's work career, but often the move to a temporary, semiskilled, or unskilled job while he was still in his forties or early fifties. As workers grew older, they tried to hold on to their jobs by trading their skills and expertise for physical assistance from young apprentices, who were often their relatives. It was not uncommon for young workers in the shop to share the workload of "Old Spence" or "Old Joe" in order to keep him going. By the 1920s, however, the efficiency movement had won out in most industrial concerns, and tasks were assigned according to age.

The labor unions tried to solve the problems of the aging worker by establishing the principle of seniority, a principle that caused considerable conflict with corporations. Because management saw seniority as inconsistent with the requirements of efficiency and individual initiative, the unions were unsuccessful, at least in the beginning. Thus, insecurity in old age, particularly among the working class, came to culminate a career that had already included exhausting labor, unemployment (especially in middle age), and insecurity at every age through the constant threat of industrial accidents and other illnesses. The 1900 census reported 28.3 percent of all workers in manufacturing and mercantile occupations as having been unemployed for from three to six months of that year. A study by the Massachusetts Commission on Old Age Pensions in 1909 found that approximately 24 percent of the population of that state who were sixty-five years of age or older were dependent on charity. Robert Hunter, an early social investigator of poverty in the United States, following E. S. Rowntree's studies of poverty in England, showed in 1904 that working-class families generally slipped in and out of poverty throughout life, but were most likely to fall below the margin at two particular stages: as young parents, burdened with numerous children too young to work, and in their middle or later years, after the children had left home and the parents remained without a steady income.[22]

The insecurities and vagaries of old age, intensified by unstable employment and recurrent poverty at earlier ages, made collective economic strategies imperative for the family unit. The functions of old people in the late nineteenth and early twentieth centuries can be better understood within the framework of the family economy. Work careers and family organization were clearly intertwined, and reciprocity among family members along the life course was essential for survival in old age. Exchanges across generations were critical for the survival of old people, particularly in the working class, as an intensifying industrial system was gradually ousting them from their jobs without providing public-welfare mechanisms for their support.[23]

Family Orientation and Functions

The family organization and ideology of nineteenth-century society, and in particular the strong interaction of family and kin, enabled older people to maintain active familial roles as they gradually withdrew from the labor force, even if they were not living with their adult children. Research has clearly established that families in the past tended to reside in nuclear units and that the coresidence of three generations was even then extremly rare. This rejection of the myth of the extended multigenerational family should not be misconstrued, however, to mean that old people lived in isolation. Solitary residence was most uncommon throughout the nineteenth century in all age groups. Except for Western frontier communities and mining towns, only about 3 to 5 percent of the population were found to be living alone.[24] Old people strove to remain in charge of their own households. Rather than moving in with their adult children or other kin, they took relatives or strangers into their own homes. In 1850 only about one in ten persons over the age of sixty-five was not the head of a household or the spouse of a head. By 1880 the proportion had risen to about one in eight. The trend accelerated in the United States into the twentieth century: in 1953 the ratio was about one in six, and in the late 1960s it approached one in four, reflecting the present large percentage of old people who live alone or share accommodations with nonrelatives.[25]

The supposed isolation of the nuclear family in urban, industrial society has frequently been cited as the explanation for the present plight of the elderly. Talcott Parsons has provided us with the classic formulation of this view: "In the first phase, the most important single distinctive feature of our family structure is the isolation of the individual conjugal family." Mathilda Riley and her associates have pointed out that the trend has not been so much toward the isolation of the nuclear family as toward a subdivision into two nuclear families: the young couple with their dependent children and the middle-aged or aged parents. Parsons's generalization has been further revised by a number of sociologists who have documented the existence of elaborate patterns of assistance and social interaction among members of the nuclear family and other kin in contemporary society.[26]

The relationships of mutual support and exchange of services that old people had earlier entered into with their kin carried greater significance before the introduction of Social Security and other forms of public old-age assistance. Except in cases of infirmity or extreme poverty, they engaged in reciprocal support relationships with their kin which simultaneously allowed them to maintain their autonomy. Close contact and mutual exchanges among parents, their adult children, and other kin persisted throughout the nineteenth century and survived to a large degree in the lives of working-class families into the twentieth. In the later years of life, parents expected their grown children to support them in exchange for a variety of services which they themselves had rendered earlier in life. Such exchanges among parents, their children, and other relatives were based on calculated needs and expectations, particularly insofar as parents relied on future support from their sons and daughters as a source of social insurance. Societal values and norms governing children's obligations for parental aid provided an ideological reinforcement for these reciprocal relationships.[27]

Migration did not contribute to the isolation of old people to the extent that was previously assumed; the argument that geographic mobility during the nineteenth century tended to separate grown children from their parents and from kin is gradually being disproved. When people moved, they tended to migrate into areas where other relatives had already settled, and after sons and daughters had established themselves, they often sent for their parents.[28] Even if migration did separate parents from their children, or brothers from sisters, surrogate familial arrangements were developed by taking strangers into the household. About one-third of the men and women in their twenties and thirties in nineteenth-century American urban communities boarded with other families; this would suggest that these surrogate relationships had great strength and pervasiveness. For young men and women in a transitional stage between their departure from their parents' homes and the establishment of their own families, boarding offered familial settings without parental pressures. For older people, particularly for widows, it provided the extra income needed to maintain their own residence, and it also helped to stave off loneliness after the children had left home. These arrangements helped balance and distribute resources, and they often fulfilled the function of what Irene Taeuber calls "the social equalization of the family."[29]

The separation of the workplace from the home wrought by the industrial revolution was by no means complete by the end of the nineteenth century. Among the urban working class as well as the rural population, work and family roles continued to be mutually reinforcing. For these groups, work entailed a contribution to the collective effort of the family unit. This meant that family members functioned as interchangeable components of a larger work unit. For example, the work of wives in the textile industry helped stabilize the family's income while husbands risked taking higher-paying, but less permanent, jobs. During slack periods, the men who were laid off took care of the house while their wives continued to work: housework and child care were not regarded as demeaning; they were valued as important contributions to the family's resources. During periods of economic constraint, families thus balanced their resources through the allocation of tasks and responsibilities among their members. In this setting, old people could also continue to perform valuable services. After they were too old to work, they took care of the children of working mothers, helped with the housekeeping, and, if necessary, shared housing space with younger family members in exchange for economic support.[30]

This integration of work with family life in the nineteenth century should not be construed as an ideal situation. The system often placed considerable constraint on individual careers and generated tension and conflict between aging parents and their children. Nevertheless, in the absence of institutional buttresses, instrumental relationships were a pervasive and realistic response to the pressures that economic exigencies imposed on individuals and families. They prevented familial fragmentation and segregation by providing a basis for interaction among people in different age groups and at different stages in life by exchanging services, even as they were pursuing individual careers. Such interdependence also exposed children and youth to greater responsibility toward older people and to a fuller view of life and a broader range of experience than is common among them today.

The major changes that have led to the isolation of older people in society today were rooted not so much in changes in family structure or residential arrangements, as has generally been argued, as in the transformation and redefinition of family functions. Changes in functions and values—especially the erosion of the instrumental view of family relationships—and the resulting shift to sentimentality and intimacy as the major cohesive forces in the family have led to the weakening of the role and function of extended-family members. In middle-class families particular, affective relationships have gradually replaced instrumental ones.

This shift occurred first in the middle class, around the mid-nineteenth century, but it soon affected the working class and its various ethnic groups, as growing conformity introduced middle-class values into working-class lives. Since then, the emphasis on domesticity and childrearing as the major preoccupations of the middle-class family—and especially on the role of women as custodians of domestic intimacy—has tended to insulate middle-class urban families from the influence and participation of aging parents and other relatives.[31] From the 1830s on, middle-class urban families became avid consumers of popular childrearing and advice-to-parents literature, not because older relatives were not present to offer such advice, but because guidance based on personal experience and tradition was gradually rejected in favor of "packaged" information. This transition added to the loss of power and influence of the old people in the family.

The ideology of domesticity that emerged during the first half of the nineteenth century also enshrined privacy as a major value in family life. The home was glorified as a retreat from the world and, at the same time, as a specialized child-nurturing center. Philippe Ariès succinctly summarized these changes for Western European society: "The modern family . . . cuts itself off from the world and opposes to society the isolated groups of parents and children. All the energy of the group is expended in helping the children to rise in the world, individually and without any collective ambition: The children rather than the family."[32]

Through a process of differentiation, the traditional family surrendered many of the functions previously concentrated within it to other social institutions. The retreat and growing privatism of the modern middle-class family drew sharper boundaries between family and community and intensified the segregation of different age groups within the family, leading to the elimination of the older people from viable family roles. The transfer of social-welfare functions, once concentrated in the family, to institutions in the larger society further contributed to the segregation of older people. The care of the dependent, the sick, the delinquent, and the aging, which had been considered part of the family's obligation in the preindustrial period, was gradually transferred to specialized institutions, such as asylums and reformatories. The family ceased to be the only available source of support for its dependent members, and the community ceased to rely on the family as the major agency of welfare and social control.[33] In the nineteenth century, some childless old people, especially widows, were already expecting to end up in institutions in their later life. Mrs. Kelleham, for example, a widow in Westcote, New York, in the 1850s, had had ten children, several of whom had died in childhood, and "in those who remain the poor woman seems to take little comfort." The woman for whom she worked as a domestic servent reported in her diary: "She says, the mother's joy has never measured with the mother's care. She will not be a burden to her children. She will work while she can work, and when she can no longer she will go to the old ladies' asylum near New York."[34]

But these early institutions and asylums, although they were to become more specialized in the second half of the nineteenth century, segregated people because of poverty, not because of age. "Poor farms," houses of refuge, and mental hospitals were not differentiated by the age of their inmates. The old were simply treated as a variety of dependent poor. The first to be institutionalized by age (during the second half of the nineteenth century) were children—a reflection of the recognition of childhood as a life stage—but special institutions for the elderly based on age rather than on destitution did not appear until later.[35] They began toward the end of the nineteenth century, with the segregation of the infirm, the destitute, the mentally ill, and the retarded from the "respectable" old, who needed help only because of their age. At that time, the intent was not so much to segregate age groups as to separate "deserving" dependents from paupers, and it involved the institutionalization only of those who were unable to take care of themselves or to obtain assistance from their relatives. Reformers depicted many homes for the aged in the second half of the nineteenth century in terms similar to social investigators' descriptions of the "death camps" they find in nursing homes today. One inspector of a state institution in Pennsylvania reported in 1920:

> There was no genuine homelike spirit. Most of the inmates looked sullen and wore depressed and downcast mien. Practically all were eager to get out of the place. . . . This feeling of depression is augmented by the fact that in no homes in an attempt made to segregrate the old people—who have been compelled to go to the almshouse through no fault of their own—from the feeble-minded, and in some cases even the partially insane. In many places they are compelled to eat at the same table and sleep in the same dormitories with the latter groups.[36]

This practice of institutionalizing the old people of the lower classes was subsequently extended to the "warehousing" of old people from the middle and upper classes as well. By the end of the nineteenth century, there were some institutions for middle- and upper-class people that were more respectable and inhabitable replicas of the asylums for the aged poor. The stigma attached to institutionalization persisted, however, as a carry-over from the earlier institutions, even with respect to these middle-class "retirement homes."[37]

The difficulties for the aged in modern American society have been compounded by contradictions inherent in the welfare system. The process of differentiation by which institutions in society assumed functions of social welfare and old-age support previously held by the family has never been fully rationalized in the United States. Even in Great Britain, where the public-welfare system is broader, old people have generally tended to rely on familial support along with their public assistance. In the United States, the level of public support for the aged under the Social Security system has been minimal, providing only basic subsistence. Old people have to fall back on their own resources or rely on their families for assistance, for services, and particularly for sociability. At the same time, however, the state has not provided the kind of support that would enable families to carry out these obligations. The American public welfare system has been designed to support individuals rather than families. As was the case with the nineteenth-century poor laws, it tends to disrupt families in need of assistance rather than to support the family as a unit.[38] Nor has the welfare system provided substitutes for the sociability and social integration that kinship ties offered to old people in the past.

In trying to understand the problems of old age in modern American society, it is important to remember that while the poor are most vulnerable, some of these problems are no less persistent among the middle class. The growing privatism of the modern middle-class family has tended to diminish the kin network as a viable framework for economic and social interaction. Geographic segregation has been compounded by suburbanization, which has drawn young and middle-aged couples into the suburbs and led the elderly into retirement communities or left them behind in the central city. These changes have been accompanied by the development of what Erving Goffman has called the "spoiled identity" and others have referred to as the "mystique of the aged." The characterization of the aged as "useless," "inefficient," "unattractive," "temperamental," and "senile" accompanied the gradual ousting of people from the labor force at age sixty-five and barred them from a variety of occupations even earlier.[39] Such negative stereotypes had already begun to appear in popular literature in the United States during the later part of the nineteenth century. Their emergence should not be misconstrued as causing an immediate decline in the status of older people, but it did reflect the beginnings of an increasing tendency to denigrate the aged in society.

Some people have attributed the emergence of a negative image of old age to a "cult of youth" in American society, but while there is undeniably a connection, one cannot be construed as an explanation of the other. The glorification of youth and the denigration of old age are both aspects of far more complicated processes. They are results of the growing segregation of different stages of life—and of their corresponding age groups—in modern American society. The socioeconomic changes of the past century have gradually led to a segregation of work from other aspects of life and to a shift from the predominance of familial values to an emphasis on individualism and privacy. These changes have affected each stage of life: they have resulted in the segmentation of the life course into more formal stages, in more uniform and rigid transitions from one stage to the next, and in the separation of the various age groups from one another.

The problems of older people in American society are in some respects unique to this age group, but in others they reflect in their most acute form problems experienced by other age groups and other stages of life as well. They illustrate the personal and social discontinuities that Erik Erikson sees as major problems in modern American society.

> As we come to the last stage [old age], we become aware of the fact that our civilization really does not harbor a concept of the whole of life. . . . Any span of the cycle lived without vigorous meaning, at the beginning, in the middle, or at end,

endangers the sense of life and the meaning of death in all those whose life stages are intertwined.[40]

Notes

1. G. Stanley Hall, *Senescence: The Last Half of Life* (New York: D. Appleton, 1922), p. 366.

2. George Beard, *Legal Responsibility in Old Age, Based on Researches into the Relationship of Age to Work* (New York: Russells, 1874).

3. "Apology from Age to Youth," *Living Age* 193, 14 January 1893, p. 170. For a discussion of the popular and medical literature on aging in the late nineteenth century, see W. Andrew Achenbaum, "The Obsolescence of Old Age in America, 1865–1914," *Journal of Social History* 8 (1974): 48–62.

4. I. L. Nascher, *Geriatrics* (Philadelphia: P. Blakiston's Son & Co., 1914).

5. Hall, *Senescence*. See Abraham Epstein, *Facing Old Age: A Study of Old Age Dependency in the United States and Old Age Pensions* (New York: A. A. Knopf, 1922); Paul H. Douglas, *Social Security in the United States* (New York: McGraw-Hill, 1936); Pennsylvania Commission on Old Age Pensions, *Report* (Harrisburg: J. L. L. Kuhn, 1919); Wisconsin Industrial Commission, *Report on Old Age Relief* (Madison: n.p., 1915).

6. Clark Tibbitts, "Origin, Scope and Fields of Social Gerontology," in *Handbook of Social Gerontology*, ed. Clark Tibbitts (Chicago: University of Chicago Press, 1960); Michel A. J. Philibert, "The Emergence of Social Gerontology," *Journal of Social Issues* 21 (1965): 4–13. On theoretical developments in gerontology, see Robert Kastenbaum, "Theories of Human Aging: The Search for a Conceptual Framework," *Journal of Social Issues* 21 (1965): 13–37; Orville Brim, Jr., and Ronald P. Abeles, "Work and Personality in the Middle Years," *Items* 29 (September 1975). An exception to this is Mathilda White Riley and Anne Foner, *Aging and Society*, vol. 1: *An Inventory of Research Findings* (New York: Russell Sage Foundation, 1968), which integrates the various aspects of aging.

7. The historical discovery of stages of the life cycle was first conceptualized by Philippe Ariès in *Centuries of Childhood: A Social History of Family Life*, trans. Robert Baldick (New York: Knopf, 1962). John Demos has explored this question in *A Little Commonwealth: Family Life in Colonial Plymouth* (New York: Oxford University Press, 1970); and see also Kenneth Keniston, "Psychological Development and Historical Change," *Journal of Interdisciplinary History* 2 (1971): 329–45; Tamara K. Hareven, "The Discovery of Childhood in American History" (Paper presented at the Annual Meeting of the Organization of Amer-

ican Historians, April 1969); Robert H. Bremner, John Barnard, Tamara K. Hareven, and Robert Mennell, eds., *Children and Youth in America,* 3 vols. (Cambridge: Harvard University Press, 1970–1974), see particularly vol. 1; John and Virginia Demos, "Adolescence in Historical Perspective," *Journal of Marriage and the Family* 31 (1969): 632–38; Joseph Kett, "Growing Up in Rural New England," in *Anonymous Americans,* ed. Tamara K. Hareven (Englewood Cliffs, N.J.: Prentice-Hall, 1971), pp. 1–16.

8. On the middle years, see Bernice L. Neugarten and Nancy Daton, "Sociological Perspectives on the Life Cycle," in *Life Span Developmental Psychology: Personality and Socialization,* ed. Paul B. Baltes and K. Warner Schaie (New York: Academic Press, 1973).

9. The term "life course" is used here, rather than "life cycle," because I shall consider not only the stages of the individual life cycle, such as those formulated by Erik Erikson and his followers, but the synchronizations of individual development with the collective experience of the family as it moves through its life course. The "life course" is more encompassing than the individual development and the collective organization of the family as individuals move through life.

10. The term "cohort," rather than "generation," will be used throughout this paper because it refers to a specific age group with a common experience; "generation" is less precise and can also have connotations of kinship. See Riley and Foner, *Aging and Society,* 1: 8–10.

11. Reuben Hill, *Family Development in Three Generations* (Cambridge, Mass.: Schenkman Publishing Co., 1970), p. 322. The most important formulation of the life course as it changes over time is in Glen Elder, Jr., "Historical Changes and the Life Course," *Journal of Family History,* forthcoming.

12. See Kett, "Growing Up in Rural New England" and John Modell, Frank Furstenberg, and Theodore Hershberg, "Social Change and Transitions to Adulthood in Historical Perspective," *Journal of Family History* 1 (1976): 7–32.

13. Philip Greven, Jr., *Four Generations: Population, Land, and Family in Colonial Andover, Massachusetts* (Ithaca, N.Y.: Cornell University Press, 1970); Daniel Scott Smith, "Parental Power and Marriage Patterns: An Analysis of Historical Trends in Hingham, Massachusetts," *Journal of Marriage and the Family* 35 (1973): 419–29.

14. Peter Uhlenberg, "Cohort Variations in Family Life Cycle Experiences of U.S. Females," *Journal of Marriage and the Family* 36 (1974): 284–92; and "Changing Configurations of the Life Course," in *Transitions: The Family and the Life Course in Historical Perspective,* ed. Tamara K. Hareven (New York: Academic Press, 1978). See also Paul Glick, "The Family Cycle," *American Sociological Review* 12 (1947): 164–74; Alice Rossi, "Family Development in a Changing World," *American Journal of Psychiatry* 128 (1972): 1057–66.

15. Modell, Furstenberg, and Hershberg, "Social Change and Transitions to Adulthood in Historical Perspective."

16. Tamara K. Hareven, "Family Times and Industrial Time: The Interaction Between Family and Work in a Planned Industrial Town," *Journal of Urban History* 1 (1975) : 365–89; John Modell and Tamara K. Hareven, "Urbanization and the Malleable Household: An Examination of Boarding and Lodging in American Families," *Journal of Marriage and the Family* 35 (1973) : 467–78.

17. Howard P. Chudacoff, "Newly Weds and Familial Extension: First Stages of the Family Cycle in Providence, R.I., 1864–1880," in *Family and Population in Nineteenth-Century America*, ed. Tamara K. Hareven and Maris Vinovskis (Princeton: Princeton University Press, forthcoming).

18. U.S. Department of Commerce, Bureau of the Census, *Twelfth Census of the United States, Occupation,* Special Report (Washington, D.C.: Government Printing Office, 1904), pp. cxix–cxx.

19. Robert and Helen Lynd, *Middletown* (New York: Harcourt, Brace and Co., 1929), p. 34.

20. Edward T. Devine, *Misery and Its Causes* (New York: Macmillan Co., 1909), p. 125.

21. Amoskeag Company, Grievance Files, Baker Library, Harvard University, Cambridge, Massachusetts.

22. Robert Hunter, *Poverty* (London: Macmillan and Co., 1904).

23. Hareven, "Family Time and Industrial Time"; Tamara K. Hareven, "The Dynamics of Kin in an Industrial Community," in *Turning Points,* ed. John Demos and Sarane Boocock (Chicago: University of Chicago Press, 1978); Tamara K. Hareven and Randolph Langenbach, *Amoskeag: Work and Life in an American Factory City* (New York: Pantheon Books, 1978). For an analysis of economic strategies of the family, see John Modell, "The Fruits of Their Toil," in Hareven and Vinovskis, *Family and Population in Nineteenth-Century America.*

24. A cumulative body of historical research on the family has documented the continuity of nuclear households from preindustrial to industrial times in Europe and America. See Peter Laslett and Richard Wall, eds., *Household and Family in Past Time* (Cambridge: Cambridge University Press, 1978), and Tamara K. Hareven, "The Family as Process: The Historical Study of the Family Cycle," *Journal of Social History* 7 (1974): 322–29.

25. M. F. Nimkoff, "Changing Family Relationships of Older People in the United States During the Last Fifty Years," in *Social and Psychological Aspects of Aging,* ed. Clark Tibbitts and Wilma Donahue (New York: Columbia University Press, 1962).

26. Riley and Foner, *Aging and Society,* 1: 167–68. Talcott Parsons, "Age and Sex in the Social Structure of the United States," *American Sociological Review* 7 (1942): 604–16. For a sociological critique, see

Marvin Sussman, "The Isolated Nuclear Family: Fact or Fiction," *Social Problems* 6 (1959) : 333–47.

27. For a formulation of instrumentalism as an important theory of kin relations, see Michael Anderson, *Family Structure in Nineteenth Century Lancashire* (Cambridge: Cambridge University Press, 1971).

28. Robert E. Bieder, "Kinship as a Factor in Migration," *Journal of Marriage and the Family* 35 (1973) : 429–39.

29. Irene Taeuber, "Change and Transition in Family Structure," in *The Family in Transition, Proceedings of the Fogarty International Center* (Washington, D.C.: U.S. Government Printing Office, 1969), pp. 29–53; Modell and Hareven, "Urbanization and the Malleable Household."

30. Hareven, "Family Time and Industrial Time"; Modell, "The Fruits of Their Toil."

31. Demos, *A Little Commonwealth*; Greven, *Four Generations*.

32. Ariès, *Centuries of Childhood*, p. 404.

33. Robert H. Bremner, *From the Depths: The Discovery of Poverty in the United Sattes* (New York: New York University Press, 1956); David Rothman, *The Discovery of the Asylum* (Boston: Little, Brown & Co., 1971).

34. Diary, 1850, Cornell University Archives, Ithaca, New York.

35. Bremner, *From the Depths*.

36. Pennsylvania Commission on Old Age Pensions, *Report*.

37. James Leiby, *Charity and Correction in New Jersey* (New Brunswick, N.J.: Rutgers University Press, 1967); Epstein, *Facing Old Age*; Walter K. Vivrett, "Housing and Community Settings for Older People," in Tibbitts, *Handbook of Social Gerontology*, pp. 549–623.

38. On this point see Frances Fox Piven and Richard Cloward, *Regulating the Poor* (New York: Pantheon Books, 1971); and Richard Elman, *The Poorhouse State* (New York: Pantheon Books, 1966).

39. Rosalie Rosenfelt, "The Elderly Mystique," *Journal of Social Issues* 21 (1965) : 37–43.

40. Erik Erikson, *Insight and Responsibility* (New York: W. W. Norton, 1964), pp. 132–33.

3 AGING AND DEATH AS UNIVERSAL EXPERIENCE

LITERARY AND ARTISTIC PERCEPTIONS

LEON EDEL

PORTRAIT OF THE ARTIST AS AN OLD MAN

Socrates: I consider that the old have gone before us along a road which we must all travel in our turn and it is good we should ask them of the nature of that road, whether it be rough and difficult, or easy and smooth.

Plato, *The Republic*

In his conversations with Goethe, the meticulous Johann Ecker-mann records a ride to Erfurt on an April day in 1827.[1] Goethe, then seventy-eight, looked attentively at the landscape and re-marked, in passing, that nature is always filled with good inten-tions, but—one had to admit it—nature is not always beautiful. By way of illustration, the master then began a disquisition on the oak. Sometimes an oak, crowded by other trees, grows high and thin, spends it freshest powers "making it" to air and sunshine, and ends up with an overblown crown on a thin body. Then there is the oak that springs up in moist and marshy soil. Overin-dulged and squat, it is nourished too quickly into an indented, stubborn obesity. Its unfortunate brother may lodge in poor, stony soil on a mountain slope; lacking free development, it becomes knotty and gnarled. Such trees, Goethe said, can hardly be called beautiful—at least they are not beautiful as oak trees.

Then Goethe described to the recording Eckermann the perfect oak. It grows in sandy soil, where it spreads its roots comfortably in every direction; it needs space in which to feel on all sides the effects of sun, wind, rain, light. "If it grows up snugly sheltered from wind and weather," said Goethe, "it becomes nothing. But a century's struggle with the elements makes it strong and power-

ful, so that, at its full growth, its presence inspires us with aston-
ishment and admiration."

The author of *Faust* was speaking a piece of autobiography
as his eightieth birthday drew near: he had been one of the
fortunate oaks of literature. Indeed, few can claim such favored
circumstances; still fewer survive to full growth; if they do, they
consume many years struggling toward light and sun, or are
undernourished like the mountain oak, or grow obese from the
effects of a soil too moist, a nature too lush. Nature has its own
ways of inhibiting and stunting art, of forestalling the ripeness of
age. Many artists, mere saplings of promise, are cut off in their
precocious youth. And those who survive often remain aging
versions of what they have been during their earlier years—that
is, individuals who repeat their performances and grow rigid and
stale. They have consumed their originality. We can count on our
fingers the few artists who surpassed themselves when old, as
Goethe did. Among painters, Rembrandt comes to mind. His
autobiography, begun early, is spread over many canvases—
those marvelous paintings of himself. They show him in jaunty
youth, all plumes and velvet jacket; in middle years, with increasing disorder in costume, but the face powerful and arresting;
and finally we look upon a watery-eyed and bedraggled old man,
but what a magnificent old man! How sure and fine is his self-
realization as he confronts his visage in old age! The early
swagger gives way to a mixture of resignation and resentment;
as an old man he paints himself with an ever greater honesty; the
feather and cape have long ago been set aside. There remains
only the truth. The artist addresses himself to his truths: the
truth of appearance and the truth of feeling, the reality of
wrinkles, the delicacy of the bulges under his eyes as they catch
the light, the face now set in irreversible lines, yet suggesting
wisdom and experience, the acceptance of all life, the recognition
that it is usually the journey, and not the arrival, that matters.
The artist as an old man knows that life will not offer him any
better chance. There is only one chance, and his art has been
that chance.

In looking at the splendid finished oaks—in visual art, Le-
onardo or Michelangelo, Titian or Tintoretto; in music, Bach or

even the gnarled Beethoven—we must remind ourselves that some of these men did not live as long as men live today. But art has its own lifespan. A finished Mozart died in his unfinished thirties. One thinks of Rimbaud, whose growth as poet came to a stop before he was twenty, although he lived on in the world of commerce; or of the Romantics, such lively saplings, who withered or were suddenly cut off close to the ground. The portrait of the artist as a young man is usually the picture of an unfinished artist, one who may not end up as an artist at all. I am convinced that the fictional Stephen Dedalus, arrogant and poised for flight, in his coldness, secrecy, cleverness, had in him nothing but a potential virtuosity.[2] He was all anger; he was mindless with rage. He wrote a single poem, not a very good one, but he called himself an "artist" and wanted the world to give him its bounty before he had given the world any proof of his worth.

Portraits of artists as young men speak to us with what Henry James called a hungry futurity.[3] The portrait of the artist as an old man, on the other hand, is that of the finished oak, standing strong and sometimes beautiful in nature, with a developed and nourished past. Most questions have been answered. The storms and stresses are over. The pain of growth, the anguish of aging, have been surmounted; the radiance and suffering have ended in triumph and fulfillment, even if sometimes in penury and want. Biographers of the young are in a forest of saplings; biographers of the old stand in clearer land, amid a finished forest—a beauty of maturity. All is not perfection; but then nature, as Goethe has taught us, is unsymmetrical, prodigal, often a game of chance.

In literature there are many kinds of aging. One thinks of Coleridge's genius spread in incompleteness and steeped in opium; of Landor's dramatic senility; of Browning in London, prosaic and drowsy after the great poetry of his early years; or of Carlyle's rage and dyspepsia and brilliance. Let me sketch the portraits of three writers—two novelists and one poet—who bridged the nineteenth and twentieth centuries. Let us look (as far as biography ever can) at what each represented. Each is a special case, as artists are bound to be. In our empirical way, we might find in these transcendent cases some common aspects of artistic experience, some crises of the imagination and of being, often observed in men of high resource and development. These may permit us to understand, perhaps in a heightened way, some of the human drama and human values in aging.

I

I choose as my first case a Russian master, Count Leo Nikolay-evich Tolstoy.[4] He was born in 1828 and died at eighty-two in 1910. He seems at first glance one of Goethe's splendid oaks. He grew up on a large estate, a nobleman, with full opportunity to sink his roots deep into native soil. The young Tolstoy, as well as the old, revealed certain traits and conflicts that embodied the most characteristic struggle of man: the struggle between instincts, which demand freedom, and civilization, which insists upon controls.

Tolstoy never knew his parents. His mother was to him dim and ghostly, probably a screened remembrance, for she died before Tolstoy was two. His father seemed large and authoritative, but he disappeared when Tolstoy was eight. French and German tutors, a series of maiden aunts and cousins, and the life on his estate provided the future writer with an enormous sense of freedom, yet a freedom hedged with emotional restrictions. Tolstoy had the privileges of a young aristocrat at large in an accepting world. He had a life of ease that is reflected in all his works—in the lives of Pierre and André and Levin. Yet how deeply troubled a spirit he was, a spirit brooding and confused. It is a cliché that the nineteenth-century Russians were "melancholy Slavs"; certainly the articulate among them gave the world a sense of yearning and weariness, a chronic soul sickness. "What is life?" they all seem to ask. "What does it mean?" And they give troubled and deeply human answers. Tolstoy had an aloofness that enabled him to see more clearly than most. He also had the egotism of his privileges, and a curiously low self-esteem, so that his art gave him no solace. It seemed to him a plaything. He was a novelist who wanted to be a philosopher. He wanted systems—for by systems alone could emotion and impulse be given a semblance of control. When young, every time he encountered any subject he experienced an urge to write a treatise on it. Whatever came to hand—religion, music, philosophy, history, conduct—required rules: rules of life, rules for himself and his busy, compulsive, driving mind, and of course rules for everyone else. Some vast inner reservoir of personal grief and insecurity, some strange fear of allowing himself to feel, although he was extraordinarily aware of the feelings of others, made him a prodigy of self-prohibitions, which were, in the aristocratic way, promptly undermined by self-indulgence.

The child Tolstoy was brought up by a clan rather than by emotionally identifiable parents. While that practice is highly successful among some primitive peoples (making children feel that every home is their home), it gave this aristocrat a sense of drift in his youth, even of rootlessness. And how difficult to be a realist who prefers lofty, abstract thoughts about God and society! How exact, how accurate, were his observations when he walked into a room! He could note the button on a cloak, and it could tell him things about the wearer; he could capture fleeting expressions on faces, see the fumbling finger, the jerk of the shoulder—he could see *into* people, and their lives, and how they handled their affairs, and could remember all they said. He loved nature, the sensible, visual world, although he lacked a style in putting down what he saw on paper. Yet how could he reconcile all these realities with a kind of inner despair, a God who made life seem arbitrary?

By sixty Tolstoy was world famous, the author of *War and Peace* and *Anna Karenina* as well as of many tales and tracts on how to lead a good life—according to Tolstoy.[5] He was a Thoreau grown old, a foreshadowing of the future Gandhi, all for nonviolence and passive resistance and self-immolation; the Kingdom of God, he said, was in man. He preached simplicity and chastity, yet could not escape the call of passion in the large bed at Yasnaya Polyana where he fathered thirteen children. After his passionate middle years, sex was still imperious; but when passion was spent, he tended to see his wife as a temptress, and blamed himself for his weakness. He entered old age with the step of a patriarch—the long beard, those world-weary wrinkles, a flat nose like that of a prizefighter, a gnarled oak of a man with lively eyes that looked searchingly, always seeking. This man, who seemed to have all the fulfillments of life, somehow felt a lack—of what? Something was missing, as seen in the frown, the rages, the enthusiasms, the prophecies of this rustic primitive genius at large on his lands amid his peasants and disciplines. "*Jak chto zhe nam dyelat?*"[6] That was also the title of one of his major essays: "What then must we do?" What *was* there to do? Endowed with abundance, could he give away his property? Put his copyrights in the public domain? Recognize that money is not important? Be a vegetarian? Have no part in the exploitation of man by man? Forswear smoking and self-indulgence? Lead a life of chastity?

He was a bundle of strivings, as Thoreau might have said, but somehow he always checkmated them. "I tell others what to do," said Tolstoy, "but I don't know what to do myself?"[7] Some sense of worthlessness, some need to hold himself in low esteem, gave him also a brooding fear of his mortality. He was afraid of death —this man who could understand and feel so much of life. He was the aristocrat in spite of himself, jealous of his prerogatives, yet also insisting he was the friend of the people, at heart closest to his *muzhiks*, his peasants, who never understood what he talked about and suspected his generous impulses. The young Chekhov, visiting Yasnaya Polyana, remarked that Tolstoy's idea was to put himself on the level of the plebeians; what was necessary, said Chekhov, was to educate the plebeians to a higher plane.[8] Tolstoy was indeed a bundle of strivings and contradictions. He was an ardent Slavophile, but he also loved the West; he was hostile to private ownership, but he kept up his estates and added to them, living as a man of wealth. In his youth he was a compulsive gambler, like Dostoevsky; but he repaired his losses ultimately with vast royalties from his writings. He never questioned the fact that so many peasants worked for him and his large family. He abhorred the eating of meat, but he could spend long days hunting. He ate vegetables and grains, but had sudden spurts of gluttony. He lectured his peasants on the evils of tobacco, and dug a ditch and made them throw their pipes into it. Then, returning to his study, he reached for a *papirossa*, a cigarette. He was orthodox and devout, but he defied the church and was ultimately excommunicated. In *The Kreutzer Sonata* he told the world it must be chaste; he quoted Christ and said that a man who lusts after a woman commits adultery deep in his heart. But at that very moment he made his wife pregnant with her thirteenth child.[9]

We must not dismiss Tolstoy as a hypocrite, any more than we would Thoreau for building his hut in a symbolic loneliness, less than a mile from his mother's home.[10] Something more profound is at work in such a genius. His sense of chaos and his sense of order are mixed. His feelings are too strong, at times overwhelming, driven by a constant depression from which there seems to be no escape. That depression is written into Tolstoy's fiction. In *War and Peace*, for example, André, a nobleman filled with despair, goes off to the Napoleonic Wars and is wounded. Lying on the battlefield, he looks up into the great immensity of blue sky (who, reading that page, can ever forget it?) and feels the futility of existence. He has an extraordinary yearning to die, and when he returns to his father's estate, he abandons life; it is a kind of abandonment of the life struggle, the life will. The other side of Tolstoy is in the ever-questioning Pierre. A gambler—anarchic, dissipated, made serious by war and suffering—Pierre wants to reform everything, to transform a cluttered world into a rational order. One side of Tolstoy has to die; the other lives and suffers. Anna Karenina—the feminine side of Tolstoy—throws herself under a train when her great passion has run its course. Passion must be punished. But Levin, like Pierre, goes on living. So Tolstoy sought to kill the art within himself and to live on in a kind of existential brooding, an eternal muddle. Levin, too, considers killing himself, but decides he must make the best of God's world. His meditations on suicide are taken almost verbatim from Tolstoy's personal journal, in which he wrote:

> I was unwilling to act hastily, only because I had determined first to clear away the confusion of my thoughts, and, that once done, I could kill myself. I was happy, yet I hid away a cord, to avoid being tempted to hang myself by it to one of the pegs between the cupboards of my study, where I undressed alone every evening, and ceased carrying a gun because it offered too easy a way of getting rid of life, and yet there was something I hoped for from it.[11]

What strikes us in particular is Tolstoy's psychological sagacity; he understands how people feel, and he has a gift for novelistic detail. But in his life he does not apply this sagacity to himself. Even when he says he wants to die, we see that he doesn't really want to—he must put his thoughts in order first. A gun is too easy; apparently he must find something more difficult. This is a man who wants martyrdom, wants someone else to kill him; a soul caught between the empyrean of speculation and a drive to exactitude, yet in reality a soul struggling with passivity, self-indulgence, egotism, unable to reform itself—asking for external forces to deal out justice. From this we may understand how unhappy was Tolstoy's old age. In the midst of his great fame, a world hero, he was a fount of despair. His quarrels with his wife and children are legendary. The Countess Tolstoy was a long-suffering woman of much ability, and Tolstoy's deep dislike of women often emerged in their struggle. In his later years he dwelt, as always, on death, but never believed he would die; and although he wrote, on the one hand, his later masterpiece "The Death of Ivan Ilyich," he also wrote the novel entitled *Resurrection*. Life was a purge. Purged, one had to be resigned—until the caldron within boiled over again.

Tolstoy's power as a writer did not diminish with age, but it did not grow. He discovered himself always in his work, yet got no comfort from it. He had no faith in art, no belief in his uniqueness. While in his search for a faith he chose a primitive form of Christianity, he recognized he could not practice his preachings. He tried. And when he broke his own rules there were remorse, self-laceration, and ultimately blame to be placed on the world around him. Again and again he told himself that a man of his beliefs had to live them—that he had to leave his cushioned ease, his servants, his home, and go forth and lead a saintly life. Still, the aristocrat in Tolstoy could not bring himself to become one of God's athletes, a missionary, a martyr. When he finally left home, it was too late. He was eighty-two, and his departure was a symbolic act of death. He became ill as he journeyed with his youngest daughter by train. He died in a railroad station, like his heroine Anna Karenina.

Tolstoy's patterns of life reverse the usual patterns of the aging artist. For example, he wrote his autobiographies at the beginning instead of the end of his career. *Childhood, Boyhood, Youth*, his fictional trilogy, made him famous in his twenties, as if he had, in the full force of his manhood, to relive his beginnings. Middle age embodied the years of his richest life—indeed, they had a plenitude that would have sufficed for most men, most artists. The Russian writer raised a large family, experimented with education and farming, and wrote his world masterpieces with consummate power, if not always with an economy of art. But his inner melancholy, his indulged self, brought him to crisis and, as we have seen, to fantasies of suicide. His old age was in reality a chronic crisis that he never resolved. Edmund Wilson argued that his proclaimed love of mankind and his particular religion seem "an arid self-directed exercise that simply raises the worshipper in his own self-esteem."[12] Tolstoy was an angry, forbidding man of high gifts, a Jeremiah—perhaps a supreme example of an artistic power that did not suffice. In tune with the realities of most humans in the crowded scenes of his existence, Tolstoy could not be in tune with the realities of his self.

II

To leap from continental Russia to continental America for our second writer is to take a great leap indeed. Yet while environment and circumstances may differ, artists are made of similar stuff. Henry James, who was born when Tolstoy was fifteen, lived to be seventy-three, dying six years after Tolstoy's death. Looking at their parallel lives, we see that whereas Tolstoy came out of feudal Russia, Henry James was a grandchild of the Enlightenment that placed America on the road to a kind of unenlightened egalitarianism. His grandfather had made a fortune in Albany, New York, and James, like Tolstoy, had a spacious childhood. Tolstoy grew up in a family clan; James had loving parents, but he had awareness of clan, both in the big grandmotherly house in Albany and in teeming New York City, where as a small boy playing in muddy streets he saw pigs rooting in the gutters and chickens walking in Washington Square. The novelist's father was like a Tolstoy in reverse. Tolstoy wanted rules and regulations to curb his freedom; Henry James's father defied the rigidities of Calvinism and preached the joys of a sensual life as against religious restraint. But in the way of puritanical Americans, the elder James's sensory adventures were tame and intellectual. Simple joys sufficed. Tolstoy had chastening experiences in the Crimean War; Henry James, the future novelist, shrank from the violence of the Civil War, suffering more from a case of nerves than from physical disability. He was exposed early to European culture, acquiring a cosmopolitan spirit without ever having had to be a provincial. Although allowed to enjoy his senses, he also inherited an idea of duty and possessed a desire for fame, fortune, and glory, which he would win by the pen, like Balzac. James did not have Tolstoy's exposure to all kinds and conditions of men in war and peace. James came to life through literature; Tolstoy came to literature through life. Such an epigram, however, would overlook the fact that an artist with a "grasping imagination" and an observant eye can often feel all life, and see it, more powerfully than the one who plunges himself into it.

What I find significant is that while Tolstoy in his twenties wrote his first novels out of early memories of childhood and youth, James wrote his first novel (at thirty, after ten years of apprenticeship) out of maturity. It deals with a young artist who feels he has to choose between art and passion, and is defeated by passion. Tolstoy had gratified his sexual needs from the first, with mistresses or in brothels, but he was a clumsy lover. Sex for the puritan-conditioned James was suppressed, controlled, turned into a problem of conduct—made a part of the art of life. James feared mistresses, and read about brothels in French novels. From the first, his concern was not what to do with the world, which Tolstoy wanted to change into a pastoral, simplified Christian world, but how to make it into a work of beauty and art. James's philosophy was that of a man in search of aesthetic freedom; Tolstoy's was that of a man who feared freedom and legislated for himself out of his own intelligence. James, like Balzac, accepted life—he wasn't the least bit philosophical. In an early essay, he is specific about this. Life, he writes, is a battle.

Evil is insolent and strong; beauty enchanting but rare; goodness very apt to be weak; folly very apt to be defiant; wickedness to carry the day; imbeciles to be in great places, peoples of sense in small, and mankind generally happy.[13]

But there was also for James one singular reality:

> the world as it stands is no illusion, no phantom, no evil dream of a night; we wake up to it again for ever and ever; we can neither forget it nor deny it nor dispense with it. We can welcome experience as it comes, and give it what it demands, in exchange for something which it is idle to pause to call much or little so long as it contributes to swell the volume of consciousness. In this there is mingled pain and delight, but over the mysterious mixture there hovers a visible rule, that bids us to learn to will and seem to understand.[14]

The world was a spectacle, supplying abundant raw material for art. All the writer had to do was to be artist enough—self-critical, exigent, sentient. The rest was a matter of craft.

With his sexual drive channeled into his art, James felt no need to marry. He was secretive, private, intimate; even his notebooks are impersonal and professional. The young artist kept strict watch on his passions. He preferred to make love to his obedient and yielding muse. His early novels are novels of society, of the world, of art; they do not deal with love. His first masterpiece, *The Portrait of a Lady*, is about a young American woman, richly endowed when compared with her European sisters, trying to "affront"—that is James's word—her destiny. But it is her American destiny to be affronted; she is too innocent, too ignorant, too unfinished. James made himself the historian of the unfinished American woman and the American girl, and won early fame. He worked hard; he fled loneliness by mingling in society; he lived an intense, busy London life, a perpetual student of "society." Middle age came upon him unobtrusively. And with it he experienced the first crisis of his aging.

As with Tolstoy, something remained unfulfilled in spite of success. We can see this in James's turning to naturalism and trying to write deterministic novels in the manner of Zola. He wrote *The Bostonians, The Princess Casamassima, The Tragic Muse*: novels in which the inner statement is that the world is unkind to sensitive young persons; it is a brutal, philistine world that expends its gifted children and discards them. When these novels failed, he told himself that perhaps he would do better as a playwright. Certainly he would make more money. He tried for five long, busy years to write for the theater. This brought him into backstage reality, a corner of life concerned in a practical way with illusion; and James, the man of the writer's study, felt out of his element. One play was produced, and was a modest success. The second, on which he placed all his hopes, was ill received by a rowdy gallery. James himself was booed when he came out to take a bow. January 5, 1895, was the night that marked a fundamental break, a crucial turning point, in James's life. He was fifty-two, and at that moment his world broke in two.

In the ensuing five years we can read what seems to be characteristic of the history of every great artist—that moment when latent depression smothers the creative individual. In this crucible the artist faces his test: he survives or goes under. It came to T. S. Eliot early, and he wrote *The Waste Land*; it was a chronic state with Tolstoy, never resolved. It came to Henry James in the moment of high drama when the gallery howled at him (as he said) like a bunch of savages. We need not rehearse the stages of his depression. He did not write about it; perhaps he was aware of it only peripherally and intermittently. He went about London performing his "forms of expression" as if nothing had changed. But the changes are revealed in what he wrote. He wrote a series of short stories about authors who are private successes and public failures—one called "The Death of the Lion," another "The Next Time." His authors in these tales are always "too good" for their public. The public does not understand them. Then, during these years, James wrote a dozen ghost stories. He lived in a ghost world. He talked of the "black abyss" of the theater, spoke in images of drowning, of trying to keep his head above water. He wrote a novel about a child murdered by drowning. Now, in middle life, he did what Tolstoy did at the beginning: he went back to childhood and set down a series of stories about children victimized by an adult world that appreciates neither their delicacy of feeling nor their fresh perceptions. James's middle-age crisis fascinates us by what his imagination brought forth; the great thing about his despair was that he did not stop writing.

To understand Henry James's old age, we must learn one thing more. In this period, in which his emotions regressed to his childhood, a past of ghosts and extrahuman happenings, he cured himself by his work. Each story released some of his anxiety, discharged his anger, made him feel strong again. In this healing process of art, he opened himself at last to love. He had been a bachelor, a man for whom physical drives were submerged in a drive to power; now, meeting a young American sculptor in Rome, he was able to love him. It was a new experience, a tense and deeply felt moment, and a bitter one. His egotism of art was breached.[15]

He was then fifty-seven. Isn't it "too late, too late?" he asked himself. In his notebook he wrote. "Youth, the most beautiful word in the language." But his youth was gone. He had believed that he had passed the time for passion—and yet at last he felt its meaning. He felt the pain, the pity, the absence of the beloved. The great thing about Henry James is that, face to face with a truth, he was able to accept it. He did not rebel like Tolstoy and try to drive passion out as if it were the devil. He wrote his novel on the theme of "Live all you can," and called it *The Ambassadors*—the story of an elderly American like himself who comes to Paris to take a young man back to America, to his mother, but decides the young man is better off living his own life abroad. In his novel he comes to the question of determinism. He doesn't ask, "What is life?" He accepts life. The question he asks is how much of life one can live within the restraints of civilization. One may not be technically a free man; one may be a slave of instincts, drives, conditionings. One is formed by heredity and environment, but one has *the imagination of freedom*, or, as James calls it, "the illusion of freedom." In his old age James was prepared to live by that illusion.

After *The Ambassadors* came *The Wings of the Dove*, a novel in which a young heiress, knowing she must die, feels that she will have "lived" if she can allow herself to love. It is the heiress's fate to be deceived, but she does, in a manner, live. And finally James writes *The Golden Bowl*, his last novel, summing up his experience and his wisdom. In this ultimate work he sees civilization as a series of grandiose myths created by man to mask his rapacity, his deceit, his cruelty, his ability to tell himself falsehoods. The myths themselves are often beautiful falsehoods, designed to hide primitive, cruel things. In living by myth—that is, by imagination—man opens the way to knowledge, to codes and forms of life that impose decency, honor, generosity, love.

While writing his last novels, James recognized and faced his solitude. Without a wife, without children, spending long months in a rural retreat, he could say to a young man who asked him about the art he practiced, "It is a solitude, an absolute solitude." He did not mind growing old, he said. "I quite love my present age [he was fifty-six], and the compensations, simplifications, freedom, independences, memories, advantages of it. But I don't keep it long enough—it passes too quickly." He also added that it takes a whole life to learn how to live, "which is absurd if there's not to be another in which to apply the lessons."

When a younger friend pressed him about his life and asked him what had been its "point of departure"—from what point had he indeed set sail?—he answered:

> I am face to face with it, as one is face to face, at my age, with every successive lost opportunity and with the steady swift movement of the ebb of the great tide—the great tide of which one will never see the turn. The gray years gather; the arid spaces lengthen, damn them!—or at any rate don't shorten; what doesn't come doesn't, and what does does. . . . The port from which I set out was, I think, that of *the essential loneliness of my life*—and it seems to be the port also, in sooth, to which my course again finally directs itself! This loneliness (since I mention it!)—what is it still but the deepest thing about one? Deeper, about *me*, at any rate, than anything else; deeper than my "genius," deeper than my "discipline," deeper than my pride, deeper, above all, than the deep counterminings of art.[16]

The answer for James was not a return to the melancholy of the spirit from which he had suffered. He returned instead to America, after an absence of twenty years; he revisited his childhood and youth. He wrote then his moving record, *The American Scene*, mingling memory and nostalgia with prophecy, predicting city blight, waste, ecological ruin, showing in this work an acceptance of himself as old and as having the clairvoyance of his years. He wrote short stories until he was almost seventy; and only then did he embark on his autobiographies, after the death of his brother and emotional rival, William James. He revised minutely his major works for the New York edition, as if he were attempting to live his creative years all over again. He brought together his travel essays. His last ten years were a kind of shoring up of all his writings.

His supreme statement as an old artist is to be found in a letter that he wrote at seventy to Henry Adams. He had sent the second volume of his autobiography to Adams, who for years had been sour with age and disillusion, a disappointed member of a great clan. James's words to Adams ring out as a summons not to bend before the infirmities and physical insults of aging:

> You see I still, in the presence of life (or what you deny to be such), have reactions, as many as possible—and the book I sent you is proof of them. It's, I suppose, because I am that queer monster, the artist, an obstinate finality, an inexhaustible sensibility. Hence the reactions—appearances, memories, many things, go on playing upon it with the consequences that I note and "enjoy" (grim word!) noting. It takes doing—and I *do*. I believe I shall do yet again—it is still an act of life.[17]

For Henry James, aging was "still an act of life" and there was no surrender. "Art makes *life*, makes interest, makes importance," James wrote, exalting the transfiguring imagination. When he lay dying, he insisted on dictating certain reverberating phrases, and when unconscious, in his last hours, his hand still moved spasmodically over the sheet, as if he were writing. He died in full belief in his art, its power, its beauty.

III

That idea of art, of great art, as being a supreme form of life brings me to my third portrait of an artist as an old man. William Butler Yeats is the very archetype of a late flowering and late power, and a towering, controlled rage,

> What shall I do with this absurdity—
> O heart, O troubled heart—this caricature,
> Decrepit age that has been tied to me
> As to a dog's tail.[18]

He is writing at sixty-one:

> Never had I more
> Excited, passionate, fantastical
> Imagination, nor an ear and eye
> That more expected the impossible . . .[19]

We are beyond the miseries of Tolstoy, the active acceptances of Henry James. This is a rage of art and a use of this rage to make poetry. In a letter to Olivia Shakespear, written when he was fifty-seven, Yeats described his feelings: "I am tired and in a rage at being old. I am all I ever was and much more, but an enemy has bound me and twisted me so as I can plan and think as I never could, but no longer achieve all I plan and think." Where is such mental energy to go when the body refuses to follow? Yeats accepted aging, but he also defied it and *used* it. He insisted on finding new crystallizations of thought; his anger pushed him to overcome physical lag by a great luminescence of thought and feeling:

> That is no country for old men. The young
> In one another's arms, birds in the trees
> —Those dying generations—at their song.
> The salmon-falls, the mackerel-crowded seas,
> Fish, flesh, or fowl, commend all summer long
> Whatever is begotten, born, and dies.
> Caught in that sensual music all neglect
> Monuments of unageing intellect.[20]

We can paint a large portrait indeed of a man who could insist upon "unageing intellect" even while seeing himself as a comic pathetic figure,

> An aged man is but a paltry thing,
> A tattered coat upon a stick, unless
> Soul clap its hands and sing, and louder sing
> For every tatter in its mortal dress.[21]

Yeats sang. He sang the tatters in a kind of revenge upon the indignities heaped upon the body. Wherever we turn in those last immortal poems in *The Tower* and *The Winding Stair* we find the old man surpassing anything he had written in his younger years.

We encounter the symbols of his old age and the images of his old age; they are not repetitions of images called up by his younger self. They speak out of awareness of the past, his deep national feeling, his sense of himself within his race and as seer and singer. He writes of spirals, gyres, staircases to be climbed, a freedom and loftiness that defy horizontal decay. In his youth he had sung high romance and the Celtic twilight. Hands were pearl-pale, water was foamy-oozy, the dawns were passioned and shod in gold. Beauty there was in abundance, and his lyric sense had a tapestried splendor. His later style is free of book language and romantic convention. The poet uses the spoken word: belly, bum, sop, pun, bowels, randy, codger, leching, warty. He is free in describing passion and sex.[22] He no longer finds euphemisms for the flesh; it is no longer made ethereal. He undergoes one of the fashionable gland operations of that time, the Voronoff monkey-gland graft that promised rejuvenescence, but one wonders whether Yeats needed such a literal step-up of his hormones.

To arrive at such power of utterance, and such heights of vision, Yeats had passed through struggles as profound as those of Tolstoy and James; one might almost say such struggles belong to the laws of art. In his reveries on his childhood and youth (he wrote his autobiographies at fifty), we can read of his years of uncertainty, his wavering between action and dream that we find in so many poets. Like James and Proust, he worked through his childhood in middle age. He had the sexual inhibitions of his Protestantism and a natural fear—it has been called shyness— of women; he had his saturation in the myth and folklore of Ireland, derived in part from his mother; he had the extraordinary clarities of his father, who was a painter—that is, an artist aware of his son's vocation. There had been years of melancholy and depression, and an obsessive love for the beautiful Maud Gonne, who was hard and conspiratorial and revolutionary, as only the Irish can be. Yeats saw her beauty; it blinded him, in a poet's dream of ideal love. In middle life when he was writing his autobiographies—seeking, as it were, the inner sources of his life—he married (in 1917 at fifty-two). With this settling influence and with parenthood (and the end of the First World War), he entered upon the fulfillment that we can read in his verse. It was not a question for Yeats, as it was for James, of "too late, too late?" but rather one of facing and using the growing truth that his body could not keep pace with his surging mind. He made his verse and prose and his plays instruments of intellectual assertion as powerful as any we have had in our time. He had by degrees (and long before his marriage) overcome his sexual fears. And he had by degrees (one can read it in the books about him and in his own autobiographies) found a course between action and dream. The truths of poetry confronted the truths of life. Yeats's marriage led to his writing a book called *A Vision*—a strange search for the meaning of the occult, the invisible spirits of his unconscious guiding him to his newfound destinies; a search in which his wife, who had the talents of a medium, participated. For all his belief in some of the old wives' tales of spiritism, Yeats's essential strength lay in his constant ability—and need—to cut through to reality. "We make out of the quarrel with others rhetoric," Yeats wrote, "but of the quarrels with ourselves poetry." His was, we can now see, the most powerful voice in English in our time speaking in behalf of life's mysteries as against scientific realism—the old battle of the naturalists and the symbolists raised to the plane of high poetry. *A Vision* must be taken seriously in spite of its mystifications, for with each insight Yeats seems to be touching, in his poetic way, truths given us in other forms later by Freud and Jung— above all, his recognition of the power latent in the unconscious. Yeats in his terminology describes this as "an energy as yet uninfluenced by thought, action or emotion."[23] We might say he is here defining the id. So, too, Yeats understood the nature of the personal myth each man and woman creates, the persona, "the image of what we wish to become, or of that to which we give our reverence." He was touching the borders of self-belief and self-concept. He defined the creative mind as "all the mind that is consciously constructive" and called the environment, the general state of physical being of humans, their "body of fate"— a packed, deterministic statement, even if not so intended, in which another might discern the built-in societal and moral values we forge as ego and superego.

I have a memory of Yeats one evening in Montreal, at his hotel: the shock of white hair, the clear, questioning eyes, the restless animal-pacing in his room, the vigor—the boundless vigor—the pounce of an animal all instinct and superb control, control of everything he said. We talk of Joyce and D. H. Lawrence; he wishes to see the best in both. It takes a long time, he says, for a poet to be understood: "we wear our metaphors and rhythms . . . poetry grows slowly, the novel reaches the public with immediacy."[24] Yeats the public figure was but a surface; he spoke in his verse by a sounding of primitive depths— like Conrad, he could tap his unconscious. It is the old Yeats, filled with the pride of his animal power, who could conjure up the beating wings, the shudder in the loins, the earthly visitor from Olympus:

> God guard me from those thoughts men think
> In the mind alone . . .[25]

and he prayed

> That I may seem, though I die old,
> A foolish, passionate man.[26]

He wanted "an old man's frenzy." He was ready to remake himself, till he would be Timon or Lear or Blake beating upon the wall—"an old man's eagle mind." The image of the old man reduced to a coat, a tattered garment, the clothes of a scarecrow, comes to us always as a bit of outraged defiance, yet Yeats feels it to be "a comfortable kind of scarecrow."

> You think it horrible that lust and rage
> Should dance attention upon my old age;
> They were not such a plague when I was young;
> What else have I to spur me into song?[27]

When he went to Stockholm to receive the Nobel Prize, Yeats looked at the medal that came to him with Sweden's bounty; it showed a young man listening to the Muse. Yeats thought: "I was good-looking once like that young man, but my unpracticed verse was full of infirmity, my Muse old as it were; and now I am old and rheumatic, and nothing to look at, but my Muse is young. I am even persuaded that she is like those Angels in Swedenborg's vision, and moves perpetually 'towards the day-spring of her youth.' "[28] Let us remind ourselves that when the Angels of Swedenborg kissed, the kiss was a burst of flame.

Yeats flamed and the flames were brighter for his being old. He had never flamed as much in his youth.

A Russian, an American, an Irishman—three towering writers— one coming to us from an old feudalism, the second from a new ill-at-ease egalitarianism, the third from a land in chronic revolt. Their lands made them; but their personal beings offer us certain general truths that belong above nationality to the universality of the emotions, out of which poems and novels are made. They had in common, all three, the melancholy and despair so often height- ened in the lives of artists; each of them had large funds of the egotism of art; they shared man's libidinal drives—sated yet never controlled in Tolstoy, repressed and channeled into art in James, liberated by middle-aged domesticity in Yeats. Tolstoy wanted to be always virginal; James late in life accepted passion as feeling and learned the meaning of love; Yeats recognized the sexual drive and its power by reference to man's primitive state, saying that Christianity had substituted a virgin womb and an empty tomb for the more inclusive phallicism of earlier religions. In their fundamental attitudes toward freedom, we can see in James and Yeats a struggle against the shackles society imposes. They speak of art as the greatest freedom—or, as James put it, the "illusion of freedom"—to be cultivated by man. Tolstoy, coming from a land that was only beginning to learn the meaning of freedom, was a man of rules, laws, precepts. What John Butler Yeats, the father of the poet, once said seems applicable to our three artists: that poetry embodies an *absolute* freedom in which the inner and outer self can expand in full satisfaction, but that in religion "there is absent the consciousness of liberty."

If we look at these states of being in all three men, we recog- nize that aging and creativity are closely linked, that there exists a creative aging. In certain instances, aging is a way of crystalliz- ing and summarizing the life of art and the achievement of art. And when—amid the new despair that aging brings—the artist has experienced fulfillment of certain old unfulfilled needs, then he finds an expanding power of mind and utterance that can bring him to the supremacies of art. When staleness, drink, drugs, or mere cessation does not occur—for these are often common among the younger and middle-aged artists—when the artist has endured and suffered and transcended his sufferings, he becomes one of the transcendent beings of art. Without fulfillment there is misdirected rage: this was Tolstoy. With fulfillment there can be a rage of doing: this was Henry James. And a rage of power, renewed and enlarged by the very process of aging, which becomes in itself the creative force of the old artist: this was Yeats.

Of our three artists it was Tolstoy, so superb in his art, who was incomplete in spite of his outer aspect of venerability and his enormous vitality. Melchior de Vogüé said of Tolstoy that he was "a queer combination of the brain of an English chemist with the soul of an Indian Buddhist." A rum mixture, no doubt—a confusion of specifics with universals. I am haunted by the image of that railway station, of Tolstoy setting out on a literal journey at an age when most artists have already completed their journey. Tolstoy's end was death at a wayside station; Yeats's was a sailing forth to Byzantium, into the glories of the imagination; and in James's final works we find the imagery of voyage and exploration, Columbus and Amerigo—and the narrative of Arthur Gordon Pym. Out of the sadness and decrepitude of aging, Yeats and James, and those who believe in art, make a hymn to life; they sing life where Tolstoy sang despair; they sing acceptance where Tolstoy sang repudiation. They acknowledge despair, they acknowledge their instincts and their feelings, and grow old without the rigidities of aging. Within the tattered coat upon the stick there is a radiance—the same radiance as in the self-portraits of Rembrandt grown old.

> Endure what life God gives and ask no longer span;
> Cease to remember the delights of youth, travel-wearied
>   aged man;[29]

and, as you travel, say again with Montaigne: "It is not the arrival, it is the journey which matters."

Notes

1. Johann Peter Eckermann, *Gespracht mit Goethe in den letzten Jahren seines Lebens* 1823–32, 3 vols. (Leipzig: F. A. Brockhaus, 1836–48). See *Conversations with Goethe* (London: Everyman's Library, 1930), pp. 192–93.

2. James Joyce, *A Portrait of the Artist as a Young Man* (New York: B. W. Huebsch, 1916). The "young man" in Joyce's novel is Stephen Dedalus. See also Joyce, *Stephen Hero* (New York: New Directions, 1944).

3. James's description of nascent "Bloomsbury." See Leon Edel, *Life of Henry James*, vol. 5, *The Master* (Philadelphia: Lippincott, 1972), p. 392.

4. I have drawn the biographical facts principally from Henri Troyat's *Tolstoi* (Paris: Fayard, 1965).

5. Troyat, *Tolstoi*, p. 564.

6. *What Then Must We Do.* For an account of this book see Ernest J. Simmons, *Leo Tolstoy* (Boston: Little, Brown, 1946), pp. 452–54.

7. Troyat, *Tolstoi*, p. 668.

8. Ibid., p. 686.

9. Ibid., pp. 575–80. See also Simmons, *Leo Tolstoy*, pp. 485–95.

10. Leon Edel, "Walden: The Myth and the Mystery," *American Scholar* 44 (1974–75): 272–81.

11. Troyat, *Tolstoi*, p. 456.

12. Edmund Wilson, "Notes on Tolstoy," in *A Window on Russia* (New York: Farrar, Straus and Giroux, 1972), p. 183.

13. Henry James, *French Poets and Novelists*, ed. Leon Edel (New York: Grosset & Dunlap, 1964), pp. 250–51.

14. Ibid.

15. Leon Edel, *Henry James: The Treacherous Years, 1895–1901*, vol. 4 (Philadelphia: Lippincott, 1969), deals with this "middle-age crisis."

16. *Treacherous Years*, p. 350.

17. Leon Edel, ed., *Selected Letters of Henry James* (New York: Farrar, Straus and Cudahy, 1955), pp. 173–74.

18. W. B. Yeats, *The Tower* (New York: Macmillan, 1928), p. 4.

19. Ibid.

20. Ibid., p. 1.

21. Ibid., p. 2.

22. Richard Ellmann, *Yeats: The Man and the Masks* (New York: Macmillan, 1948), pp. 181–82.

23. Edmund Wilson, *Axel's Castle* (New York and London: Charles Scribner's Sons, 1969), pp. 57–60.

24. Yeats was in Montreal for a lecture 27–28 November 1932.

25. Yeats, "A Prayer for Old Age," in *Collected Poems* (New York: Macmillan, 1951), p. 281.

26. Ibid.

27. "The Spur," in *Collected Poems*, p. 309.

28. Yeats, "The Bounty of Sweden," in *Autobiographies* (New York: Macmillan, 1955), p. 541.

29. Yeats, "From Oedipus at Colossus," in *Collected Poems*, p. 222.

ROBERT F. SAYRE

THE PARENTS' LAST LESSONS

One of the common experiences of people in their early forties, which they seem to need to talk about, is having parents who are in their sixties and seventies. The situation itself is only a biological and statistical inevitability, at least in contemporary American culture. But I have been surprised, just the same, at the frequency with which discussion of parents now comes up among people I know. Ten years ago, when we were in our early thirties, we talked about our children—about pregnancies and births, bottles versus breast-feeding, how to get "them" to sleep through the night, and then about toilet-training and schools. We were primarily parents, and our own parents were secondary subjects. They were just grandparents and in-laws who were or were not helpful or demanding, visiting, vacationing, or whatnot. Only in the last four or five years, I realize, have I been telling and hearing stories about *parents*, usually with friends, but sometimes with people I have just met, if they are my age.

This is, I suppose, one of the features of a "mid-life crisis," as the psychologists call it. But I will call it by its older name— "middle age." I now realize that I am in that period because I am in the middle, between my children, who are six, eight, and ten, and my parents, who died in 1974, in their late seventies. In fact, maybe beyond the middle, for as my brother and sisters and I observed to one another at my mother's funeral, we are now the oldest generation. *Our* children know no Sayres who are older than we and our cousins.

Therefore, I would like to talk about my parents and my great-aunt, who lived in my parents' family when I was young, and about my own perceptions of their "aging" now that I, too, am "aging." Four persons in three generations. It is, by definition, a senescent topic. It won't have much appeal to that large "youth audience" we used to hear about! For, as I just noted, talk about one's old or recently dead parents is mostly for the middle-aged and beyond.

The reasons why we in our early forties talk so much about our parents are, I think, two. First, we suddenly bear a responsibility for them which we never expected to have. All through our own childhood and even our early adulthood (though I realize that the extent of this period can vary widely), we usually thought of ourselves first. Our lives were full of problems, theirs were predictable and secure. They knew what they were doing, because they were telling us what to do. Only on rare occasions did we worry about them or for them—when they were very sick or when a father lost a job. Unless we were very foresighted or unless *they* told us, we did not anticipate the day when we would have to tell *them* what to do. So the burden of a sick or indigent or incompetent parent is a surprise. And it is sometimes a heavy burden, financially, psychologically, or both. Second, as we see them grow old and die, we realize as we never did before that we are mortal, too. What is happening to them will, in a few short decades, happen to us. Time is different when you are forty, and you know that in a short while you will be sixty or seventy yourself. And so you look to your sixty- or seventy-year-old parents for your last lessons: how to go on living and how to die. If they are healthy and active and contented, you are happy for them and you seek to imitate them. If they are miserable, you try to help them, but you also hope that you will not imitate them. One way or another, they are your inheritance: your blessing or your curse.

The case for my brother, sisters, and me is one of exactly this ambivalence. Our father, Harrison Sayre, lived to be almost eighty. On the evening of 15 May 1974, he went over to our sister Dixie's house for supper. He had a drink with her and praised the view he liked so much from her living-room windows—the lawn, the trees, the sunset over the city. Then, as he frequently did, he lay down for a nap, while Dixie prepared supper. When she tried to wake him, she could not. May 21, six days later, would have been his eightieth birthday; and we had been planning a large celebration for him. Instead of the party, we had a memorial service. But it was not a gloomy one, for he had died, as a friend said, "easily and with dignity—the way he lived." "It makes you realize," my brother said, "that death can have dignity."

Mother died on 19 October, five months later. She was seventy-seven, and for six years she had been in rest homes, excluded from a normal life because of a relentless decline in her memory. She had an obscure neural ailment known as Alzheimer's disease, and though it was not what killed her (the "cause" was pneumonia), it had brought on her slow death to the world. At first, back in the late 1950s and early 1960s, she had begun to forget friends' names. Then she began doing daft things like going out to deliver something to a friend's house and getting lost. A companion-housekeeper was hired, but the disease continued. By the time she was in the first rest home, she could not remember her grandchildren's names. Later she barely recognized us children. When told of her husband's death, she only asked, as if she had never heard of him, "Hal?"

I think that anyone can see the extremes of dignity and degradation represented by these two fates. Given the choice, one would prefer to grow old and die like Harrison Sayre: no senility, no decline in his mental faculties, and only a slight reduction in his physical strength. The few ailments that he had had were skillfully treated by expert doctors, and he then maintained his health by regularly taking his pills, carefully watching his diet, and getting plenty of mild exercise. Finally, by dying quickly and painlessly, he even cheated the doctors and the hospitals of those expensive fees for terminal care. Mother's rest-home care, on the other hand, cost between ten and fifteen thousand dollars a year, and if it prolonged her life, it did so for what? She was happy, in a simple, childlike way. She was warm and well fed. She had nurses to look out for her, and put her on the toilet and change her diapers. She watched television and talked in a polite, vacuous way with the other patients. When we went to visit her, we sang old college songs and World War I patriotic tunes. She apparently did not even recognize her own pitiable state. But I know that her condition gave Dad and the rest of us a great deal of sadness. Had we been right to put her in the rest homes? Was there anything we and she could have done in the years before to have prevented this depressing end?

The assumption of most men and women is that how we age and how we die must be consequences of how we live. A plane crash, a virus, a bullet, or one slip of the wheel on a narrow road—these may happen to anyone. But they cannot destroy this basic faith. Those people who are leading satisfying, healthy lives normally expect to go on with them. When doctors and actuaries tell them that their life expectancy is seventy or seventy-five, they believe it. People who smoke and drink excessively, who are tense or overweight, and who feel generally dissatisfied and gloomy are likewise assured that they run higher-than-average risks of cancer, heart disease, and the other causes of early death or old-age distress. Thus, most people at the age of thirty-five or forty-five begin to feel some responsibility for their later fate. They diet, exercise, get annual physical examinations, and try to be more moderate in their habits. This, as I myself realize, is one of the major causes of that legendary middle-aged conservatism. If you want to live to seventy, to see the maturity of your children, and to complete the goals you have set for yourself, you cannot go on living like Lord Byron or Scott Fitzgerald.

Therefore, the questions which I have repeatedly asked are: where was Mother wrong, and Dad right? If we are responsible for our old age, in what ways did Dad prepare for it, and in what ways was Mother irresponsible? For even though Mother's Alzheimer's disease may have been unavoidable—an accident like a plane crash or a congenital defect like her colorblindness (which I share)—I would still prefer not to think that I am helpless before the same fate. As I have learned to live with the colorblindness by looking very carefully at stoplights, I would also like to circumvent Alzheimer's disease. Such precautions may ultimately be as vain as those of Oedipus's parents, but doing nothing is obviously not the answer either.

Mother grew up in Columbus, Ohio, and lived there all her life. She was an only child, but her parents, James White and Maude Hanna White, seem to have been related to half of the city. As I imagine them, they were all members of that Middle Western business middle class: McKinley Republicans, American Victorians, who confidently believed that America was the best country on earth, Ohio the leading state, and Columbus the best city. They had their local aristocracy of old and leading families, to which Mother looked up, and they had their rigid Victorian customs and taboos, which were honored as "good taste." But Mother's generation was perhaps the first to belong to what Thorstein Veblen called the "leisure class." She had time for tennis tournaments (as a girl she was a city champion), for dances and parties, and she eventually went to Vassar College to prepare for her later roles in the YWCA, the Junior League, and other volunteer groups and charities. When I was a child, Mother's stories of her childhood, including the little electric car her parents gave her when she was only twelve, all seemed long, long ago. But today I realize that the differences between her childhood and mine were superficial, not essential. Neighborhoods and addresses changed, like fashions, but neighbors and family life did not. The secure complacency, the supposed good breeding, the comfort and conformity, and the energetic pleasures in which she was raised endured in the Columbus in which I was raised, too.

Dad's childhood in Newark, New Jersey, was several steps lower economically, and more old-fashioned culturally. Before the First World War, Newark was a small town. His father and mother belonged to its plain, Presbyterian majority. Sayres had been in northern New Jersey since the early eighteenth century, but Dad's own relatives had not prospered. Both of his grandfathers had died before the end of the Civil War, so that both his father and mother were raised by widows. Neither of his parents, he said later, was much aware of the changing industrial world of their times. The stories he heard as a boy were family stories from the American Revolution. He grew up serious and thrifty. Poor eyesight kept him out of sports, though as an adolescent he was over six feet tall. He went on to work his way through Wesleyan University by selling aluminum cooking ware. In three years he graduated, Phi Beta Kappa, and stayed an extra year as a high school debating coach and an assistant in philosophy. He was a lieutenant in the First World War, and then moved to Columbus, Ohio, to be a salesman in his cousin Fred Freeman's bond brokerage business.

He and Mother married in 1921, and with money from Mother's family, Dad was able in 1923 to buy an interest in the American Education Press and become an editor of its small line of teaching materials for junior and senior high schools, the most important of which was *Current Events*. Preston Davis, the manager and major owner of the company, was a perceptive but retiring man who gave his close associates encouragement in developing their own ideas. One of Dad's, which had been suggested to him by the teachers he visited, was a weekly paper like *Current Events* that could be used in lower grades to teach reading. In 1928 he and Preston Davis started *My Weekly Reader*, and it became, as Dad said, "a children's favorite, a publisher's miracle." Its subscription price was only twenty cents a semester, so low that each child could have his own copy—and no competitor could undercut the company. It became Depression-proof. Editions were added to supply all the lower grades, and each autumn an avalanche of orders poured in. "Following the successful launching of the *Weekly Readers*," Dad recalled, "Preston doubled my salary, recommended my name for inclusion in *Who's Who in America* . . . and nominated me for presidency of all three companies in our corporate complex. . . . Dividends from the Educational Printing House were so liberal that I never asked for another salary increase. In return, Preston gave me free hand to do the community work—which after 1931 I felt was all-important."

His was an American success story, but with some subtle variations. In 1931 he was only thirty-seven years old—very young for a businessman to decide that "community work . . . was all-important," even if he considered his income sufficient. Benjamin Franklin, whom he often regarded as a model, did not retire until he was in his mid-forties. To be sure, Dad had not retired. He remained president of the American Education Press until it was sold to Wesleyan University in 1949. But in 1931 the Japanese invasion of Manchuria and the failure by the League of Nations to oppose it looked to him, he said later, like terrifying omens. Perhaps in these later reflections he was boasting a little of his foresight, but he did genuinely believe by the 1930s that there was no security for him or for other people which was not dependent on world order. And feeling ineffectual in promoting world order, he concentrated his energies, time, and ability on promoting the health and betterment of the communities in which he lived. He was what people in Columbus called "community-minded," and the words "community" and "citizen" had profound meaning to him. Thus, he was not a typical businessman, rushed, tense, and absorbed in daily affairs. His nearest modern equivalent might be one of those vice-presidents for public relations, as some companies call them, who devote most of their time to comumnity service. Such service does not bring in business, but it does enhance the company's reputation and bring a different voice to the boardroom. Ideally, such men have wide interests and a sense of history. They are not moles; they are eagles. Not only did Dad believe in this kind of work; it also brought him great satisfaction. He grew in it, and I think that it contributed to the greater patience and mellowness he developed in his sixties and seventies. He was definitely not the kind of businessman who works hard till age sixty-five and then retires to play golf and raise roses.

Had someone looked at him and Mother in 1940, however, when they were still only forty-six and forty-four, respectively, it would have been much harder to see this about him or to see what was so different about her. I raise this point because obviously none of us can yet look back on ourselves. Our lives are in process, and therefore we should try to understand the lives of our parents as they were at our own present ages, not just as they later reconstructed them from the position of age sixty-five or seventy-five. This is all the more important with Mother because her loss of memory prevented her ever having that retrospective view of herself, whereas Dad took time in his seventies to perfect his. He wrote his autobiography, in the form of three hundred pages of disjointed chapters which he called *Random Recollections*. And though these are a great help to me in reconstructing his past, I have nothing like them for Mother. Nor is she mentioned much in his *Recollections*. He found it painful to think about her, and he did not like dwelling on her failures (though I know he thought about them often).

But as a means of recapturing Dad and Mother in the late 1930s and early 1940s, I have looked at several reels of old home movies which Dad took; and they are magical recreations. For instance, they show me at age three or four playing in the sand on the beach at Point O'Woods, New York, where we went in the summer. They show my twin sisters, Babs and Jean, at age nine or ten, dressed to go to an evening movie or children's dance; and they show our big brother and sister, Jimmy and Dixie, sailing the eighteen-foot Cape Cod Knockabout that was bought in 1938. Characteristic glimpses "as we were," and as Mother and Dad liked to see us. But these proud parents also took a few shots of themselves "as they were," and these are the most precious, because until I saw them I had forgotten (or never known) how youthful Mother and Dad—Harrison and Mary Sayre then were.

Some shots of Mother show her in a bathing suit, reading in the shade of a beach umbrella. Her figure is trim, her hair a dark brown just turning to black, and her motions quick and a little shy, camera-shy. She waves a hand in front of her face, and I can hear her saying, "Oh now, Hal, now really! Point that at the children, not me." But the camera does not move, and she soon smiles, a lovely and satisfied, shy, girlish smile. She is/was a warm, gentle person.

Dad is not photographed on the beach. (Perhaps he wanted no one else's wet and sandy hands to grasp his expensive gadget.) But about five o'clock one afternoon, he was caught in his white shirt and white-duck slacks as he and Mother were off to a party. He stands on the boardwalk in front of the cottage, grinning like a monkey and grotesquely chomping his jaws. For a moment I cannot figure out what he is doing. But then I see. He is mocking the motions of some of us children chewing gum! Chewing with our mouths open! "Close your mouth when you chew" was something he frequently told us at dinner. And if that command failed, he got sarcastic. He mocked us, as here! He was very funny; but he was also a little frightening. As a child (and long after), I was as much afraid of his mockery and sarcasm as I was of his ordinary reproofs. At that time I never felt close to him.

In these old films, I find the revealing (if extremely selective) evidence that Mother in her mid-forties was the more pleasant person. Had someone taken bets then on which would live the longer, more joyful life, I suspect that most people would have guessed she would. He was twinkly, but also a little nasty. She seemed naturally happy. He had to work at it. He clowned in his light moments, but he also teased. And his teasing seemed to suggest the suppressed criticism, the dissatisfactions with the people around him. He was, I imagine, as displeased by habits in Columbus City Hall and the world at large as by children chewing with their mouths open—and made equally strenuous objections to both. The more cynical or worldly of his friends probably regarded him as an idealist. "Hal Sayre," I hear them saying, "is a perfectionist, while Mary is good-natured. Oh, they are an attractive couple," the voices go on, "religious, honest. Neither drinks; they serve no liquor in their home. But they are not Prohibitionists—just staunch Presbyterians. It's hard to know which is the more determined on this. I guess it's Mary, since Hal will have a beer now and then. But in most ways she is the light-hearted one. She's nervous sometimes, but when she relaxes she is lots of fun. She has more fun at parties without tasting a drop than other people do on three highballs. He has some interesting ideas, but he wants to change the world!"

Studied from this perspective, Mother's premature senility and the dignity of Dad's old age are hard to explain. This view also makes Mother's degradation even more pathetic. How could life turn on someone who seemed to love it so much? Everything that was youthful and happy in Mary Sayre appears, in the end, to have folded back on her and turned her into a helpless child all over again. Where his life was a rising diagonal line, hers was a circle. She went from youth into a still-vivacious middle age, and then back into a dependent, timeless childhood.

But there are more things which must have been on Mother's and Dad's minds when they were in their middle age. Wouldn't they, indeed, have thought sometimes of *their* parents just as I am now thinking of mine? I know they did, for in 1936 Mother's mother, Grandmother White, died, and soon afterward Dad's maternal aunt, Miss Adelaide Browne, who had briefly lived with Grandmother, came to live with us. She would have been a constant reminder to him of his parents and his ancestry. In 1942 he researched and privately published a slim volume of genealogy called *The Descendants of Ephraim Sayre*. He was thinking not just of his parents but of all his ancestors. And I remember trips which he and Mother made a few years later to country towns and villages in eastern Ohio from which Mother's father had come. They may have even planned a White-Hanna genealogy to match the Sayre one. Being only ten or so then myself, I was not interested in this. It bored me. But now I have sympathy for what they were doing.

Both of them, moreover, must have had fears like mine. Mother's mother had been afflicted with "hardening of the arteries" and high blood pressure, and in her final years she lost her memory. One of her habits was to ask all her grandchildren for a kiss; and one day she kept repeating this demand to my brother, Jim, who was about eight or ten. "But Grandma," he said, on each new demand, "I just kissed you."

"Oh that doesn't matter," she answered. "Kiss me again."

But on the fifth or sixth request, he stayed where he was and said, sweetly but firmly, "I'm all out of kissing juice." The story was repeated in the late 1950s, when Mother was losing *her* memory and asking for repeated kisses from *her* grandchildren.

Dad's ancestral fear came from his father, and though *he* had died much earlier, in 1915, it was probably an even heavier burden. He never told us about it until 1968 or 1969, when he was working on his *Random Recollections*. His father, Joseph Sayre, had had epilepsy, which in the nineteenth century carried all the awful superstitions we are aware of from Dostoevsky and was believed to be hereditary. The possibility of seizures was so great that Dad, as a little boy, used to have to accompany his father on business errands around Newark. And he was so afraid of passing the curse along to his own children that before he and Mother married he made a special trip to New York to get expert advice. The doctor told him not to worry; and neither he nor any of us has ever had the disease. But the consequence of watching his father in those terrifying fits was "a lifelong distaste for losing consciousness." "I fainted while making a speech in high school once," he wrote in the *Recollections*, "and, on the doctor's advice, willingly abstained from red meats for more than three years. I saw enough drunkenness in the streets of Newark and heard enough about it among family connections to make me prefer sobriety. I dislike the thought of anyone's losing control of himself." And control himself he did, all his life. Mother had nothing near his firm resolution and steely self-discipline.

But Mother also had different responsibilities. While Dad in the early 1940s was a little like his exemplary Benjamin Franklin, a successful tradesman whose income permitted him to work for Columbus as Franklin had worked for Philadelphia, Mother still had all the daily chores of managing a large household. This Dad readily acknowledged. He called her "the manager," and he always deferred to her on household matters. But what was especially difficult for her was the care of Aunt Adelaide, who was a model of old-age vitality to Dad but a competitor and a burden to Mother. Thus, Aunt Adelaide's story seems to belong here, too, because it further illustrates how generations respond to one another.

Aunt Adelaide Browne, Dad's mother's unmarried younger sister, was born in 1857. For thirty-three years she was a missionary in India, where she founded an orphanage which grew into an elementary school, a middle school, and eventually a high school for hundreds of children. In 1937, when she came to live with us at 264 North Drexel, she was already 80 years old, and I do not imagine that anyone expected her to live more than another five years. She was barely five feet tall and very frail-looking. But she was alert and peppery, and she lived on and on—for twenty-two years. She did not die until 1959, at nearly 102. For most of that time Mother could never leave the house, whether for a vacation, a weekend, or, toward the end, an afternoon, without making sure that someone was on hand to be with Aunt Adelaide. Before the Second World War, when servants could be hired for five dollars a week plus room and board, this was not so hard, but by the 1950s, when live-in "help" was no longer available—yet needed all the more for Aunt Adelaide—this was a constant worry. Mother thought that she had to keep someone on hand every hour of the day. In the morning a maid or one of us brought Aunt Adelaide breakfast in bed. Mother was downstairs by 7:00 or 7:30 to have breakfast and plan the day. At lunch Dad was downtown eating with his men friends. Mother was usually eating at home with *his* Aunt Adelaide, hearing unending stories about distant Sayre and Browne relatives or about retired missionaries. After lunch Aunt Adelaide napped. Then

Mother tore out of the house to meetings, on errands, to pick up children, or maybe just to get away. At dinner, we could seldom have a raucous family fight. No one, as far as I remember, ever got mad or loud, or blew up, as I eventually discovered other families did. Sitting on one side of the table was always that calm, saintly missionary. Every dinner was like a Sunday-noon dinner, with the minister present. The aunt who came to dinner stayed twenty-two years.

Dad, all this time, had no cause for exasperation with this amazing little woman. He knew only her jolly wit, her kind and clever flattery, the lessons of her experience, and an unceasing devotion verging on the maternal. I think I only now see what a peculiar advantage he had from her, from Aunt Adee, as he boyishly called her. From his mid-forties to his mid-sixties, he still had a doting mother-stand-in who praised his every achievement. For a time I think she even kept a scrapbook about him. But she was no simpleton of a protective, fawning mother, but a wise and accomplished person, who had lived abroad, learned another language, and once had the responsibilities of a school headmistress. Thus, any interesting news or perplexing decision could be discussed with her more easily—and probably more profitably—than with Mother. He, an educational publisher, had a retired expert teacher right there at home. Yet I am sure she never intruded, for I know that her way of teaching was always to say little until asked and then to answer with her own questions. "Well what do *you* think? What are *your* reasons?"

It is also interesting that even living in American luxury, this bright, quick person practiced a kind of Oriental asceticism. She liked to say, with a little sassiness, "A third of what you eat keeps you alive; the rest is for the doctors and the undertakers." But she was not withdrawn from society. During the war she knitted over one hundred heavy wool sweaters for soldiers and refugees. Every fall Saturday, she listened to the radio broadcasts of Ohio State football games. She cared about her favorite players, though she never saw them, as if they were her own distant students. Her cries over touchdowns and fumbles were so intense that people sometimes thought that the long-expected heart attack had suddenly come. ("Hundred-Year-Old Missionary Dies Listening to Michigan Game" would certainly have been the Columbus headline.) And with all her piety and scrupulosity she was never much troubled, as far as I could see, over the scandals of recruiting, secret payments, riotous fans, and the rest of the seamy side of the game. "No one can live in Columbus without an interest in football," she woud say, in a tone that was so matter-of-fact that it was at once beyond irony and the very essence of satire. She had a saint's power to delight in the good and coldly ignore the bad.

Yet, like Dad, she had a sharp tongue when she wanted to use it. Her scorn for Franklin Roosevelt when he ran for a third term was expressed in two words: "Mr. Indispensable." I remember her pointing to his picture on the cover of a *Life* magazine that came in the fall of 1940. It was the first time I had heard the word "indispensable," and I had no idea what she meant. "But that's Roosevelt," I said in my seven-year-old's voice. "He's the President of the United States," I kept repeating. "That's Mr. Indispensable," she repeated, "and no one's Indispensable. No One's Indispensable." I was just more confused. Did No One now have a name, Mr. Indispensable? How could the President of the United States be No One? I'm sure that she eventually gave me a simple explanation, for I did at least realize that she was saying that none of us is so useful or wise or precious that the world cannot get along without him. But this shows how stubborn she could be, too. At eighty-three, teaching herself that *she* was not indispensable, she would not give in easily. She stabbed at Roosevelt's nose as if her finger were a dagger. "Mr. Indispensable."

Aside from a few memories like this one, I could never really see, as a child, what was so amazing about her. She used to help us with our spelling lessons. She would invite us to her room and give us candy (especially peppermint Life Savers), and she would praise me when I later did little things like fix a lamp cord, or "fix" her radio by plugging it in. But she also had a contrariness that was unpredictable. If you were late in doing something she had asked, she would keep after you. She combined extremes of selfless humility and proud conviction. She once showed me a dime that she said had been given her by Mr. Rockefeller. I by then knew who he was and asked, "Only a *dime*, with all his money?" She answered that he gave much more money away than that. She seemed to like having actually met the richest man in the world. Or was it that she had that thin sliver of his fortune? Millions for him, a dime for her, and it made no difference to her. But I particularly remember how one of Dad's and Mother's maids used to be amazed every summer at Aunt Adelaide's way of protecting raspberries from the birds. In a long white dress she would sit beside the bushes for hours on end with her knitting and the family cat, undaunted by the heat and sun. Edith Daniels, the maid, perspired buckets herself and, having grown up on farms, had a sensible respect for the Midwestern summer sun. "That Miss Browne," Edith would say. "I don't know how she does it." "Oh, I used to live in India, you know," was her answer. And so the next day she would be back at her post, a little living scarecrow, happy and laughing, proud to be doing her duty, however humble.

Having this presence in the house for twenty-two years was hard on Mother. Aunt Adelaide could wear Mother's cast-off dresses and look fine in them. The most intelligent guests would come to Sunday dinner, then go upstairs and spend an hour or more being enchanted by Miss Browne and have to be dragged out to join other people. Later they would praise Mother's hospitality, but Aunt Adelaide's company. In those years, I think, Mother was most interested in details and things, in family plans, furniture, and all the business of running a house (she had to be); Dad was most interested in projects and improvements of society—in ideas; and Aunt Adelaide was most interested in people. In her idiosyncratic way, she defined "personality" as meaning "an interest in persons." And she had it. Quarterbacks, missionaries, Indian students and professors visiting the United States, my sisters' boyfriends, distant relatives she could only write to—she followed them all. People reciprocated with an interest in her, and she was like the unknown guest from out of town who stole all the dates. Ninety, ninety-five, and finally one hundred years old, with her wrinkled face and her white hair held up in pearl-colored pins, with her mohair shawl and dresses below her knees, she had more essential charm than any debutante who ever danced till dawn.

But Mother never learned to share in Aunt Adelaide's popularity. Mother, unfortunately, had not only to arrange sitters and meals for Aunt Adelaide, but also to compete with her. The good side of the competition may have been that for these twenty-two long years, Mother had to stay young. Youth and beauty and energy were her assets against the charm and serenity and occasional sharp tongue of a woman twice her age. So Mother stayed in control: if Mother got sick, Aunt Adelaide might secretly begin taking over the household. Keeping her household (and her husband) seemed to require being the manager and nursing the rival. Aunt Adelaide was elderly. Aunt Adelaide must have breakfast in bed. Would someone please take up her tray? Aunt Adelaide must have naps, quiet, a nice room, care and consideration. And when I think of the strain this must have put on Mother, I wonder at how she did it. She seldom cracked, seldom broke down and pampered herself, though when she did she would verge, I think, on the hysterical. Then she had to have breakfast in bed, naps, doctors, enemas, special diets, and the whole panoply of Victorian neurasthenic care. For Mother sick was a demanding, petulant person, even more powerful, in a way, than Mother well. No one, not even Dad, could overrule her whining fury and senseless whims. But these moods came only after she had been driven to desperation. Most of the time she suppressed this urge to pamper and baby herself by pampering Aunt Adelaide. It was Aunt Adelaide who was frail and weak. Mother was young and strong.

The further consequence, however, was that when Aunt Adelaide finally died, Mother, at age sixty-three, no longer had to keep this battle going. Nor had she had the opportunity to begin to relax her nerves and prepare for her own old age. There was no longer Aunt Adelaide against whom to be young and active and beautiful. Mother's aging began, fast. We children had grown up and left her, and having fewer of the outside interests that absorbed Dad, she had little to do. She suddenly became that saddest of sights, the overprotected middle-class grandmother in an age of two-generation families where grandmothers have no function. Of course, she was proud of being "Mama." In the early 1960s she and Dad had thirteen grandchildren, and at every holiday she wanted "a family reunion." But when the children came, they made her nervous. Dad, on the other hand, began imitating the old Aunt Adee tricks. He gave chess lessons, taught puzzles and word games, and always kept a big jar of licorice drops near his desk. Mother admired his skill, but did not have it herself. She had belonged to a culture where nurses fed the children, brought them in for one respectful "goodnight from Grandmama," and then hustled them off to bed.

It would be an oversimplification to imply that the long burden of Aunt Adelaide and the sudden change after her death were the only things that brought on Mother's senility. After all, many people have had elderly relatives living with them, even in this age of the two-generation family, and though some may have suffered from the experience, others have enjoyed and learned from it. Dad loved Aunt Adelaide not simply because she was his relative. Nor did Mother resent her only because she was *not* her relative. The point is, rather, that Aunt Adelaide was a kind of catalyst, an agent who brought out opposing tendencies in each of them, and the same or nearly the same tendencies would probably have come out anyway. In fact, as we could see later, Mother's response to grandchildren was pretty much the same—they were darlings and so on, but they made her nervous. Her response to some of Dad's friends, particularly if they were involved in work she did not understand, was cold and formal. She did not try to understand their work and regarded meeting them merely as an obligation. The older she got, the greater her resistance to change. It shocked her that her daughters came back from the hospital only six, five, three, days after delivering babies. Her confinements had lasted two weeks, and that was the "right" way. If we took coaches rather than Pullmans, we endangered our health. When we began to stop taking any trains and took planes, we seemed to Mother to be taking horrendous risks.

Dad's reactions to these failures in Mother made matters worse. I remember one day before Christmas in the middle 1960s, when Dad was in bed with a cold and Mother was trying to locate a box of handkerchiefs which she had bought to give a friend. She knew this was an instance of her loss of memory, and she was distraught. "Hal," she kept saying, as she circled in and out of their bedroom, "where *did* I put those handkerchiefs?" I helped her, but could only follow her aimless quest. Dad meanwhile sat in bed, increasingly impatient with her. "Think, Mary," was all he could say. "Where did you put them when you brought them home?" He did not console her by telling her patiently that the handkerchiefs would turn up, and not to worry. He did not understand what had really happened. He was utterly frustrated with her and scowled at her as if she were a dumb schoolgirl. She just needed to "think." Then, with a groan, he got out of bed and joined the search, while she cried that he shouldn't, that he was sick. They were working against each other like two motors turning in opposite directions. He thought her problem was a mere failure of will, and his severity just made her the more flustered. Finally Mother and I went to another room to wrap other presents, forgetting the handkerchiefs and letting Dad go back to bed.

In September of 1968 Dad had a stroke, and in the ensuing treatment the doctors discovered a heart fibrillation. We children flew to Columbus from all directions and had a conference. When and if Dad recovered, we decided, he should not go back to the big house at 264 North Drexel. He and Mother alone did not need so much room, and maintaining the house was a burden. The trouble was that Mother was so attached to the old house— after thirty-two years—that she would not want to move. We had to choose between her wish to stay and Dad's need for something more manageable (for she was no longer "manager"). Moving might dreadfully unsettle her; staying might soon bring him another stroke.

What clinched the decision, at least for me, was the proposal, supported by Mother's doctors, that she go in the meantime to a psychiatric rest home. There she might have tests to determine exactly what her disease was and the treatments to arrest it, if possible. While she was there, the house would be sold, and Dad would move to a large apartment, with room enough for Mother should she recover. The decision was harsh, but I think it was the right one. As I watched Dad in his hospital bed, seeing him in tears one moment and telling jokes the next, I had an overwhelming sense of his determined will to live. He would readily accept any changes, do anything to be well and back on his feet. Mother, I had to recognize, scarcely knew what had happened to him. And when I recalled that absurd and dreadful fuss about the handkerchiefs, I recognized that separating them might save them both. With their currents working against each other, an overload, a short circuit and blackout for both, seemed inevitable.

So the decision was executed, and while Mother was in the

rest home, Dad underwent a miraculous operation in which his heart was stopped and then electrically stimulated to set it again in a normal beat. Dixie and Babs, the two sisters living in Columbus, went to work, methodically clearing out 264 North Drexel, emptying its dozens of closets and drawers and cupboards, basement to attic, of the accumulations of several generations—our old toys and sailing trophies; Mother's and Dad's clothes, books, furniture, dishes, and so on; and heirlooms of Whites and Hannas, Sayres and Brownes. This was not just a sale and a move, it was the end of an era. And Dixie and Babs proceeded so efficiently and carefully that Dad scarcely needed to do anything. He just sat in the library, gleefully sending off bundle after bundle of his once-prized papers and speeches to the trash. He was being reborn. And he loved it.

By the spring of 1969 he was begun on his new life. His apartment had been beautifully furnished with the best of the things from 264, and he entertained proudly. He kept Mother's nurse-companion for a time, in gratitude for what she had done and in case Mother might return. But when that was seen to be impossible, he let her go. Alice Brown, his and Mother's former maid, came in daily to clean and prepare some meals; but he got on very well alone. He was constantly going out to meetings, to luncheons, and to dinner parties, and I think he wore his distinguished tuxedo more in those last five years than in the previous twenty.

But most gratifying to him was the growth of the Columbus Foundation, the focus, finally, of all his decades of community service. He had started this civic foundation long ago in 1943, with some money from Preston Davis, and for twenty years or more it grew modestly, acquiring more good will than money. But in the late 1960s it began to receive bequests of a staggering size, some of over a million dollars. Its long-awaited success and the prospect of the numerous civic projects which it could support gave him immense gratification. There was nothing that contributed more to his culminating sense of usefulness to his city.

As he told me one night of the foundation's latest bequests, I asked him how he had first heard of the idea. I knew the story, but I liked hearing it. He told it well, and it illustrated how a seed would root in his mind and maybe not flower for years, but then bloom like an orchard in May. So he repeated the story of how, shortly after he and Mother were married, they went to Cleveland to visit Freda Goff, a friend of Mother's from Vassar. Her father, Frederick H. Goff, was a lawyer and banker and had recently started the Cleveland Foundation, the first community foundation in America. Dad listened to Mr. Goff's persuasive arguments for this new institution, which was more versatile than the separate charities to which people usually made bequests and yet could still be used to support them; and Dad resolved that if the opportunity ever came, he would help start one in Columbus. But as he told this story, what suddenly struck me was that Mother had been the essential intermediary. Without her friend-ship with Freda Goff, he would never have met Mr. Goff. So I asked what Mother had thought of the idea and whether she had had any part in its development in Columbus.

No, he said, she hadn't. She had never taken much interest in it. "What a pity," I said, "because if she had, you and she would now share this reward." My suggestion seemed to strike him like an arrow, making him involuntarily give up something he had long been holding back. He had privately thought of such a shared final purpose with Mother, I think, but when it did not occur, he did not talk about it. Typically, he kept his disappoint-ments to himself. So, after a dark moment of hesitation, he looked up at me and said, in an earnest, husky voice, "Your mother is thought-less."

He seemed so close to tears that I hesitated to continue. But he had said something that pained me. Mother *thoughtless?* A person who had spent twenty-two years taking care of *his* aunt, who had raised us five children, run his house for him, and been generous, considerate, and self-sacrificing until she was ex-hausted . . . ? "I always believed," I told him, "that Mother was very thought*ful*. I can't think of any word which is less appropriate!"

"No," he answered, repeating himself very slowly. "She is thought-less."

"You mean now?" I replied. "That may be true now—and how ironic, when you think of what she was."

"No," he said. "I mean before, too. Your mother has always been thought-less."

He would say no more. And after a while I perceived his

emphasis and the meaning he was giving to the word. He meant that Mother did not *think*. She never *thought*—thought deeply, thought ahead, planned her life—in the profound philosophical way that he did. And so from his perspective the Alzheimer's disease was no accident or unpreventable disability. It was a fulfillment of her tragic flaw. "What a cold person he could be," I exclaimed to myself. And what suffering he endured because of his coldness! For it was now plain to me how much he had wished to make Mother thoughtful, in his passionately rational way. But the more he tried, the more exhausted she must have become, and so the more futile her efforts, to her. Yet as a Christian, he loved her still. So he tried to refrain from judgments. He held to faith in his way, hope that she would see it, love for her nevertheless.

And refraining from judgments was right. For in judging her, he implicitly revealed and commented upon himself. But he knew the Scripture better than I: Judge not that ye be not judged. So neither of us said any more.

LESLIE A. FIEDLER

EROS AND THANATOS: OLD AGE IN LOVE

I want to talk about certain myths of old age—or rather about a myth central to our culture of Old Age itself. I propose to deal not with official mythology, which is to say, the Scriptures of a sect, much less official mythography, which is to say, scholarly interpretation of such Scriptures—but with literature both popular and high: song, story, and drama, including movies and dirty jokes. In these forms, the myths and their meanings with which I am concerned remain covert, implicit, and pass therefore into the deep imagination, influencing behavior and perception, without ever posing the problem of belief. If, then, we hope ever to understand how the old see themselves and are seen by others, at a level so far below the lintel of full consciousness that no effective rational challenge is possible, we must augment the insights of behavioral and medical science with the kind of illumination that only such myths can provide.

More particularly, I want to talk about myths of old men in love (I shall confine myself to males not just because I am one, but because our patriarchal culture is concerned chiefly with them): "Dirty Old Men," we have come to call them, for reasons which I shall try to make clear. The plight of mythic old men represents in extreme form the tension between Eros and Thanatos, carnal love and physical death, which determines the basic rhythms of our entire lives; and thus any meditation on that plight leads us to a heightened awareness of an absurdity underlying both comedy and tragedy: an absurdity which arises out of the conflict between the desire we cannot deny without denying the very wellspring of our existence ("We cannot cross the casue why we are born," says Shakespeare, who will be much on my mind here) and the fragility of the flesh upon which the satisfaction of that desire depends. Such a perception of absurdity cannot be transcended without either the total renunciation of passion or a leap to faith, or both—if, indeed, it can be transcended at all.

The desire which represents one pole of this dilemma is typically represented in myths by the desirable Youth: the fatally beautiful Maiden or the irresistible Ephebe; and the weakness of the mortal body by the Old Man: the tremulous and decrepit greybeard, who though he stands on the verge of death seeks to forget it in the intoxication of a carnal embrace with such a maiden or ephebe. In a culture like ours, which has traditionally endured repression and prized sublimation in the name of reason and self-control, the flight to the anodyne of sex has long been considered a second-best for those of any age, and for the old totally inappropriate, especially when the desired partner is extremely young: since we do not merely quite properly ask that the old be treated with dignity, we (more dangerously) demand of the old that they behave with dignity, impose decorum on them as a burden and a chore.

Such unions are felt by all of us nurtured on such myths (and who among us is not?) to be not only in principle taboo, but also likely in fact to prove ill-fated, since they represent a sin against ongoing life, which demands that the young marry the young—while the older generations withdraw from sexual competition and prepare for death, learn, in short, to be *properly old*. Even the most enlightened among us are likely to share this feeling, though we do not like to confess it, when we talk from the top of our ideological heads, rather than out of our viscera or the myth-ridden depths of the psyche.

To be sure, we can all cite cases where the ancient taboo has been broken with impunity, not only in the legendary or historical past, but right now; and not only by certain grizzled veterans, exempted by genius from what restricts ordinary men, like Picasso or Charlie Chaplin or Henry Miller, but by our own neighbors, our selves. Yet when we fantasize or dream or relax into that unguarded receptivity into which mythic literature compels us, we hear again deep within the old saws, the old songs, "Crabbed age and youth cannot live together."[1]

And we remember or half-remember—I remember or half-remember (and going to my shelves pull down to check out) phrases and scenes from favorite books of my own youth, some of which I have devotedly read and reread ever since, some that have long gathered dust. In Malory's *Morte d' Arthur* or in Tennyson's *Idylls of the King*, I encountered at age eight or nine the form of the myth that returns to me first: the story of Merlin, the aged Wizard of King Arthur's Court, who was charmed out of life though not into death, because he yielded to the erotic charms of Nimue or Nineve or Vivien. The name of his beloved scarcely matters, varying from one version to another. What counts is that she be forever Young, even as he is eternally Old: "Half-suffocated" (Tennyson describes him) "in the heavy fell of many winter'd fleece on throat and chin"; and that entwined in her snake-like arms, he betray to her his ultimate magic. Falling so inappropriately in love, he dooms himself to eternal imprisonment in a cave in Cornwall, or the depths of a magical forest: symbols of the senile impotence from which not even death itself can deliver him.

From the melancholy of Arthurian Romance I then turn, as I turned in my growing up, backward in historical time to Plautus and Terence, whose plays I learned as a college freshman to render into halting English. And I remember how we all laughed together in class, with a heartlessness appropriate to our age, even as the Roman audiences had laughed long before us with a heartlessness appropriate to theirs. And what joins us is a common pleasure at the discomfiture of the *Senex*: the Old Man (presented this time not as a revered Sage, but as a pompous householder, a foolish father, a buffoon) robbed by the wiles of his parasite and his son of some teen-age Prostitute, for whom he had foolishly lusted. Indeed, the popular audience still laughs whenever that stock plot of the Defeated Dodderer is borrowed again by some contemporary hack, just as the Romans had borrowed it earlier from the Greek playwright Menander. What else, indeed, is *A Funny Thing Happened on the Way to the Forum*: a hit on Broadway and, in its movie version, in every small town in America?

That New Comic plot embodies a true myth of the eros of the aging: a myth of the Old Man defeated in his final hybris, as ancient as the culture of what we call the West—and as stubbornly long-lived. Even as I write these words, a scrap of some lost play of Menander is perhaps being dug up from the sands of Egypt; and in some second-run movie house of Buffalo or Milwaukee or Newark, Zero Mostel runs through the streets of a Hollywood version of Rome to cheat the *Senex* of his inappropriate bride, while the satisfied audience chuckles and guffaws. And if those among them clutching the stubs of Golden Age tickets in arthritic hands are somehow disturbed, they scarcely dare admit it even to themselves—lest in so doing they admit that they are the real occasions for the merriment around them.

They may, indeed, feel their own plight as more pathetic than comic; but most men in most times have considered comedy the proper mode for rendering the foredoomed defeat of Old Age in love. It was certainly Chaucer's preferred mode; though in his best-known treatment of the theme, "The Merchant's Tale," he presents it as the comedy of the old husband betrayed rather than that of the old father fooled: a version that still delights audiences, as certain scenes in Richard Lester's recent *The Three Musketeers* attest. January and May, Chaucer allegorically names his ill-assorted pair: a reformed roué of more than sixty and the girl of less than twenty whom he has ill-advisedly chosen as the companion of his declining years. Like Lester, he conceals the pain of cuckoldry in farce—but he also tempers the farce with irony, thus doubly distancing the cuckold's distress. In "The Merchant's Tale," he maintains that ironic tone and the detachment it makes possible by telling his story through an obtuse misogynist who totally identifies with the aging husband.

Yet somehow, behind his unsympathetic back, Chaucer lets us surmise how it felt to the young bride to be possessed by so superannuated an erotic overachiever—primed for the act by all the recommended aphrodisiacs and a desire to prove his unflagging powers. Though we are spared the details of their actual love-making, we learn how it seemed to her to wake and feel his half-shaven bristles on his cheek, and sitting up, to look down on his worn and withered frame. The real as well as the fictional narrator of the tale, however, was not a woman, young or old, but an aging man. And in the end, therefore, we must read the reactions attributed by Chaucer to May as projections of the unconfessed self-hatred and *Schadenfreude* experienced by an old man viewing himself in the mirror of a beloved young girl's eye.

I did not, indeed, realize reading "The Merchant's Tale" at age sixteen what shame and guilt underlie Chaucer's presumably lighthearted tale—and how deep a yearning for self-punishment prompts the final scene of a cuckolding actually witnessed and improbably explained away. Yet just before that scene, as if to give us a clue, the King of Hell and his raped child-bride, Persephone, appear. It is child-rape, then, for which, at the level of fantasy and myth, the Old Man blames himself; though at the level of fact, he may only have seduced or persuaded or bought his bride, who on that level is a woman full-grown, however junior to himself. And in the popular mind, such fantasies become full-blown paranoiac nightmares of the Dirty Old Man luring toddlers into back-alleys with a lollipop.

Nor are such nightmares confined to bar-room or *kaffee klatsch* gossip. Writers close to the mass mind, like Dickens and Dostoevsky, have in novels like *The Old Curiosity Shop* and *The Possessed* turned them into enduring literary images of terror. And in the world of politics, Goebbels helped prepare the German people psychologically for the extermination of the Jews with a series of cartoons in which the dread figure of Father Abraham and the image of the aged violator of children are blended in a horrific unity. For so ultimate an offense, indeed, cuckoldry seems an insufficient punishment. It is death that is demanded, like the awful death of Quilp, the aging pursuer of Little Nell through the pages of *The Old Curiosity Shop*; or more commonly, since the archetype we are exploring seems to have a special affinity with farce and burlesque (even Quilp is finally a comic character), a death in bed, as lust proves too strong for the aging body it suits so ill.

"What a way to go!" male hearers of such tales are likely to comment—but behind their sniggering, there is a shudder, too. A shudder and a laugh. I must confess, indeed, that like everyone else, I, too, even as I approach sixty, find myself laughing at such jokes; since that is one way of pretending that they are about someone else. Nor is it pretending only; for the other at whom we laugh is dead, is he not, and laughing, we know that we are not. Not yet. It is harder, however, to pretend amusement at the version of the myth—almost as common as the one I have been describing—in which the burden of guilt has been shifted from Age to Youth, from Him to Her: the Old Man presented not as Victimizer but Victim.

Not that it is necessary, in order to remain inside the comic frame, for the girl involved to be completely exculpated (obviously in Chaucer she is not), merely that the *Senex* be presented as the chief offender: contemptuous of the conventions by which our society has traditionally dignified both life and death. Comparatively, however, the girl must seem worthy of the Happy Ending which both the *fabliau* and the New Comic versions of the myths provide: the Young in one another's arms—whether in casual intercourse in a flowering pear tree, as in Chaucer; or in the matrimonial bed till death do them part, as in Plautus and Terence. Only the Old Man stands alone—or rather *knows* he stands alone, as, indeed, he should have from the start. At that point the audience, satisfied by the ritual reaffirmation of the generational roles their own deeply buried lusts call into question, rise satisfied, to embrace each other in renewed innocence and laugh all the way home.

But it is quite otherwise in works embodying a myth in which the young girl bears the chief onus of blame—having functioned as a kind of second Eve in the new Fall of Man, irrevocable this time for having occurred in the evening rather than the morning of life. The Legend of Merlin and Nimue, at which we have already glanced, is obviously a prototype of such tales, moving us to tears rather than laughter. And it is perhaps for this reason that it did not really come into its own in the tradition of literature in English until sentimentality had replaced irony and satire as prevailing literary modes. Malory had made very little of it in his fifteenth-century retelling of the Arthurian Romances; but in Victorian times, Tennyson moved Vivien and Merlin to the very center of a long poem on the same theme.

And that archetype has continued to obsess us, particularly as recast in certain popular movies made between World War I and World War II, in which the figure of Vivien blends with that of the "Vamp": that female creature of the Night, who, like her

male predecessor, Dracula, sucks away the life of victims of the
opposite sex. Such films are replayed even now, in part because
some of them can be considered, on formal grounds, "classics";
but in even greater part because the mythic material they contain
seems to us ever more relevant as more and more of us live
longer and longer—sometimes long enough to outlive our original
mates, more often long enough to exhaust the passion that orig-
inally brought us together. For such aging survivors, what we like
to call the new "sexual permissiveness" brings confusion rather
than freedom; since by downgrading traditional ideals of con-
tinence and fidelity, it compels the elderly, when death draws
nearer and physical beauty fades (in themselves and in their
original mates), to keep performing the ever less convincing role
of lovers with ever more incongruous partners.

The Blue Angel is for me the most memorable of such films,
for in it the figure of the young Vamp (elsewhere degraded into
the comic-strip stereotype of the Golddigger mercilessly milking
her mindless Sugar Daddy) is raised by the acting of Marlene
Dietrich to the highest archetypal power, so that the original
frisson of the myth is preserved. And it is similarly preserved
beneath all the horseplay of the movie made from Vladimir
Nabokov's *Lolita* (though the age of his heroine has been
changed from thirteen to sixteen, thus losing one main significance of the novel). The astonishing success of Nabokov's book
(his only bestseller, because alone among his books it evokes
archetypal material available to the largest audience) is due, I
am convinced, to the fact that in it he challenged, travestied,
inverted, the horror at the heart of the Myth of Old Age in Love,
the nightmare of child-rape—by making the nymphet the seducer,
and the old (or at least aging) male a double dupe for having
believed to begin with that he was victimizer rather than victim.

At any rate, one function of both these films is to allay by dis-
placement the guilt felt by elderly lovers; but, as it turns out, the
guilt only and not the *shame*. Recalling *The Blue Angel*, I am
aware how beneath its surfaces of misogyny, beneath even the
fear of sexuality which that misogyny is intended to disguise,
there persists a bittersweet celebration of the contempt felt—not
so much by the sleek Sirens with unfallen breasts to whom it is
attributed as by Old Men themselves, contemplating the ruin of

their bodies, which our culture has taught them so extravagantly to prize, and on which therefore their self-definition as males depends.

The passage in which that self-hatred and the obscene joy felt by the author recording it is most vividly expressed is to be found in Thomas Mann's *Death in Venice*, a prescient little book published when he was not quite forty. From it I cannot resist quoting at length, in the hope that that quotation will be reinforced by recollected images out of Visconti's rather heavy-handed film version, which in this scene at least, seems all the more effective for its lack of subtlety. "In the light of the sweet youthfulness which had done this to him," Mann writes of his aging protagonist, who at this point knows he is hopelessly, irrecoverably in love with a beautiful and indifferent young boy, "he detested his aging body. The sight of his gray hair, his sharp features plunged him into shame and hopelessness. It induced him to attempt rejuvenating his body and appearance. He often visited the hotel barber."

And then Mann renders one such scene with the barber, in which Aschenbach is persuaded to disguise the fading of his flesh with cosmetics.

> And like someone who cannot finish, cannot satisfy himself, he passed with quickening energy from one manipulation to another. . . . In the glass he saw his brows arch more evenly and decisively. His eyes became longer; their brilliance was heightened by a light touching up of the lids. A little lower, where the skin had been a leatherish brown, he saw a delicate crimson tint grow beneath a deft application of color. His lips, bloodless a little while past, became full, and as red as raspberries. The furrows in the cheeks and about the mouth, the wrinkles of the eyes, disappeared beneath lotions and creams. With a knocking heart he beheld a blossoming youth.

But, of course, Mann's victim-hero cannot grasp the elusive phantom of youth and beauty in a grotesque mask of youth and beauty that dissolves (as Mann never troubles to tell us, but Visconti makes explicit) under the heat of the plague-ridden city through which he pursues the boy. Not until he learns what he—painted not like a lover but a corpse—has really been pursuing, can Ashenbach attain his true desire. He last sees the madly desired youth on a sandbar, separated from where he sits in a beachchair by a strip of water,

> a strongly isolated and unrelated figure with fluttering hair—placed out there in the sea, the wind against the vague mists. . . . And suddenly, as though at some recollection, some impulse, with one hand on his hip he turned the upper part of his body in a beautiful twist which began from the base—and he looked over his shoulder toward the shore. The watcher sat there, as he had sat once before when for the first time these twilight-gray eyes had turned at the doorway and met his own. His head, against the back of the chair, had slowly followed the movements of the boy walking yonder . . . it seemed to him as though, removing his hand from his hip, he were signaling to come out, were vaguely guiding toward egregious promise. And, as often before, he stood up to follow him. Some minutes passed before anyone hurried to the aid of the man who had collapsed into one corner of his chair . . .

It is a conclusion tranquil and almost religious in tone, quite unprepared for, it long seemed to me, by the grotesqueness and horror of the immediately preceding scenes. Yet it is, at the deepest levels, satisfactory and even credible, like the improbably Happy Endings of Shakespeare's last plays: true, if not to fact, at least to the wish that cues our dreams. Shakespeare, however, in spite of his own homoerotic sensibility, never granted to any of his homosexual lovers (think, for instance, of the two Antonios in *The Merchant of Venice* and *Twelfth Night,* closed out by the Happy Endings of everyone else, and abandoned on the empty stage without lines) the benison of a peaceful death. Indeed, the only equivalent I know to the last pages of *Death in Venice* appears in Ronald Firbank's now almost forgotten novel, *The Eccentricities of Cardinal Pirelli,* published in 1926. Dead at the age of thirty-nine, but obsessed always by the eros of old age (the heroine of his first novel is 120), Firbank, like Mann, deals with the passion that drives a reverend and aged man vainly to pursue —in this case through the aisles of a baroque church—a teasing and heartless boy. We last see his obsessed Cardinal, dead at the foot of an altar, but beatific and presumably blessed, though stripped naked of all his regalia except for his mitre, and (we are led to surmise) unrepentantly erect to the end. "Now that the ache of life," Firbank tells us, "with its fevers, passions, doubts, its routines, vulgarity, and boredom, was over, his serene unclouded face was marvelous to behold. Very great distinction and sereneness was visible there, together with much nobility, and love, all magnified and commingled."

It is an ending which suggests that the most outrageous of loves—breaking those mythologically reinforced taboos which in our culture forbid the consummation he sought on the grounds of holy celibacy as well as the identity of sex—can itself be a sacrament: self-transcending, so long as it debouches not in penetration and orgasm but in frustration and death. For a closed circle of upper-class English aesthetes to which Firbank belonged in the years just after World War I, so paradoxical a conclusion may have worked; as it may work again for future generations, whose deepest fantasies and guilts have been radically altered by the Gay Movement and the revolt against the celibacy of the clergy. But how could I have responded to it: a good Jewish boy from Newark, New Jersey, headed—I was certain—for a life of heterosexuality; and convinced that only the kind of Dirty Old Men who otherwise exposed themselves to little girls at play or sat with hats in their laps at pornographic movies could contemplate a union with a fellow male young enough to be their child. Indeed, for me, pederasty doubly compounded the heinousness of the act—as I suspect it still does, in their deep psyches, for most of those who will read this paper.

That this was not always the case, I knew well enough even then. And Mann reminds us of this when he permits Aschenbach to call his beloved Tadzio, in the privacy of his own head, "Phaedrus", a name which refers us back to the Platonic dialogue that opens with a discussion about whether it is better to be a lover, which is to say, old and wise like Socrates, or the beloved, which is to say, young and desirable like Phaedrus. And thinking of Plato, we are likely to remember the *Symposium* and the ancient Greek myth of Two Loves: one heterosexual, earthbound and leading to marriage; the other homosexual, "heavenly" and eventuating in a relationship in which the older lover repays the younger for his carnal favors by instructing him in dialectic and a knowledge of the "true gods." Even for Plato, however, that second or "higher" kind of love still binds the lover to the material world, until he learns to transcend his attachment to a particular individual and, indeed, to the flesh itself, by lusting only for the Ideal Form of Beauty, Beauty in the abstract.

In Judaeo-Christian culture, however, it is forbidden even to begin the ascent toward wisdom with a pederastic attachment, and in the secular culture which succeeds it, with any passion, heterosexual or homosexual, that joins the very old and very young.[2] But *why*? Whence that basically irrational taboo? The answer surely must lie somewhere in the texts I have already evoked; but to unriddle them further I must go deeper—back to more primal forms of song and story: back to the fairy tales that preceded them in history as well as the personal experience of us all.

Long before we read Malory or Tennyson or Shakespeare, much less, Thomas Mann or Ronald Firbank, we were exposed to those Old Wives Tales in which some nubile girl is sealed into a tower, or set high on an unclimbable hill, or kept from marriage with someone of her own age until an improbable task is accomplished or a riddle answered: kept, in short, in the power of the Old Man, *her* Old man, who, indeed, proposes that task or asks that riddle. The incestuous base of such restraints is, though clearly implied, typically not made explicit in fairy tales, in which, despite their lack of secondary elaboration, a kind of primary censorship is at work. And, in any case, what chiefly concerns the tellers of such tales is not the cause of the life-inhibiting taboo with which they begin, but the means by which some Young Lover breaks through to the Happy Ending in which Boy gets Girl—which is to say, the Son wins the Daughter from the Father.

There are, of course, a few stories in which the Father-Daughter incest which cues the plot is stated overtly, most notably *"Peau de l'ane,"* "The Ass's Skin," a favorite always of the French. Not only was it included in the first printed collection of such material, Perrault's seventeenth-century *Tales of My Mother Goose*; it was also turned into a movie for the Parisian Christmas trade in the early 1970s. And the märchen subplot in Shakespeare's *Pericles* reveals that the riddle asked by the wicked King Antiochus of the suitors for his daughter's hand deals precisely with their long-continued incest, for which, in due course, both father and daughter are burned to death by fire from Heaven. Indeed, Claude Lévi-Strauss argues (and I, for one, believe) that all fairy-tale riddles, whatever their manifest content, conceal the same guilty secret. "Between the puzzle solution and incest," he writes, "there exists a relationship, not external and of fact, but internal and of reason."

Moreover, when Sigmund Freud recast such mythic stuff as psychohistory in *Totem and Taboo*, he turned it into an account of the creation of the Nuclear Family by the imposition of an incest-taboo. In his latter-day fairy tale, the Ogre-Father-Chieftain is overcome by his sons, bent on depriving him of the right to breed new daughters out of his own daughters and daughters' daughters for as long as he survives. And to prevent such girls' ever falling back into the hands of that "single powerful violent and suspicious Old Man" (the description comes to Freud from Darwin), those son-brothers ban him from possessing *any* young female in his power. But it is precisely such taboos which actual Old Men seem to threaten by reaching out to take—by dint of wealth or power or cunning accumulated in time—actual girls young enough to be their daughters. (Think, for instance, of the horrific scene in Norman Mailer's *Deer Park* in which the Movie Producer, the Old Man on his executive throne, forces some barely nubile starlet to kneel between his legs and satisfy his aging desire.)

Nonetheless, the lust of aging males—still fertile at an age when the women with whom they have grown old have ceased to ovulate—draws them, despite themselves, toward fertile girls they might have fathered; so that not merely the fantasy, most often punished in dream and story, but the fact, more often than not undetected and unpunished, of father-daughter incest persists still in many parts of the world. It must be, then, its analogy with this abhorred yet irrepressible relationship that makes the passion of Old men for Young girls both suspect and alluring. But if this is the only, or primary, cause of the taboo we have been examining, why should their lust for Young boys be felt as equally or more dangerous? (Not even Freud at his most flagrantly mythopoeic has suggested that father-son incest was once a part of human life.) James Joyce says on this subject a word from which it is hard to demur:

They are sundered by a bodily shame so steadfast that the criminal annals of the world, stained with all other incests and bestialities, hardly record its breach. Sons with mothers, sires with daughters, sesbic sisters, loves that dare not speak their name, nephews with grandmothers, jailbirds with keyholes, queens with prize bulls . . .

In light of this, it seems to me that the father-daughter incest-taboo represents not an ultimate ground of explanation for our fear of intergenerational sex, but only another metaphor for the ultimate yearning of aging males to recapture simultaneously those beloved women of their youth whose flesh has withered with their own, and the mother they have never really known, the Virgin Mother, lost forever with the act of love to which they owe their own begetting, except as reborn in the Virgin Daughter, their sisters or their own female children. The latter fantasy is captured with confusing religious overtones in Ingmar Bergman's *Wild Strawberries*, and rendered more nakedly manifest in "The Ass's Skin," in which a Fairy Tale King promises to his Queen dying in childbirth to remain faithful to her memory until he meets a woman as beautiful as she—who turns out to be, of course, the very daughter whose birth has meant her death.

But also, and even more poignantly perhaps, the eros of old men yearns to repossess that ambiguous beauty they themselves once possessed—or come at least to believe in age they did possess in youth—attractive to male and female alike. If it is this perhaps imaginary lost androgyny they long to recapture, young males on the border between boyhood and manhood might well satisfy their desire better than any girl. But the kind of union between consenting adults of the same sex permitted these days by enlightened communities will not do. Only pederasty, a relationship between an older man and a boy, is an appropriate equivalent. The Judaeo-Christian tradition, however, has imposed upon that relationship a taboo even more fearsome than that which forbids incest. "He who has offended the least of my little ones, it were better for him that a millstone were about his neck and he were cast into the sea." No wonder, then, that in the hierarchy of mythological horrors, the rapist of little boys ranks even lower than the violater of small girls.

And yet a hunger so deeply implanted in us that it can be

denied only by denying our full humanity demands to be rescued, not only from rigid and obsolescent morality, but from the historical process in which archetypes, subtle and ambiguous, have turned in time into gross stereotypes, in which the aged man in love, that is, undignified and out of control, is vilified and caricatured. Such stereotypes serve to reinforce the indignities visited upon the aged by those whose perceptions of them are hopelessly warped by contradictory impulses in themselves with which they never quite come to terms. And worse, they reinforce the self-hatred of the aged themselves. Is there, then, no positive, life-enhancing way to get out of the trap—to transcend the conflict between the imperiousness of carnal desire and the fragility of the flesh to which I alluded at the beginning of these remarks?

In more traditional societies, ritual has presumably served such ends, myth ceremonially performed rather than expressed in secular song and story. But my one brief encounter with a surviving rite of this kind has left me unconvinced that such a strategy could ever have made possible the degree of transcendence we nostalgically attribute to it. Or perhaps in present-day Nepal—where only a few years ago I paid my rupee with her other worshippers and saw the seven-year-old Living Goddess plain—the ritual has become decadent as well as commercialized. In that time-trapped country, at any rate, an Avatar of the Goddess is still selected, when the occasion arises, from a list of girl-children born to certain qualified families. The candidates must be, first of all, very young, with many years left still between them and puberty, at whose onset their reign ceases; and they must also be able to look on unflinching as scores, even hundreds, of sheep and goats are ritually slaughtered in an enclosed courtyard, where the blood of the sacrifice finally mounts up over their feet.

The girl finally chosen is ceremonially robed, her face painted in a mask-like simulacrum of something sexually alluring, though rather equivocal in gender. She is then confined for as long as her tenure lasts to the Sacred Chambers, where she can be looked at by many (for a fee, through a window and from below) but touched only by the aging Priests, who practise with her, on her, certain Tantric sexual rites, about which much is whispered by the uninitiated but little precisely known. What is ceremonially re-enacted in such rites seems to me to be the fantasy of child-rape, the erotic myth of female innocence possessed by male experience. It is all, however, if not exactly chaste, at least genitally ambiguous and satisfactorily sterile, since the Girl-Goddess is prenubile (at the first emission of menstrual blood she is dethroned and her successor selected), and the Priests who possess her have been trained to withhold their semen in the act of love. Indeed, such retention of the seed is for the followers of the Tantric Way a supreme form of spiritual *askesis,* as well as a source of earthly delight: unendurable pleasure indefinitely prolonged—in this case, between the Old Man and the Child, the dying human and the immortal Goddess.

But the reigning Avatar is only ritually, mythologically divine, even before menarche, so that when recently the seven-year-old incumbent was visited by a journalist (a young woman, by the way) from India, she gave the ritual game away. At first the Living Goddess spurned in dignified silence the candy with which her interviewer had hoped to bribe her into speech. But at the very last moment, she grabbed it, crying to that interviewer's departing back, "Next time bring me a doll," which is to say, a symbolic baby to mother and nurse. But even after she has been declared empty of the Divine Presence and released to the secular world, the ex-Avatar—despite the fact that it was the onset of fertility which ungodded her—is unlikely ever to have a real baby. Whatever the Old Priests may declare, she remains for ordinary males forever taboo, precisely for having performed over and over with those Priests the nightmare of child-violation. Indeed, the two Avatars who preceded the reigning Goddess are, at the present moment, working the streets of Kathmandu as prostitutes, which seems to me somehow fair enough. Are not whores, after all, no matter how young and attractive, available to all men with their price in hand, no matter how old and hideous? And do they not, therefore, represent in fallen form a ritual more ancient even than that of Nepal, in which on the steps of the Temple of the Great Goddess, her acoltyes honored with their bodies all males still potent and willing, no matter how close they stood to death.

And that ritual persists among us still, does it not, though it has grown ever more degraded as the whorehouse replaced the

Temple; and the act once considered sacred has become, therefore, a dirty joke. Reflecting on the theme, I find myself recalling
(in a conjunction odd but somehow appropriate) scenes from my
earliest adolescence in Newark, New Jersey, when—in the same
candy store where "eight pagers," erotic parodies of current
comic strips, were peddled under the counter, and the corner
cop was nightly implored to lay his magnificent *shlang* on the
table to be wondered at by all—two old lechers called, like a pair
of burlesque comedians, Klein and Schlein (how incredibly
ancient their sixty-five or seventy years seemed to me at fourteen
or fifteen) would talk, making the only poetry in their power,
about some young girl they had bought the night before, moist
and open as their wives no longer were: some fabulous *shikse*
"with a *tuchas* as white as gold." And how could I know—any
more than they—that it was an Avatar of the Goddess whom
they sought in parody. I only despised them then as Dirty Old
Men, believing that, so close to their own deaths, the heyday of
their blood should have been long since tamed.

Ignorant kid, I had not yet learned (and what would I have
done with the information in any case?) that the Triple Goddess
in her third and final form is called not just Persephone but *Kore*,
meaning the Daughter; and that in this form she presides over
the laying out of the dead—stands, in fact, for Death itself:
Death as Love, Love as Death, the Daughter as Death, Death as
the Daughter. Such a theological interpretation of the myth, I
warn you, however, is not, for me, a satisfactory ending to my
search, only another metaphorical simplification of the mystery:
a way of achieving peace, not by a true resolution of warring
Eros and Thanatos, but by the elimination of one of its poles. "If
the eye offend, pluck it out." It is to a poet, therefore, rather
than a prophet or a priest that I propose to turn in conclusion—
to Shakespeare, who all his life long wrestled with the problem
of "crabbed age" in love with youth, and who in *The Tempest*
came as close as any man can to transcending the dilemma that
relationship figures forth.

From the beginning of his career, Shakespeare confronted the
dilemma in its two primary mythic forms, as pederasty and incest:
the love of an older man for an unattainable boy, and the strange
unwillingness of fathers to release their nubile daughters to mar-

riage and motherhood. About the former, the society he lived in was equivocal; for though the Church condemned it and the State exacted the death penalty for practicing it, overt homosexuality was the preferred erotic mode of much of the aristocracy and of James I himself, while the neo-Platonic Academies of the time called on the *Symposium* to justify their contempt for women and their preference for each other. Besides, the theater of Shakespeare's day was a constant provocation, with boy actors playing sometimes boys and sometimes girls, but especially girls pretending to be on stage the boys they really were off it: boy-girls, girl-boys—fit symbols for youthful beauty and the unlimited possibilities of polymorphous perverse pleasure.

Yet in the most confessional of all his works, the *Sonnets*, Shakespeare makes it clear that even the notion of a "pure" or Uranian Love, which is to say, homosexual love without final physical consummation, is a delusion and a trap, a way to mutual betrayal and self-deceit, since what it really embodies is a desire to end all begetting: which is to say, total death. And in the mouth of Antonio—his surrogate in *The Merchant of Venice*, who in his heart wants to abort the Happy Ending of the play by keeping Bassanio for himself—Shakespeare passes sentence on all in his own heart which is similarly inclined. "I am a tainted wether of the flock," Antonio says, "meetest for death." But even Antonio's desire to die for his beloved youth Shakespeare seems to find a last sentimental self-indulgence. And he grants him, therefore, no such consummation—only abandonment and a continuing life alone, when at the close Bassanio gets Portia, or rather, she him.

With the meaning of father-daughter incest, however, especially in its typically attenuated form of "All right, marry then, if you have to, but not *him*," or "Say at least that you love your papa more," he apparently had more difficulty in coming to terms. Whatever sympathy he expresses for those of his young heroines who flee their fathers for their lovers' sake, he seems to have found it hard to let them escape scot-free. Some, to be sure, he permits conventional Happy Endings, when the New Comic form of his inherited material offers him no alternative. But he condemns as many more to death, when the plot can be wrenched to allow it; not only in tragedies like *Othello* ("She has deceived her father and may thee," Iago says, preparing for the bloody dénouement), *Hamlet* and *King Lear* (in which Shakespeare actually changed the ending of his source in order to give Cordelia her due comeuppance), but even in that odd failed comedy, *Romeo and Juliet*.

Only late in his life, when he is writing *Pericles*, does Shakespeare become fully aware that what had seemed to him earlier, in the continual father-daughter crises of his plays, chiefly the fault of the strong-willed daughter is primarily, or even solely, the responsibility of the father. Like those fictional fathers, Shakespeare was for a long time unable to realize the implications of the reluctance he presumably shared with them to relinquish his child to someone of her own generations, whom she might love more dearly, and who would in any case outlive him. But contemplating the mythic materials in the old legend of Apollonius of Tyre, on which he drew for *Pericles*, he seems to have learned that the desire to keep the daughter implies also the desire to beget on her new daughters, and on them new daughters still, which in turn implies an unwillingness to accept one's own death, a delusive dream of immortality in the flesh. The mythic meaning of father-daughter incest seems, then, to be in one sense the opposite of that of pederasty. But in another, deeper sense, they are complementary, two sides of a single coin, since both the dream of embracing death in the form of a beardless boy and that of forestalling it indefinitely in the arms of an ever-renewed bride represent a refusal to grow old, to accept man's fate. "We must endure our going hence even as our coming hither," Shakespeare had already written at this point; but that wisdom both the pederast and the incestuous father deny.

Not so Prospero, of course, who at the beginning of *The Tempest* has been granted by a series of events beyond his control the dream of all concupiscent fathers: finding himself as old age approaches the sole human male on a desert island with his nubile daughter. To be sure, there is also Ariel, a spirit of air and fire, which is to say, a duplicate *anima* figure to Miranda, and one almost equally dear to him. Indeed, Prospero bestows more endearments on him than on her, for Ariel is a "he," a boy-actor, in fact, though he plays only female parts in the little plays which Prospero mounts within the larger play, and is usually portrayed by a woman on the modern stage. He symbolizes, in short, the fulfillment of the pederast's fantasy in which the beloved boy is no heartless flirt, but a slave subservient to his master's every wish.

And finally, there is that grosser spirit, Caliban, the would-be rapist of Miranda, whom Prospero from time to time forgets, wants to forget, since he stands for dark incestuous wishes in himself which up to the last possible moment he resists admitting. It is, however, the unexpected reappearance of that phallic monster which disrupts his Wedding Masque: the pageant which so improbably evisages a union of male and female, fertile and long-lasting but without passion. And the unforeseen interruption reminds him therefore not only of the absurdity of his Futopian vision of marriage, but also (for reasons which should be clear at this point) of the fact that he has grown old and feeble, and must therefore complete his tasks without delay. "Bear with my weakness," he says to his prospective son-in-law, "My old brain is troubled. Be not disturbed with my infirmity."

And what remains to do in the little time left him is precisely to destroy the self-serving double dream of earthly bliss with which the play begins: to disenchant his enemies, and give away to one of them (the chosen lover of the daughter belongs always, mythologically speaking, to the Enemy Camp) his beloved Miranda; then to free his "chuck," Ariel; and by abjuring the potent magic which can make reality conform to wish, or seem to ("I'll break my staff . . . And deeper than did ever plummet sound/I'll drown my book . . . "), insure that his return to the real world of Naples and Milan can never be revoked or reversed. In that world he foresees himself not just presiding at the marriage, the going away of the daughter he so long feared but finally, with only token resistance, allowed, but beyond that, devoting his last days to meditating on his impending and now accepted end: "And hence return me to my Milan, when/Every third thought shall be my grave."

Only Caliban canot—even at the moment of reconciliation and acceptance—be given away to another, or remanded to the elements from which he came; for unlike Miranda and Ariel, that rebellious creature dreaming the daughter's rape is bound to Prospero till death do them part. "This thing of darkness I/

Acknowledge mine . . ." Prospero is driven at last to admit, thus confessing that the uncontrollable sexuality which has threatened both his own dignity and the innocence of his daughter is something neither monstrous nor alien, but human and his own. And what, then, is left to add, as he stands alone with this hard-won wisdom on a stage deserted by all the other characters, except the even more difficult truth, which that first confession has somehow made easier to confront—

> . . . Now I want
> Spirits to enforce, art to enchant,
> And my ending is despair
> Unless I be relieved by prayer . . .

Notes

1. There are, to be sure, literary works in which the marriage of Youth and Age is presented as a viable Happy Ending: in certain late novels of Dickens, for instance, and—at the very last moment—in Shakespeare's *Measure for Measure*. But such wishful projections have never assumed the status or ubiquity of true myths, that is, widely shared communal dreams.

2. In this paper I have limited myself to a consideration of the myths of the Old which bear on this taboo. For a treatment of the complementary myths of the Child which reinforce it, I refer the reader to Philippe Ariès *Centuries of Childhood: A Social History of Family Life*, trans. Robert Baldick (New York: Knopf, 1962), and to my own essay, "The Invention of the Child."

FRANCIS V. O'CONNOR

ALBERT BERNE AND THE COMPLETION OF BEING: IMAGES OF VITALITY AND EXTINCTION IN THE LAST PAINTINGS OF A NINETY-SIX-YEAR-OLD MAN

I have been busy painting and struggling with its many problems which afford much fun and a challenge. [23 May 1960] I thank you two old friends for helping and teaching me to see things to paint—and so many things that go with painting and things to avoid—at 86 years—painting and sketching keep me busy and interested—always with a desire to improve—*always* —what will Carolyn and Carl say of this or that picture just finished and often sweated over. You can understand how much your opinion means to me? [20 August 1963] To the studio—to wrestle and swear—paint things over, dozens of times—hoping for a good reasonable result—It's great fun. [15 July 1964] I am sure the art world will be put into a spasm of mayhem—even—*silence* [when a painting of his appears in the Cincinnati Art Club exhibition]. It's fun to be alive and contributing something, however little, *but still something.* [19 September 1966] I have been painting—almost daily—the paintings are strong, even powerful, different in composition, color and what have you—no old man's stuff—laff at this— However—I love to paint—it's part of my life—but after finishing a canvas—I always hope—the next one will be better. Still so much to learn. [10 August 1969] When asked—I say— I am not an amateur nor a professional—nor a hobbyist or a Sunday painter—I'm a free lance and paint because I love it so. [23 June 1971] I paint one masterpiece a day—could do more but must not tax my strength. . . . I slap on the paint—it looks like an oil—and I just love to paint. Sometimes I can hardly believe that an old duffer now in his 97th year can love to paint. [3 October 1973]

> Excerpts from letters by Albert Berne, aged eighty-three to ninety-six, to his friend and teacher, Carl Zimmerman, and his wife.[1]

The happy old man who wrote these letters to his painting teacher died at the age of ninety-six on 22 December 1973. He would often tell his family, "I think that these paintings may mean something to someone some day."[2] What Albert Berne contributed to our understanding of the last phase of the human life cycle and of the painting process he loved is the subject of this study.

Biography

Albert Berne was born on 9 August 1877 in Cincinnati, Ohio, the only child of Rudolph John and Thecla Mosser Berne. As a young boy he was drawn to music, and in 1895, at the age of eighteen, he enrolled in the Cincinnati Conservatory of Music. After graduating he taught voice (he was a baritone) and piano at small colleges in his native state and at the Conservatory. About 1902 he went to Germany (his first language was German), where he studied piano in Berlin with the famous teacher Heinrich Barth. A fellow pupil was the young Artur Rubinstein. He was an avid traveler in Europe, sometimes taking off for months on walking tours through Germany and Switzerland. He loved to climb in the Alps—an experience reflected, as we shall see below, in the compositional matrix of his last paintings. He would also have been aware in his travels of the radical ferment in the arts—especially painting and music—in Europe during the years before the First World War. He returned to Cincinnati and resumed his singing and teaching, introducing German lieder into the standard repertory of his city's concert halls. During the war years he lived in New York. In 1923, at forty-six, he married Lucile Kroger, the daughter of a wealthy Cincinnati merchant. Thus, for the last fifty years of his life he was financially secure, with homes in his native city and at Chatham, Massachusetts. He had two sons: Albert, Jr., and John Henry. His wife died in 1932. The next year, on the advice of a physician, Dr. Rockwell Coffin, who thought it would ease his loneliness and bereavement, he began to paint. He was fifty-six. He studied first under the illustrator Harold Brett on Cape Cod and later at the Cincinnati Art Academy with Frank Myers. During the early 1940s he worked with the Cincinnati painter Carl Zimmerman. His training was essentially academic, and until the end of his life he would lay out a full palette before begining to work and, the next day, study what he had done in a frame for "retouching." His earliest paintings were, as might be expected, representational, carefully composed, meticulously rendered landscapes and still lifes—the subjects an academic amateur selects. As he grew older, however, his paintings became more intense, progressively more abstract, though never renouncing reference to nature. It was his habit to paint one work each day, a ritual which grew more and more set as he aged. He showed his work locally in Ohio and in Province-town, Massachusetts, during the summers he was at Chatham.

As he stated in the letter to Zimmerman quoted above, he did not view himself as either an amateur or a professional artist. He did not paint for money. He would not permit a price to be placed on any work of his exhibited. Neither did he have any thought of becoming a famous artist. He was, simply, a "free lance" in the purest sense of the dictionary definition of the term: "A person who acts on his own responsibility without regard to authority." He traveled from canvas to canvas, conquering each for the sake of the struggle and the challenge of it all. He painted because he loved to paint and for no more purpose than he dreamed. Indeed, having these canvases is comparable to having the record of a ninety-six-year-old man's concluding dreams, and it is in this context that we will consider them: the map of the unconscious culmination of a beautiful life, fully and sensitively lived, and made visually explicit at the end.[3]

During the winter of 1972–73, Berne suffered a serious illness and barely survived. In May 1973 he requested to be taken to Chatham. He tentatively resumed painting in June, creating three paintings that month. The last of these was a vertical landscape with a dark disk in the sky. It is dated 30 June and begins the sequence of paintings studied here. (See plate 1.) For the next 162 days—that is, from 1 July to 9 December—he painted 147 canvases, missing only 7 days for a trip and 8 days because of illness. He was generally so weak physically that his servants had to support him from his bedroom to his chair. His hands were so delicate that he wore protective gloves. Yet he was able to pour all his life's energy into one hour's painting a day, com-

Plate 1

pletely covering a canvas that averaged about four and a half square feet in area. Anyone who has ever painted a picture, or even tried to cover a wall with one color, can understand the remarkable feat of will performed daily by this feeble man up to thirteen days before his death.

Sometime in the course of painting these pictures, Berne told his son Henry that he was pleased that his easel had been moved from his studio, which he was too weak to reach, to an area just outside the door of his bedroom. He was grateful because he could paint, and he told his son that if he could not paint he would not have "anything to show for his time." This simple statement can, I think, be translated into Erik Erikson's rubric for the integrity of the aged: "I am what survives me." Berne had a deep conviction that what he was painting was important for others—though his son Henry, who holds a Ph.D in mythology, reports he could not articulate the symbolism of his work, nor would he happily brook filial hermeneutics. He also had the strength—and I again use Erikson's terms—to fuse the "generativity" of his maturity with the "integrity" of his old age.[4] The paintings he created to justify his last days can now serve us, and so some brief comments on their style, technique, and compositional devices, and some more extensive commentaries on their content, are in order.

Style, Technique, and Compositional Matrix

Those familiar with the styles of twentieth-century painting will recognize in Albert Berne's work the very strong "influence" of German Expressionism. This was a man who spoke German as a first language, who was thoroughly aware of turn-of-the-century German culture, and who seemed, as he grew older, to turn to the visual radicals of his youth for a stylistic vocabulary. The color and forms of Wassily Kandinsky, August Macke, Emil Nolde, and the French Fauves, who were strongly influenced by the Germans, can be found in his work.

His last paintings are on "canvas board" (that is, commercially primed canvas pasted to stiff pasteboard rather than stretched on wooden supports). He used water-based acrylic paints, which permitted a wide range of bright, permanent colors, a heavy paint quality (impasto) comparable to oils, and quick drying, which facilitated the "retouching" ritual. He systematically alternated vertical (28" × 22", or 4.3 square feet) and horizontal (24" × 30", or 5 square feet) canvases and would finish each, except occasionally for the signature, in one sitting. He was assisted by his housekeeper, who prepared his palette, washed his brushes, and, at times, "retouched" small areas and lettered in the signature under his meticulous supervision.[5]

His colors are always bright and fresh—almost Fauve in their intensity—and skillfully orchestrated between warm and cool. As he progresses through late summer into autumn to early winter, however, this color balance can be observed to evolve with the seasons: deep and lush during the summer, hot red, orange, and yellow in the fall, and cooler tonalities for winter. He was thus conscious of the cycle of nature around him on his six-acre estate and reflected that awareness in his last works. Not surprisingly, his most iconographically rich paintings occur in the autumn, when, as we shall see, he dies symbolically with nature.[6]

The formal elements of Berne's last works fall into a basic compositional matrix that he used in almost every painting. (The exceptions will be discussed later.) This basic configuration, inspired by traditional landscape painting, can be schematically diagrammed as in Figure 1.

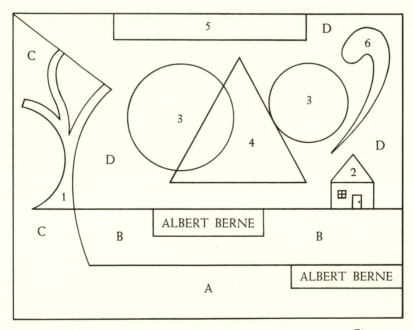

Figure 1

The basic rectangle, whether vertical or horizontal, is divided into three levels: a ground plane of earth and foliage (A), an intermediate realm of light blue entering from the right (B) to meet a traditional area at the left (C), which leads the eye to the upper half of each work (D), where it enters the most important area of the composition. This area sometimes "reads" as sky, as in traditional landscapes, sometimes as a towering mountain range seen from the opposite shore of a blue lake. Most often, however, the visual cues of ordinary landscape experience break down, and the eye enters an ambiguously situated visionary realm filled with swirling colors and hieratic, symbolic images painted with overwhelming dynamism. This imagery should be discussed in detail.

Imagery

In discussing the imagistic content of Berne's last paintings, insights from the study of children's art and from Jungian psychology's sense of the continuity of iconic material, both in history and in the individual psyche, will be employed where useful. In respect to children's art, however, a paragraph from a book on art therapy, Maria Petrie's *Art and Regeneration*, raises an important point in contrast to the method used here. A passionate argument for studying the art of children, it contains the following typical statement.

> The most fruitful object of psychological research, however, is the young child, in whom the emotional life is as yet uncontrolled by the intellect and is not yet crisscrossed with the million threads of knowledge and memory.[7]

The task here—the task of interpreting the art of old age—requires encounter with that controlling intellect and the web of erudition and recollection preserved in, and in many ways determining, the acts of the venerable individual. If the child is (for argument's sake) a *tabula rasa*, the old man or woman is the exact opposite. Where the child's acquired repertory of images is restricted by experience and kinesthetics, the ancient's is vast and complex. The difference is between discovery and discrimination—finding and selection. The intellectual dichotomy is between the "oneness" of childhood's perspective and the multiplicity of sensibility in the old—between a sense of self as cosmos and a sense of self in history and society. The psychic situation is, however, the same. The need for symbolic focus remains at both poles of life. Here the aged have the advantage of their own inner history. Their selection of images will be as rich and varied as that history. The numinosity of those images will depend on the depth of unconscious experience. The deeper, the simpler: the iconic choices are made from a wisdom which has transcended all artificial complexities. To mistake this process for the simplicities of childhood is to misconstrue and demean old age. In his masterful essay "Art and Time," Erich Neumann states that art made in the creative solitude of the Great Old Men

> no longer relates either consciously or unconsciously to any historical time; the solitary monologue of these "extreme" works is spoken, as it were, into the void. And one cannot quite tell whether it is a monologue or a dialogue between man and the ultimate. Hence the alienation of these great men from their contemporaries—they all, like the aged Laotse, have left the mountain pass of the world behind them.[8]

The images which appear in the upper half of Berne's paintings (D) are sometimes representational, such as trees (1) and houses (2), and sometimes abstract circles and triangles (3 and 4), or a narrow, dark rectangle entering from the top (5). In a few paintings, strongly delineated symbols such as phalli, boats, serpent shapes, numbers, and vestigial human figures appear.

Another important factor is the artist's signature, which travels about as a "cartouche" in areas A and B, with its usual base in the academically conventional lower right corner and its upper limit dead center in the blue area (see diagram). The signature thus becomes a dynamic formal element in each composition, waxing and waning as the symbolic situation warrants.

Berne's repertory of images takes on a generalized significance when each element is related to the broad tradition of Western iconography. The next step is to establish a meaningful context for each image.

CIRCLES AND OTHER OVALS These forms relate to the universal symbolism of the sun as the source of light and energy. These "circles of life," as I shall call them, are always some variant on the image of the circle suspended over an element—usually horizontal—below it. They are thus to be distinguished from the more internally articulated mandalas, though both images have similar symbolic overtones. The circle of life appears in the lyre-crown of the Egyptian goddess Hathor, goddess of love, music, and light. It is also found in the familiar halo around the head of Christ and the saints.

The frontality of the circle of life is a dimension of its power. I have found that this configuration of the circle over the horizontal is the symbolic matrix of the frontal self-portrait. Plane of brow and shoulders parallel to the picture plane, this image of a face staring straight out has an impact far beyond the usual three-quarter view. Artists create such portraits at turning points in life, where the total personality must literally renew itself, confirm itself—face iteslf. Artists as distant in time as Dürer and Mondriaan painted such portraits at the point of transition from youth to maturity. The same circle of life latent in these frontal self-portraits can be found in abstract paintings done at similar points of passage in the developments of any number of modern artists.[9]

The circle of life is, then, a sign of vitality. It will appear in Berne's paintings in conjunction with other similar images of life and energy to do battle wth the encroachments of death.

TRIANGLES, MOUNTAINS, AND PYRAMIDS   The traditional interpretation of the symbolism of the triangle sees it as

> the geometric image of the ternary and, in the symbolism of numbers, equivalent to the number three. In its highest sense it concerns the Trinity. In its normal position with the apex uppermost it also symbolizes fire and the aspiration of all things towards the higher unity—the urge to escape from extension (signified by the base) into non-extension (the apex) or toward the Origin or the Irradiating Point.[10]

The Expressionist painter and first influential practitioner of "abstract" art, Wassily Kandinsky—an artist who has obvious influence on Berne's style and formal relations—interprets the triangle in his classic *On the Spiritual in Art.*

The life of the spirit may be graphically represented as a large acute-angled triangle, divided horizontally into unequal parts, with the narrowest segment uppermost. The lower the segment, the greater it is in depth, breadth and area. The whole triangle moves slowly, almost invisibly forward and upward. Where the apex was today, the second segment will be tomorrow. . . . At the apex of the highest segment often stands one man. His joyful vision is the measure of his inner sorrow. Even those who are nearest to him in sympathy do not understand. . . . How long will it be before a larger segment of the triangle reaches the spot where he once stood?[11]

This dynamic conception of the triangle is a function of the symbolism of the number three. The Jungian analyst Edward F. Edinger, following the Pythagorean system, sees *three* as the sum of the unique, uroboric quality of *one* and the discrimination of opposites implicit in *two*. It thus implies the fusion of unity and duality inherent in any dialectic and, ultimately, process—as opposed to the number four's implication of goal and achievement, which will be discussed below.[12]

Mountains are high, vertical, massive, and triangular. Berne's paintings draw heavily on his visual experience of the Swiss Alps, and his mountains reach upward like Kandinsky's spiritually yearning triangles. Several of Berne's mountains have vertical "shafts" or axes. (See plate 2.)

The vertical axis of the mountain drawn from its peak down to its base links it with the world axis, and anatomically, with the spinal column. . . . But the profoundest symbolism [of mountains] is one that imparts a sacred character by uniting the concept of mass, as an expression of being, with the idea of verticality.[13]

Berne's triangular mountains also suggest the massiveness and the symbolism of Egyptian pyramids. Since elements of Egyptian iconography appear throughout his work, the symbolism of the pyramid is pertinent here.

According to the Egyptologist I. E. S. Edwards, the erection of the pyramids paralleled the development in Egypt of sun worship, and the structure of the pyramid represented the rays of the sun shining down on the earth. Indeed, the shape of the structure would seem to be derived from the "benben," or solar symbol

housed in the temple of Heliopolis. It consisted of a pyramid-shaped stone on which the sun god was believed to have revealed himself in the form of a Phoenix. This legendary bird is renowned for its ability to renew itself in fire and is a recognized Western symbol of the eternal cycle of death and rebirth. Edwards goes on to interpret the pyramid as a means by which the dead Pharaoh could ascend the rays of the sun to heaven. In at least one painting by Berne, a mountain takes on the clear shape of a pyramid crowned by the sun.[14] (See plate 3.)

Finally, a word should be said about the pyramid as the combination of the triangle (when viewed from the side) and the square (when seen or conceived from above). The number four, like the base of the pyramid, is firmly rooted in and symbolic

of the earth, of terrestrial space, of the human situation, of rational organization. It is equated with the square and the cube and the cross, representing the four seasons and the points of the compass.[15]

Plate 3

In Jungian theory, the quarternity is the basis of the mandala. Edinger points out that mandalas "emerge in times of psychic turmoil and convey a sense of stability and rest." As we have already seen, this is true of the circle of life also, in its more generalized, latent context. Edinger sees the number four as a symbol of the goal of centered rest and "structural wholeness, completion—something static and eternal"—and of course in contrast to the dynamic, vital aspects of ternary symbols.[16]

Thus, Berne's use of triangles, mountains, and pyramids in his paintings is analogous to his use of circles and ovals. They are all symbols of life and vitality and, as will be seen, join with the signature cartouche to contend against the incursion of death.

THE SHADOW OF DEATH   Of all the symbols of death in Western culture—scythes, hourglasses, skeletons, dust, worms—those of darkness, shadow, and the colors black and purple are the most generalized and familiar. Goethe's last utterance, "More light," requests what death takes away, not only figuratively but physiologically, as the eyes go out. It is therefore not surprising to find in the visual arts the formal element of the "shadow of death" appearing either directly before the death of the artist or about three years before that event, when the psyche apparently "gives up" and psychosomatic processes take over the dissolution of the body. This formal element takes the shape either of dark veils or dark rectangles, descending from the top of the picture into a bright "sky" area—as if obliterating the sun. As with the frontal self-portrait, a consistent pattern of such occurrences can be found in the late work of artists.[17] In Albert Berne's paintings the shadow of death can be found descending in 43 of 146 paintings, or about 30 percent. It is always countered by circles and triangles from below. This contention between symbols of vitality and extinction forms the basic drama of these works. (See plates 4, 5, and 6.) Berne's signature rises to its highest central point whenever the darkness from above appears. It, in effect, joins the fray, becoming a moving expression of his relentless inner battle

Plate 4

against death. It also emphasizes the symbolic significance of the tripartite lateral division of the basic compositional matrix. The ground plane (A) seems to be earth. It is always filled with swirling foliage or shell shapes, which react passively or actively to the situation above. The blue area (B), which almost always enters from the right, is the area of Berne's signature. The color blue— the color of sky and water—is usually interpreted as a "spiritual" color. Here, it is the realm of his practical self—the ego—the area of his worldly power. The upper region is a realm of ultimates (D), where his visions/dreams take place and where, it would seem, not being dead, he cannot enter with his signature. Only once does this tripartite division disappear (except of course where, as he does on occasion, he depicts a street with houses). It is on 21 November 1973, when he paints the entire foreground blue, with his signature, and a vision of a strange, vertical white element—almost a figure—appears in a richly colored setting of swirls and ovals. (See plate 7.) This seems to relate to the female, since this configuration of the tall, draped figure is found in his paintings previous to the last series, and it always refers to

Plate 5

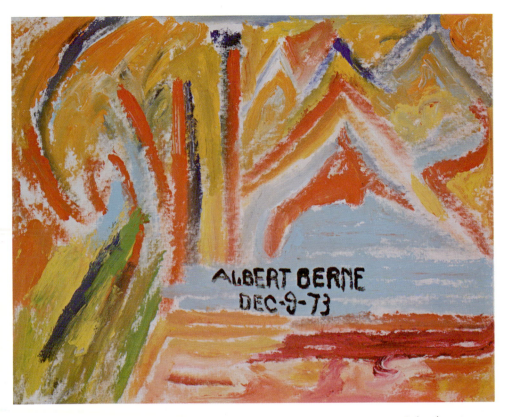

Colorplate 1

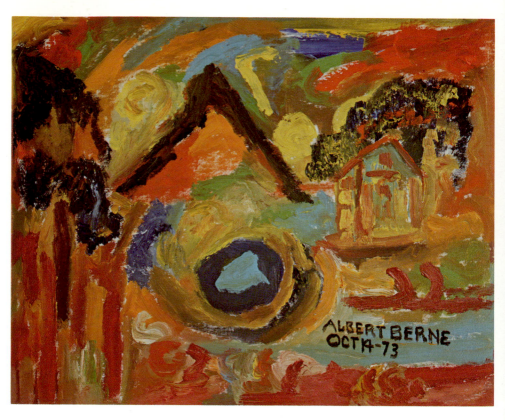

Colorplate 2

Plate 6

Plate 7

woman in nature. That the earth plane should disappear in such an instance suggests the centrality of woman—his mother and his wife—in his inner life.

MALE AND FEMALE IMAGERY   The act of painting with a loaded brush and the painterly dynamics of Berne's last works bespeak an intense masculine vitality that needs no Freudian interpretation. The wonder is to find such libido in so old a man. Explicit phallic imagery appears in the paintings of 12 and 13 October (in the latter the phallus takes the form of a five-branched tree), and the opposition of surging vertical elements to horizontals and in conjunction with ovoid shapes occurs throughout the series. (See plate 8.) Occasionally small houses (see figure 1: item 2)— traditionally interpreted as female—are depicted. In several works the figure 9 appears (see figure 1: item 6), most dramatically on 9 July and 9 August. (See plate 9.) Since Berne was born on 9 August, and was given to correcting other people's 9s to conform to his favorite version of the number, 9 obviously had a

Plate 8

Plate 9

Plate 10

special personal significance for him, over and above its traditional symbolism of triple synthesis on each world plane of the
corporeal, intellectual, and spiritual. It is also possible that it can
relate to certain agricultural symbols: shepherds' crooks (a Phar-
aonic symbol in Egypt as well as in the symbolism of a Christian
bishop), and the bending heads of grain and fruitful vines. The
androgynous aspect of this element in Berne's repertory of symbols is also significant, since the way *9* is used in the paintings
gives it clear phallic, as well as feminine, traits.[18]

Plate 11

The presence of a female figure in these paintings is problematic. In several works four vestigial human figures, rendered with no more than single brushstrokes, can be isolated. Thus, in the painting of 8 November 1973, these four elements stand in a clearly defined perspective space in what appears to be an urban setting. (See plate 10.) In the work of 28 November, four figures bow from the lower left corner toward a great circle in the visionary plane, which itself contains two white "figures" at the center. (See plate 11.) The four figures to the left in this work are rendered three dark and one light. Berne's son Henry sees these as the family constellation: the dead mother being the light element; his father and the two sons being the dark tones. All four bow toward the two figures in the circle above, which Henry Berne sees as his father's parents. Further, Dr. Berne states:

> The influence of the Feminine in my father's life was strong and constant. His mother was a major figure for him, living to the age of 89 and living in the same house with him for most of his life. His wife, my mother, was absolutely central in his life. They had as completely cooperative a relationship as I have ever seen. They depended on each other for different things, loved each other, and admired each other. He lived as a widower for 41 years after her death and never failed to say "good morning" and "good night" to her picture every day. . . . He often said, "I wish your mother were alive. She'd be so proud of the work I am doing. She was always interested in everything I did." In a large, personal sense, his paintings were done for her.[19]

On another level, his paintings were also done for the Zimmermans, as his letters quoted above clearly indicate. Berne constantly sought the approval of those who were closest to him, and his insecurity in this was essentially no different from that of the professional artist who seeks the praise of critics, dealers, and patrons. To make something is a social act; social approbation is absolutely required if the "struggle" inherent in the creative process is to seem worth the investment of time and energy. For Berne, to make a painting was also a real act of love, as he repeatedly states, and the creative process becomes for him a literal "matrix" in which to encounter the feminine principle in all the hidden implications of nature. Dr. Berne continues:

> The frequency of appearance of mountains and water indicates to me the influence of the Anima. Mountains have often been seen as feminine symbols. The breast-like shape is one obvious reason. The *mons veneris* is often thought of when mountains appear in dreams. The ocean, of course, is the Great Mother. And ponds are often thought of as symbols of the Self. The symbolism of the tree is one of the most complicated of all, but much of it is feminine. Erich Neuman speaks of the tree as feminine many times: it bears fruit, it shelters, etc.[20]

TREES Throughout Berne's paintings, bare-branched trees (see figure 1) are sometimes rooted in clearly defined landscape settings and at other times float freely in clearly symbolic settings. A tree

> is one of the most essential of traditional symbols. Very often the symbolic tree is of no particular genus. . . . In its most general sense, the symbolism of the tree denotes the life of the cosmos: its consistence, growth, proliferation, generative and regenerative processes. It stands for inexhaustible life, and is therefore equivalent to a symbol of immortality.[21]

The painter Paul Klee, in his famous essay "On Modern Art," compares the artist to a tree.

> May I use a simile, the simile of the tree? The artist has studied this world of variety and has, we may suppose, unobtrusively found his way in it. His sense of direction has brought order into the passing stream of image and experience. This sense of direction in nature and life, this branching and spreading array,

Plate 12

I shall compare with the root of the tree.

From the root the sap flows to the artist, flows through him, flows to his eye.

Thus he stands as the trunk of the tree.

Battered and stirred by the strength of the flow, he molds his vision into his work.

As, in full view of the world, the crown of the tree unfolds and spreads in time and in space, so with his work. . . .

And yet, standing at his appointed place, the trunk of the tree, he does nothing other than gather and pass on what comes to him from the depths. He neither serves nor rules—he transmits.

His position is humble. And the beauty at the crown is not his own. He is merely a channel.[22]

Berne's most dramatic tree is rootless and joins the numbers three and four to form a stark seven-branched silhouette against the cool winter tonalities, introduces his last nine paintings, created in the first nine days of December. Seven, the number of perfect order—and of pain—introduces and ends this penultimate sequence.[23] (See plate 12.) The last painting (colorplate 1), with its tall rectangle and fluid triangle flanking each other—four and three now separate but in conjunction—brings Berne's paintings to an end, on the anniversary day of his birthday, 9 December; thirteen days later he would be dead.

THE BOAT OF THE DEAD   Of all the symbolic patterns discernible in Berne's last paintings—and the major ones have been discussed above—the most unique and impressive occurs between 20 and 24 October 1973. These are preceded on 14 October by a work which seems to sum up his repertory of standard symbols. (See colorplate 2.) What is unique here are the two figures in the boat to the right, bowing in their odd way toward the intense blue circle centered in the work beneath a mountain/triangle. Here some centering ritual seems to be taking place. Six days later, on the twentieth, a large house appears with a dark entrance below, as if opening into its foundations. (See plate 13.) The next day Berne paints a boat, the masts of which are trees in full foliage (the only such in his work), which bears the sundisk. (See plate 14.) The next day this boat reappears in a brilliant golden ambiance. (See plate 15.) On the twenty-third, a great mandala

Plate 13

appears, and the next day the series ends with an even more emphatic mandala flanked by two three-branched trees. (See plate 16.) Here we find the remarkable—perhaps I should say archetypal—image of the Egyptian boat of the dead, which carried the deceased to Ra, the sun god, whose boat carried the sun through the underworld at night, never failing to reappear at dawn. Every pyramid had, nearby, pits designed to hold the wooden boats in which the Pharaohs would make this symbolic journey to the land of the dead. In Berne's work of the twenty-first, the configuration of the "shadow of death" descends in the shape of the boat and its tree-masts, to be countered by the sun-disk and transmuted into brilliant light the next day. Then the stabilizing mandalas appear to center the artist after his deepest descent into the place of death.[24]

Plate 14

Plate 15

Plate 16

Albert Berne's Contribution

When, in 1933, Dr. Rockwell Coffin suggested to Albert Berne that he take up painting after the death of his wife, he opened up a world of expressive potentiality quite different from anything Berne had experienced previously. His life as a musician and singer had been centered since adolescence in the vibrant and rationalized world of sound and song. He could reach—literally touch both physically and emotionally—an audience with music. His listeners, in turn, could touch him with applause. Thus, the social transaction of his art was tangible and satisfying. In his late years, however, a widower, his voice no longer young, he turned to the more private world of the visual image. Music takes place in time—in a scheduled environment of beat and measure. Music's measures are purely temporal. Berne's role, not being that of a composer, was also that of the interpreter of the creations of others. As a painter he could move from interpretation to creation, and in doing so move literally from time to timelessness. The creative process (whatever the art) is a timeless experience. The artist, involved in making, loses all sense of the clock. To be so absorbed in the creative process, even for a short time each day, is to exist in a timeless world of meditation, of dream, of unconsciousness, of childhood. To be so absorbed in the visual is also to exist in silence; the painting process and the painted object both exist in silence. Paintings are physically static. They speak in symbols only to the eyes. Norman O. Brown describes the process succinctly.

> To reconnect consciousness with the unconscious, to make consciousness symbolical, is to reconnect words with silence; to let the silence in. If consciousness is all words and no silence, the unconscious remains unconscious.[25]

Berne's paintings, with their evocation of the Alps, suggest that in his old age he returned, through the conscious and unconscious processes of art, to the silent mountain splendor that was the setting for his youthful and unscheduled wanderings. He returned, through them, to the timeless environment of what Erikson has called the "psychosocial moratorium," where, free of constraint, he found his center in the world. The myth of his old age, then, was to return in symbols to that origin where identity was found and destiny prophesied in the loves and fantasies of youth. If this be "second childhood," then we ought to encourage the elderly to make the most of it, keeping always in mind a careful distinction between the values of the "childlike" and the tragedy of the "childish."[26]

But if the humanist presumes to discuss humane approaches to aging in a culture bereft of universally accepted religious symbols, then it is his obligation to explore new contexts within which human beings can find a personal "myth" with which to renew themselves at each stage of the life cycle. By "personal myth" I mean a sense of origins, identity, destiny, and completion compatible with age and situation, which bestows meaning on life and enterprise. Put another way, a personal myth conquers depression by answering the questions posed in the suicidal Paul Gauguin's great depiction of the life cycle: *Where Do We Come From? What Are We? Where Are We Going?*[27] The style, character, and aesthetic quality of the answers—whether they are stoic or self-indulgent before contending forces of nature and society, or whether they find expression in the vocabularies of "high" or "popular" or "folk" culture—is not immediately important. The humanist's task is first to allow men and women of all backgrounds and educational levels to participate fully, freely, and creatively in human consciousness and in human society according to their capacities. There is no room for elitism here, especially in the face of death. The ultimate goal is to discover how to permit elderly men and women to achieve in our time, and to live with, a personal sense of wholeness and identity with which to grow toward their extinction.

Albert Berne seems to have achieved this goal. He can be viewed as a model; his is an almost ideal human situation. If this man's achievement of self-integration through painting is within the scope of human potentialities, then we can abstract from it lessons applicable to less fortunate situations. I can see no value in lamenting the plight of the aged—the physical decay, the poverty, the dogfood, the squalid nursing homes, the inhuman welfare system, the indifference of children, the culture's obsession with youth, or even the frustrating realities of trying to help (to quote Emerson) those "frowzy, timerous, peevish dotards, who are falsely old"—if we have no alternatives with which to alleviate their complex physical dependence and spiritual isolation.

Let us look to the potentialities of the visual arts for alternatives. Verbal animals, humanists (even those in the liberal arts) tend to view the visual and musical arts as forms of aesthetic embellishment and entertainment rather than as media of human introspection and revelation. Individuals tend to fixate at their highest accomplishment, and for most of us that is verbalization. The visual and aural levels of discourse have little to do with the modes of communication our culture considers normal. But these are alternative ways of communicating with oneself and others. In old age (and at other, less pressured, points in the life cycle), these modes of discourse can serve to humanize an individual's social context and to increase his participation in human consciousness. My suggestion, then, is that the visual arts can be means of psychic wholeness and practical solace for our senior citizens.

One hardly needs mention that a vast and comprehensive literature exists about the paintings and other visual expressions of our junior citizens. Children's art is a pedagogic and clinical industry. Its morphology has been analyzed, its iconography catalogued, its therapeutic utility recognized, and its aesthetic quality debated (especially by parents). No such literature exists for the art of old age. Indeed, even studies of major Western painters such as Titian, Michelangelo, or Goya—men who lived to advanced age—seldom do more than describe (the sin of art history is to describe) the "intensity" or "spirituality" of the late work. Theoretical statements are rare. Typical is this statement from the distinguished art historian Erwin Panofsky. He notes that the artist

> In the last phase . . . may either continue with the style of his maturity in a more or less mechanical way and thereby cease to be productive, or he will outgrow the tradition established by himself. In both cases this "late period" will mean a certain isolation."[28]

Beyond such art historical commonplaces, little is said or seen. Occasional, and usually inconclusive, attempts have been made to compare the early and late work of famous artists, but these are limited by the very diversity of genius in their unique "popu-lations."[29] I am not aware of any comprehensive attempt to col-lect and compare the visual creations of elderly amateurs or to study the art of old age in controlled situations comparable to those established for the study of children's art. What is apparent, unfortunately, when one finds art activities going on in senior citizen groups and old age homes, is an awful "art educationist" atmosphere. One finds the elderly given the tasks of children because their "arts & crafts" instructors, often supplied by local boards of education, see the elderly as overlarge children of no different mentality. There is only, at best, a primitive understand-ing that art activities for the old are "satisfying" in some mysteri-ous way. The intellectual and emotional factors involved in self-expression that takes place after a full life of human encounter and varied practical and inner experience is not explored, or, it would seem, imagined. The use of art in the psychotherapy of the elderly is recognized (a search of *Psychological Abstracts* found about five items in the last ten years), but it seems that nothing much is being done.

It is my hope, therefore, that by studying the last paintings of Albert Berne, we will find in them a visual Rosetta stone by which we can begin to translate the hieroglyphs of the aging psyche. Such a study should help to expand our awareness of what it is like to be both ancient and human. It will also, I hope, suggest a number of areas to be more deeply explored if we are efficiently to assist the aging to face with peace, purpose, and dignity the last of life and inevitable death.[30]

Notes

The last paintings of Albert Berne are presently in the collection of his son, Dr. John Henry Berne of Washington, D.C. It is hoped that they can form the nucleus of a study center dedicated to the art and symbolism of old age.

1. Albert Berne's letters to Carolyn and Carl Zimmerman in Cin-cinnatti were written mostly from his homes in Palm Beach and Chatham, Massachusetts. The 105 letters, dating from 1955 to 1973, give a detailed account of his working habits, his attitudes toward painting, and the vicissitudes of being old.

2. All direct quotations and biographical information have been obtained, at various times, from the artist's son, Dr. John Henry Berne of Washington, D.C. (who quotes his father here in a communication dated 14 August 1975); Albert Berne's servants, who cared for him during his last years, Paula Schettler and Robert Huber of Cincinnatti; and Dr. E. Robert Harned, his physician at Chatham, Massachusetts in a letter dated 17 October 1976. (Hereafter, respectively, JHB, PS, RH, or ERH to FVO'C.)

3. PS and ERH to FVO'C. Both state that Albert Berne consciously attempted to paint his dreams during his last six months.

4. JHB to FVO'C. See also Part II of Erik H. Erikson's essay in this volume.

5. PS to FVO'C.

6. ERH to FVO'C notes that Berne seemed most vigorous in October 1973. This would be a natural state required, and probably inspired, by the unconscious process revealed in the paintings of 14–24 October. See below and the illustrations.

7. Maria Petrie, *Art and Regeneration* (London: Elek, 1946), p. 58.

8. Erich Neumann, "Art and Time," in *Art and the Creative Unconscious,* Bollingen Series, LXI (Princeton: Princeton University Press, 1974), pp. 103–4.

9. The psychological role of the frontal self-portrait is based on evidence deduced from a survey of over three hundred members of the National Academy of Design and the National Society of Mural Painters, which I conducted while in residence as a Visiting Research Associate at the Smithsonian Institution's National Collection of Fine Arts in 1972. Of the respondents who had created frontal self-portraits, 57 percent related such works to outstanding changes or events in their lives. While these visual and statistical data remain unpublished, they have been presented in public lectures at the Smithsonian in 1972 and at the Foundation for the Open Eye in New York in 1975. They will be incorporated into a book I am writing on the dynamics of the creative and patronage processes. For Dürer's 1500 self-portrait, see Erwin Panofsky, *The Life and Art of Albrecht Dürer* (Princeton: Princeton University Press, 1955), p. 43, illus. fig. 110. For Piet Mondriaan's self-portrait of 1900, see *Modern Portraits: The Self and Others,* (exhibition catalogue, Wildenstein, New York, 1976), pp. 114–15. Abstract and semiabstract artists such as Paul Klee, Max Ernst, Arthur Dove, Jackson Pollock, and Adolph Gottlieb have all used this configuration, some, like Ernst and Gottlieb, adopting it, after its first emergence in their art, as a recurring motif.

10. J. E. Cirlot, *A Dictionary of Symbols* (New York: Philosophical Library, 1962), p. 332. I have used this reliable compendium of traditional symbol interpretation, based on a wide range of scholarship from Gaston Bachelard through Sir James Frazer and C. G. Jung to

Heinrich Zimmer, in lieu of attempting the impossible task of documenting in so limited a space the implications of each image and numerical complex discussed. The exact meaning of what each image meant to Albert Berne will never be known, though it is clear that he did not normally speculate on such matters, or attempt to interpret his dreams, on which many of the paintings are based. The importance and significance of the images he used rests in the clarity, power, and consistency of their usage. This interpretation assumes their unconscious origins and universal import. Needless to say, anyone who has not seen the complete sequence of 146 paintings or is disinclined to accept cross-cultural iconographic interpretations of visual images may find this study, of necessity, a rather arbitrary reading of complex and overdetermined data. I hope to have conveyed, at the very least, something of the human dynamism of their subject matter and to stimulate concern for the study of such iconography.

11. Wassily Kandinsky, *On the Spiritual in Art,* (New York: Wittenborn & Co., 1963), p. 27.

12. Edward Edinger, "The Three and the Four," in *Ego and Archetype* (Baltimore, Md.: Penguin Books, 1973), p. 179–81.

13. Cirlot, *Dictionary of Symbols,* p. 208.

14. I. E. S. Edwards, *The Pyramids of Egypt* (Baltimore, Md.: Penguin Books, 1947), pp. 21, 233–36. The painting is that of 6 October 1973.

15. Cirlot, *Dictionary of Symbols,* p. 222.

16. Edinger, *Ego and Archetype,* pp. 182–188.

17. As with the frontal self-portrait/circle-of-life study, the documentation for this image of descending darkness has been presented by me publicly only in lectures. See the sketch for Dürer's dream in William Martin Conway, ed., *The Writings of Albrecht Dürer* (New York: Philosophical Library, 1958), p. 145; and José Clemente Orozco's *Metaphysical Landscape* of 1948, collection: Museo Orozco, Mexico City, reproduced in Donald L. Weismann, *The Visual Arts as Human Experience* (Englewood Cliffs, N.J.: Prentice-Hall, 1974), fig. 13–11, p. 129, for the two manifestations of this image: veils and rectangles. The image also appears in work created within the last three years of the lives of abstract artists such as Paul Berlin, Jackson Pollock, Mark Rothko, and Eva Hesse. The dark rectangle also seems to appear in the work of very disturbed children. See Petrie, *Art and Regeneration,* fig. 14, p. 64; and Rose H. Alschuler and La Berta Weiss Hattwick, *Painting and Personality,* rev. ed. (Chicago: University of Chicago Press, 1969), plates 49 and 63.

18. Cirlot, *Dictionary of Symbols,* p. 223. For the 9 shape as the emblem of the goddess, see Joseph Campbell, *The Mythic Image,* Bollingen Series C (Princeton: Princeton University Press, 1974), fig. 70, p. 83; and Buffie Johnson and Tracy Boyd, "The Eternal Weaver," *Heresies* 2, no. 1 (Spring 1978), figs. 8 and 9, p. 67.

19. JHB to FVO'C, 14 August 1975.

20. Ibid.

21. Cirlot, *Dictionary of Symbols*, p. 328.

22. Paul Klee, "On Modern Art," in *Modern Artists on Art*, ed. Robert L. Herbert, (Englewood Cliffs, N.J.: Prentice-Hall, 1964), pp. 76–77.

23. Cirlot, *Dictionary of Symbols*, p. 223.

24. It would be useful to develop psychotherapeutic techniques utilizing the art of the aged as clinical data. If the thwarted child can produce the dark rectangle of death at the top of a painting (see above, note 17), and not die but for an instant, what psychic mechanisms induce it with such regularity in the last works of artists? And what other keys to psychic states exist—perhaps unique to the aging process—which remain to be discovered? Further, it would also be interesting to see if thanatologists might use diagnostically the obvious iconography of the "shadow of death" in recognizing the presence of the will to die and in alleviating the ensuing traumata. In other words, can these iconographic insights be used in a therapeutic situation to help the dying find resignation and peace in the process of the last struggle—to help others fill the boat of death with the sun?

25. Norman O. Brown, *Love's Body* (New York: Random House, 1966), p. 258.

26. See Richard I. Evans, *Dialogue with Erik Erikson* (New York: Harper & Row, 1967), pp. 53–54, as well as Erikson's most recent book, *Toys and Reasons: Stages in the Ritualization of Experience* (New York: W. W. Norton, 1977), passim.

27. Painted 1897. Collection: Museum of Fine Arts, Boston.

28. Panofsky, *Life and Art of Albrecht Dürer*, p. 13.

29. See, for example, the exhibition catalogues for *Continuity and Change* (Hartford, Connecticut: Wadsworth Atheneum, 1962) and *From El Greco to Pollock: Early and Late Works by European and American Artists* (Baltimore, Md.: Baltimore Museum of Art, 1968), which summarize the art historical literature in the field. Art historians ought to take another look at the late work of the Old Masters from Donnatello to Picasso from the point of view presented here. Such evidence might even help some of them become aware of the fact that real human beings actually make the objects they so brilliantly explicate in terms of form, color, style, and historical and literary influence. The superficiality of so much art historical writing and art criticism, the bias against biographical interpretation, the worship of the "aesthetic," and the overemphasis on the formal analysis of isolated works of art are all the result of our art writers having no coherent theoretical model of the artistic personality and of its life cycle. Since the creative process flowers most often in the second half of that cycle, an understanding of the art of old age might provide a basis for deeper insights into the dynamics

of the young and the middle-aged artist—especially those who die "before their time."

30. Perhaps evidence can be created by stimulating the development of art education techniques and opportunities designed to give the elderly access to the creative process. Such techniques would have to take into consideration the richer and more complex personalities of the aged, their senior status in society, their experience in human relations, and their self-evident difference from young children. It also goes without saying that while it is possible to find, as here, a coherent pattern of symbolic content in a single artist, the significance of that content for clinical purposes—and outside the individual biographical frame of reference—requires a wide range of comparative evidence, objectively analyzed.

CONTRIBUTORS

JOHN DEMOS is Professor of History, Brandeis University, Waltham, Massachusetts. He is the author of *A Little Commonwealth: Family Life in the Plymouth Colony*.

LEON EDEL is Professor of English, Emeritus, University of Hawaii, Manoa, Hawaii. His works include *Literary Biography*, *The Modern Psychological Novel*, and a five-volume biography of Henry James.

ERIK H. ERIKSON is Professor of Human Development, Emeritus, Harvard University, Cambridge, Massachusetts. His publications include *Young Man Luther: A Study in Psychoanalysis and History*, *Childhood and Society*, *Insight and Responsibility*, *Dimensions of a New Identity*, and *Toys and Reasons: Stages in the Ritualization of Experience*; he edited *Adulthood: Essays*.

LESLIE A. FIEDLER is Professor of English, State University of New York at Buffalo, Buffalo, New York. His works include *The Second Stone: Love and Death in the American Novel* and *Freaks: Myths and Images of the Secret Self*.

TAMARA K. HAREVEN is Professor of History, Clark University, Worcester, Massachusetts. She is the founder and editor of the *Journal of Family History*; her most recent books are *Amoskeag: Life and Work in an American Factory City*, *Family and Kin in American Urban Communities*, and *Transition: The Family and the Life Course in Historical Perspective*.

ROBERT KASTENBAUM is Professor of Psychology, University of Massachusetts, Boston, Massachusetts, and Director, Cardinal Cushing General Hospital, Brockton, Massachusetts. He edits the journals *Aging and Human Development* and *OMEGA*.

ROBERT R. KOHN is Professor of Pathology, School of Medicine, Case Western Reserve University, Cleveland, Ohio. He is the author of *Principles of Mammalian Aging*; the monograph *Aging* in the series of teaching units prepared by the Universities Associated for Research and Education in Pathology and published by the Upjohn Company; and numerous articles.

JUANITA M. KREPS is James B. Duke Professor of Economics and Vice President, Duke University, Durham, North Carolina, currently on leave while serving as United States Secretary of Commerce. She is the author of *Lifetime Allocation of Work and Income: Essays in the Economics of Aging* and *Sex in the Marketplace: American Women at Work*; coauthor of *Principles of Economics* (with Charles Ferguson) and *Sex, Age, and Work: The Changing Composition of the Labor Force* (with Robert Clark); and editor of *Technology, Manpower, and Retirement Policy*.

PETER LASLETT is Fellow of Trinity College and Reader in Politics and the History of Social Structure in the University of Cambridge, and Director of the Cambridge Group for the History of Population and Social Structure. He is the author of *The World We have Lost* and *Family Life and Illicit Love in Earlier Generations: Essays in Historical Sociology*, and editor of *Household and Family in Past Time*.

FRANCIS V. O'CONNER is an historian of art and the director of Raphael Research, a New York consulting service specializing in the fine arts. He has published a number of books about American art between 1930 and 1960, the most recent being *Jackson Pollock: A Catalogue Raisonné of Paintings, Drawings, and Other Works*, edited with Eugene V. Thaw. He is currently undertaking a research project concerning the imagery of the aging process and its relevance to both gerontology and the interpretation of the visual arts.

ROBERT F. SAYRE is Professor of English, University of Iowa, Iowa City, Iowa. His writings include *The Examined Self: Benjamin Franklin, Henry Adams, and Henry James* and *Thoreau and the American Indians*.

DAVID D. VAN TASSEL is Professor and Chairman, Department of History, Case Western Reserve University, Cleveland, Ohio, and Project Director, "Human Values and Aging: New Challenges to Research in the Humanities." He is coeditor, with Stuart F. Spicker and Kathleen M. Woodward, of *Aging and the Elderly: Humanistic Perspectives in Gerontology*.